NEXT TO HUGHES

NEXT TO HUGHES

*Behind the Power and Tragic Downfall of
Howard Hughes by His Closest Advisor*

ROBERT MAHEU

and

RICHARD HACK

HarperCollins*Publishers*

FIRST EDITION

Designed by Ruth Kolbert

Library of Congress Cataloging-in-Publication Data
Maheu, Robert.
    Next to Hughes / by Robert Maheu and Richard Hack.—1st ed.
    p.   cm.
    Includes index.
    ISBN 0-06-016505-7
    1. Maheu, Robert. 2. Hughes, Howard, 1905–1976. 3. Businessmen—United States—
Biography. I. Hack, Richard. II. Title.
    HC102.5.M22A3   1992
338.7´67´092—dc20   91-50479
    [B]

92 93 94 95 96 MAC/HC 10 9 8 7 6 5 4 3 2 1

To my wife, Yvette, and children—
Peter, Robert, Christine, and Billy

R.A.M.

To Anne and Big Joe—
the best of parents,
the truest of friends

R.H.

Acknowledgments

DURING THE PREPARATION OF THIS BOOK, I FACED MANY DISCOURaging and what appeared to be meaningless moments. The apparent and cowardly solution was always the same and very simple: "Give up the whole thing. Who in hell cares?" My wife and children cared, as did many of our friends. They gave me the courage to tell the truth about many phases of my life which I would have preferred to forget.

My mother, father, and sister Betty were always prepared to help me through adversities and not particularly anxious to indulge in the successes. They were never impressed with the power which I so stupidly enjoyed at times.

Having to file litigation against Howard Hughes was one of the most difficult decisions of my life. However, he left me no alternative. He and I became the consequences of his inability to discern between friends and foes. The true friends surfaced, sometimes at great expense to their own careers. Dean Elson, Tommy Webb,

Dr. Bob Buckley, Fanny Fox, Dr. John McGonigle, my nephew Frank Doyon, Jim Rogers, Mort Galane, Virginia and Keith Hanna, Roscoe and Missy Williams, Gene Maday, Mildred Johnson, Charles Blaisdell, John and Alleyne Mitchell, Tommy Callahan, June Brainerd, and her sister Betty Perry. Hank and Barbara Greenspun and my family were constantly by my side and always on the scene when I had given up all hope.

I could not have survived without the help of Roderick Thomson and Bill Miller.

I owe a debt of gratitude to Michael Viner for his unfailing belief in this project; my editors, Larry Ashmead and Eamon Dolan; Bennett Cohen, who did the original interviews and outlines for this book; and particularly Richard Hack, who had the tenacity and patience to cope with me. Thanks also to Les Whitten for his invaluable help.

And, yes, I thank Howard Hughes, who taught me so much about life through his own unhappiness. I have often described him as the poorest man in the world.

R.A.M.

Prologue

Thursday, November 26, 1970

THANKSGIVING DAY. I WAS POISED OVER THE TRADITIONAL TURKEY, carving knife in hand, when I heard the words that would change my life forever.

"The Man is gone."

Earlier that day I had arrived with my family at our chalet on Mount Charleston, Nevada. We had flown up in a Hughes company helicopter with Larry O'Brien, the chairman of the Democratic National Committee, and his family. Larry was working for Howard Hughes as a political consultant specializing in tax legislation. Although I'm a lifelong Republican and he was a dyed-in-the-wool Democrat, I found Larry one of the most honest, reliable, and likable men I had ever met. So when I heard that he would be in Las Vegas over the Thanksgiving holiday, I made sure he spent it with us.

And what a Thanksgiving we had arranged! Cooking is a hobby of mine, and I had planned to oversee the whole meal myself—mashed potatoes, turnips, peas, squash, boiled onions, homemade cranberry sauce, every kind of pie you can imagine, and a thirty-five-pound turkey! This was to be the kind of Thanksgiving I remembered having when I was growing up in Maine. And to be

1

honest, I was even more thrilled about it than my children were. Until the call.

I had just taken the bird out of the oven when the phone rang. It was Jack Hooper calling from Las Vegas. Jack was the head of security for Hughes's holdings in Nevada. Years earlier, Jack had been with the Los Angeles Police Department. He later retired and organized the Bel Air Patrol—a private security force that keeps watch over L.A.'s richest and most exclusive neighborhood.

Jack was tall, slender, and rarely troubled. But he was troubled now, and with good cause. He had just misplaced our mutual boss—the richest man in the United States.

"What the hell do you mean, the Man is gone?" I asked none too calmly.

Everyone was seated at the table just a few feet away from me. I was trying like hell not to yell. It wasn't easy.

"Mr. Hughes has left the penthouse," Jack explained, meaning the private hospital Howard Hughes maintained as his office and living quarters on the top floor of the Las Vegas Desert Inn Hotel and Casino. "All his aides are gone. We have no idea where they went."

For a moment I was silent. Shocked. For over four years, ever since I had moved his base of operations from Los Angeles to Las Vegas, Howard Hughes had never once stepped foot outside of his bedroom in the Desert Inn. Money, power, even his marriage to Jean Peters—Hughes had sacrificed all of that and more just to remain safely ensconced inside his ninth-floor cocoon.

On top of all that, Howard had been seriously ill for over a month. There was some mystery as to what his ailments were, but Dr. Harold Feikes, his physician, had assured me that they were severe enough that even trying to move Howard to a local hospital could endanger his life.

Yet Jack Hooper was on the phone, telling me that suddenly, without warning, Hughes and the so-called male nurses who cared for him, fed him, clothed him, and controlled all his communications, had vanished, leaving no trace of where they had gone or why.

Holding onto the phone, I had the feeling most cops get before an arrest. Neither fear nor panic. It's subtler than that. It's a little empty space in the pit of the stomach that comes from knowing you're about to face danger but not knowing *how much*. I knew I was about to face the fight of my life.

For nearly fifteen years, I had been Hughes's closest confidant, the overseer of most of his operations, and—quite literally—his alter ego. If Howard wanted someone fired, I did the firing. If he wanted something negotiated, I did the bargaining. If he had to be somewhere, I appeared in his place. I was his eyes, his ears, and his mouthpiece. I met with presidents, appeared before committees, and entertained the rich and famous. It was, to say the least, a unique arrangement. We had agreed to it over the phone while we were in the Bahamas in 1957. Howard had suggested it because of his increasingly obsessive need for privacy.

It was an arrangement that invested me with tremendous power, especially during the years in Las Vegas. By November of 1970, Hughes owned and operated seven casinos and five hotels, and was negotiating to purchase more. But the casinos and hotels were just the tip of the iceberg. After we'd arrived in Las Vegas, Hughes had begun a long spending spree, and by this point his Nevada holdings seemed endless, including airports, businesses, ranches, private homes, and most of the undeveloped land on the Las Vegas strip.

He was, in effect, the King of Vegas. And as his surrogate, I wore the crown.

It was a role Hughes encouraged me to play to the hilt. If I was to be effective as his proxy, he told me, I had to live the way people imagined *he* lived. And I did. I had jets, helicopters, and limousines available to me around the clock. I had a mansion on the golf course at the Desert Inn, and a two-story chalet on a mountaintop outside of Las Vegas. I had a wine cellar stocked for me partly by Baron de Rothschild himself, and I had parties catered by the finest chefs from Hughes's own hotels. My salary was in excess of $500,000 and my expense account was unlimited.

I never considered myself a big gambler or womanizer. But power is the most seductive mistress of all. In the late 1960s, Howard Hughes was perhaps the richest and most powerful private individual in the United States. And through Howard, much of that power was mine.

Yet the same neuroses that caused Howard to give me so much power would soon allow him and others to strip me of it. For while I may have controlled Hughes's empire, I had no control over his person. In fact, I had never seen the man face to face.

That was Howard's choice. He believed that for me to represent his interests properly, I needed to have an image of him in my mind as he had been in the 1930s and '40s—handsome, charismatic, robust—rather than the sickly, bedridden, phobic figure he became in the 1950s and '60s. So although for years we lived near each other in Las Vegas, wrote endless memos to one another, and talked incessantly on the phone, we never met.

The man who was responsible for caring for Hughes's personal needs was Frank William Gay. Every story has a villain, and I'm not afraid to say that in this story, it's Bill Gay. Tall, thin, and humorless, Gay was like Dickens's Uriah Heep—"ever so humble"—until you suddenly found yourself under his thumb.

Gay was already part of Hughes's entourage when I started working for him, but his ambitions were always being frustrated by Howard, who put little faith in his talents. During the 1960s, Hughes reduced Gay to little more than court eunuch, limiting his responsibilities to the care and feeding of Howard's wife, Jean Peters. Hughes felt Gay botched even that, blaming him when

Peters sued for divorce. But Hughes never dared to fire Gay, because Gay knew something even I didn't know—the depths to which Hughes had deteriorated both physically and mentally. Howard may have cut Gay off during the Vegas years, but the aides Gay had hired remained loyal to him, keeping him constantly informed of what was going on.

I knew Gay was jealous of my relationship with Howard and the power it afforded me, and I was fully aware of Gay's ambition. But I underestimated him. Of all the maneuvers I thought Gay might use to insert himself between Hughes and me, I never imagined he would try this.

I should have realized months earlier that something was amiss. Tensions had been growing between Hughes and me. Not that we hadn't argued before. Howard and I were both tough sons-of-bitches who appreciated a good scrap. But we also knew what was worth picking a fight over and how to resolve things before they got out of hand.

At the beginning of 1970, however, Howard started to change. No longer content with simply being reclusive, he began to become increasingly nervous. He wasn't picking fights over the big issues anymore, he was picking them over meaningless ones. And resolving each petty battle was getting harder and harder. Suddenly Howard was firing off memos questioning every minor detail of my performance. Why did I use the private jet so much? Why did I invite his competitors in the casino business, like billionaire Kirk Kerkorian, to parties held at Hughes-owned hotels? And why was I investing my own money in *non-Hughes* business ventures?

The answers were rather obvious, and I told him so in exactly those terms. I used the jet because I had to get places fast, to take care of *his* business. I invited Kerkorian, Del Webb, and other hotel and casino owners to our parties because it was polite, it was good business, and because they invited me, *as Howard's representative,* to their own parties. And so far as my investments went,

Howard knew that they never once jeopardized my work for him. The truth was, any consideration I gave to my own finances was an afterthought; something I did at two in the morning after I'd spent all day and night planning intricate stratagems to better the Hughes empire, not build one for myself. And since I couldn't invest in any Hughes enterprise (he owned all the stock in all his companies), my only options were non-Hughes investments.

As long as our channels of communication remained open, however, I had no problem handling the situation. After each complaint, I'd set Howard straight, and he'd realize that he was questioning me without cause. Even so, Howard's sudden pettiness was an annoying distraction, and I knew who was behind it all: Bill Gay.

Howard used to call Gay and his clique of followers the "Hollywood Gang" because Gay had worked out of the old Hughes building at 7000 Romaine Street in Hollywood, California. They were constantly trying to undermine Howard's trust in me; Howard himself had told me that much.

"Bob," Howard once said over the phone after we'd fought one of those skirmishes instigated by Gay, "this is another example of how those bastards are trying to wedge their way between us. We can't let them!" Yet, the growing tension with Hughes wasn't my only clue that trouble was brewing; there was also a surprising new alliance between Bill Gay and Chester Davis, Hughes's general counsel.

It's hard to imagine two people less alike than Bill Gay and Chester Davis. Gay, a Mormon, was a prim, almost feminine teetotaler who always made a great show of his purity. Davis, on the other hand, looked and acted like a sailor on leave. He was squat and muscular, and his foul-mouthed monologues ran nonstop no matter who was present, men or women.

Circumstances surrounding a 1961 court case between Hughes and TWA threw me into a fight with Chester Davis. Howard stood to lose over $130 million in the suit, which made claims that he had mismanaged the airline. A number of my sources in Washington—including Clark Clifford, who would later serve as secretary of defense under President Lyndon Johnson—felt the only way I could save Howard's case was to fire Davis. He had simply made too many enemies with his approach. By the time I took Clifford's advice, however, Davis had formed an alliance with Gay. And when I made my move, in early November, 1970, they retaliated by forcing *me* off the TWA case, claiming that the order came from Hughes.

Normally, this wouldn't have posed a problem. I simply would have called up Howard and straightened it all out, just as I'd done dozens of times. But things had gotten so bad at that point that I hadn't talked to Howard for over six weeks.

During those weeks, the coterie of aides who oversaw all of Howard's daily needs claimed that he was so sick he couldn't talk to anyone, even me. And Dr. Feikes, whom I trusted, confirmed that Howard had been losing quite a bit of blood and was sleeping much of the time.

Just two months earlier, Hughes had made me call off a trip to Europe. My second oldest son, Robert, was starting school in Germany and I'd promised Yvette, my wife, that I'd go with her to help enroll him. But Howard had interceded, demanding that I stay in Las Vegas so I could be on hand for "urgent business." After that came silence.

The frustration was terrible. I knew that if I could talk to Howard, I could work out the tensions between us—the TWA mess, the Davis affair, everything. That's how it had always been. But now the lines of communication were closed. And there was nothing I could do about it.

I had been having a recurring fantasy back then. I imagined myself in the lobby of the Desert Inn, dressed as usual, except that underneath my suit jacket I was wearing my old service revolver, an FBI-issue gun that I still owned. It was holstered the way we wore it at the Bureau—on the right hip, for an easy draw.

In my fantasy, I made my way through the Desert Inn lobby and, without calling upstairs to Howard's aides, headed for the elevator. You needed a special key to open the elevator doors on the ninth floor, where Hughes lived. Only a handful of people had them: Jack Hooper, Howard's aides ... and myself.

The fantasy was always the same. I entered the floor unannounced, walked past the security guard, and made my way down the corridor toward the hermetically sealed suite that served as Hughes's bedroom. Moving my jacket away from my revolver, I let the aides who stood outside Howard's door get a glimpse of it. I had no intention of actually using it; but I wanted everyone to know that it was there, just in case.

After flashing my gun, I pushed the aides aside, forced my way past them, and entered Hughes's own *sanctum sanctorum,* the bedroom where no one but his closest personal attendants were allowed—the men who fed him, bathed him, and cared for all his physical needs. And inside there I found ...

Blank.

The fantasy always stopped there. I had my own fears about Hughes's condition. Later I learned that nothing in my imagination compared to the horror of reality. But in the fantasy I never knew what I'd find.

I only knew that Hughes's concern over security went so deep that if I'd tried to break through it like that—no matter what the reason—he would have cut me off forever. So I never went up that elevator unannounced, never forced my way past Hughes's aides, never pried open the lid on his insanely controlled world to confront him, face to face.

Now it was too late. As Jack Hooper said, the Man was gone.

The moment I hung up with Jack, the search for Hughes began. I spent most of that Thanksgiving on the phone, ignoring my family and guests while I called people throughout the Hughes organization and checked out every possible place where Howard might have been taken. There were two houses we had rented for Jean Peters, which were now sitting empty. Howard could have been taken to either of them. There was also the Krupp Ranch, outside Las Vegas, which we had recently bought. Finally, there was every hospital in the Las Vegas area to check. And recheck. And then check again.

During all this, I was also trying to keep the story of Hughes's disappearance out of the press. It was like trying to put a pot on a tornado, but I was determined. Everything had to remain confidential, at least for a while. After all, it wasn't just the security of Howard's empire that I was worried about, it was the safety of Howard himself.

All of this was taking place at a volatile time. Assassinations and riots seemed to have their own life. The Kennedys, Martin Luther King, Jr., Watts, Chicago, and Detroit spoke of a violence we all feared. "Off the Pig" was a saying back then. I knew they weren't just talking about the police. They were also talking about the establishment: the rich, the powerful. They were talking about men like Howard Hughes.

That was not the only possibility that I dealt with that night. Some of my earliest jobs for Howard back in the fifties had been to quiet blackmailers who were trying to bleed him for cash. And only a few years earlier Frank Sinatra's son had been kidnapped in South Lake Tahoe by extortionists. After the abduction, they called Frank Sr. and demanded a huge ransom. The same thing could be happening to Hughes, I thought, and it might only be a matter of hours before I would get a mysterious call asking for a million dollars, or five million, or ten, to be dropped off on some desolate Nevada road.

I also realized that the disappearance might have nothing to do with radicals or blackmailers. It could be an inside job planned by people in the organization who wanted to cut me out. Taking Howard was the simplest way. By the end of the night, though, I had turned up nothing. All I knew then was what Jack Hooper had told me hours earlier: he was gone. And so was my "happy" Thanksgiving.

That evening, I took the Hughes chopper back to Las Vegas and headed straight for my office, a series of suites in the Frontier Hotel, across "the Strip" from the Desert Inn. For a couple of days I lived inside those suites, rarely sleeping, barely eating, aware of little but the telephone. There were really only a few leads as to where Howard might be. And none of them pointed to any person or group outside of Hughes's own circle. Even though I wasn't sure how to handle it, at least I had come to a firm conclusion. This was an inside job, pulled off by Howard's aides. And behind it were Bill Gay and Chester Davis.

My security had learned that no one *inside* the Desert Inn saw Howard or his aides leave Wednesday night, which meant they had to have gone down the external fire escape. Since Hughes certainly couldn't walk down the fire escape, he had to have been carried down nine flights of stairs, his frail body subject to the chilling winds of the wintry desert night. From what Dr. Feikes had told me, that alone could have killed him. Obviously, however, those bastards didn't care.

But being certain that Gay, Davis, and the "male nurses" were behind the disappearance was only the first step. The most important question remained: where did they go?

The possibilities were almost endless. Howard had always been consumed by wanderlust. Las Vegas, Tahoe, Phoenix, Boston, and Montreal were just a few of the cities to which he'd considered moving over the years. For a man like Hughes, considering a move didn't just mean looking in the classifieds. It meant buying land, homes, buildings, sometimes even businesses. So there were a number of cities where Howard's abductors could have gone and found an operational base ready and waiting for them.

When I learned that an unscheduled private flight had gone from Nellis Air Force Base in Las Vegas to the Bahamas the Wednesday night before Thanksgiving, I became very, very interested. Howard had been attracted to the Bahamas for well over a decade. In fact, he was considering a permanent move there in 1957 when we'd first discussed my becoming his "alter ego." He probably would have gone through with it if the islands hadn't suddenly fallen prey to political turmoil. Even so, Howard maintained a liking for the Bahamas, and had extensive financial interests there.

I had learned of the unscheduled flight from a well-placed source at McCarran International Airport. My man knew about the flight, but not who was on it or why it was so shrouded in mystery. That same week, just by coincidence, industrialist Del Webb was going to Washington, D.C., to visit his friend J. Edgar Hoover. Though I still kept the story from the press, I pleaded with Del to ask Hoover to open up an FBI investigation into the possible kidnapping of Hughes. Del did his best, but Hoover refused, claiming there wasn't enough evidence to start an investigation.

I disagreed. I had enough clues to believe I knew who had abducted Howard and where they'd taken him. I even sent Peter, my oldest son, and Dean Elson, the former head of all FBI operations in Nevada, who was then working with me in the Hughes organization, down to Miami to hire private eyes to search for the Man in the Bahamas.

Even though I'd begun to fathom the logistical questions surrounding Hughes's disappearance, other issues continued to baffle me. I wondered, for instance, now that Gay and Davis had abducted Howard—what the hell were they going to do with him?

With the exception of Gay and Davis, I had been talking to Hughes's top executives from the moment Howard disappeared, and none of them knew anything more about what was going on than I did. It seemed incredible to me that Gay and Davis would try to pull off a full-blown coup on their own, without some support from others high up in the Hughes organization.

There was a further riddle. Even at his most neurotic, Hughes was a tough s.o.b. He wouldn't simply *allow* them to take over. They'd have to keep on controlling him somehow, either with intense psychological manipulation, or through his use of drugs.

Drugs ...

In retrospect, I realize how much I had overlooked that possibility. I knew Howard took sleeping pills now and then, or maybe popped something to stay up all night when we were in the midst of negotiations on a deal. But I had never suspected that he used opiates. At the time, I had no idea at all of the sway the drugs held over him, nor of the confidence his addiction and paranoia gave Bill Gay and Chester Davis in their efforts to commandeer the Hughes empire.

But I found out just how confident they were on Friday, December 4, barely more than a week after Hughes's disappearance.

Edward P. Morgan, an influential Washington lawyer, a close friend, and an ex-FBI man like myself, had come to Las Vegas to help me locate Hughes. That Saturday around 1:00 P.M., he stopped by my office and told me he had received a call from Chester Davis. Davis and Bill Gay wanted to meet with Ed in Los Angeles. Davis didn't say about what. He didn't have to.

I figured the next time I heard from Ed, he'd be calling from L.A., with news about the meeting. But three-thirty that same afternoon, he came back to my office. In the course of that time, he had flown to L.A. by private jet, had a two-minute meeting, and returned to see me.

"I hate to tell you this, Bob," Ed started, "but I have a message from Davis to you. You must leave town before sundown ... or else." On a winter's day in Las Vegas, that left me less than two hours to clear out!

I looked at Ed for a moment, silently collecting my thoughts and considering my options.

Finally I spoke. "Well, I have a message, too. Tell Davis he can go *fuck* himself. I'll be here. And in case he can't reach me— because my personal telephone lines are now unlisted—you let him know they'll be listed by tomorrow!"

With that, the fight began. And the chaos.

On Monday, Gay's group made a public statement and word of Howard's disappearance hit the press. It was front-page news around the world. "Mystery Shrouds Disappearance of Howard Hughes," headlines read. The networks led off the evening news with the story, telling of the enormous rift that had developed between me and Bill Gay's Hollywood Gang, and of the possibility that Howard had been kidnapped.

That was just the beginning. Within days, I was embroiled with Gay and Davis in a brutal legal battle over who controlled the Hughes operation in Las Vegas. Reporters were everywhere: at the Desert Inn, at the Frontier, at my front door. There were even reporters in helicopters, buzzing my windows, trying to get candid pictures of me and my family. Finally I went on the CBS news show "60 Minutes" to quiet the speculation and let people know what was really happening.

As I was being interviewed by Morley Safer on the program, I wondered if Howard was watching. He watched television with a passion, and he enjoyed "60 Minutes" enormously. During the course of the segment, I discussed the possibility that Hughes had been kidnapped, and found myself looking directly into the camera with a simple plea: "Howard, please call me."

As crazy as things were during that time, the moment that stands out most clearly in my memory is the realization I had at home, late one night, after everyone else had gone to bed.

I wasn't sleeping much then. There were too many details I had to try to remember, and too many potential disasters I had to keep blocked from my mind. I had gone over my notes on the court case at least once when I poured myself a drink and sat down to go over them again. But as I sat there, my mind drifted from my notes and traveled back to 1954, and the very first job I found after forming Robert A. Maheu Associates.

A group of businessmen who wanted to win control of New York Central railroad had hired me to influence stockholders toward their side of the fight. It wasn't a dangerous job, and certainly not very glamorous, but it was challenging because of the subtlety it demanded. You couldn't just browbeat people into siding with you. You had to seduce them, appeal to them with a come-on that was half blarney, half factual, but totally convincing.

This meant making personal appeals to hundreds of stockholders. Obviously, I couldn't contact them all by myself, so I set about hiring assistants to canvass the Northeast. But I was picky about what sort of assistants I wanted. These men had to gain a stockholder's immediate respect, so I told the employment agencies that I would only hire bright, presentable men in their forties and fifties, who dressed well, had their own transportation, and were willing to work for just twenty-five dollars a day.

I fully expected the agencies to come up empty-handed. No one, I thought, could match my demands and still be so hard up he would work for that little. To my amazement, the agencies produced a small army of fully capable men willing to do just that.

As I interviewed the applicants, I couldn't help but ask each one why a man of his caliber was available for a twenty-five-dollar-a-day job. Almost without exception, the answer was the same: they had trusted their financial security to the whims of a single employer. Then, when the business went belly-up, or was sold, or management changed, they'd found themselves—at the age of forty-five or fifty—suddenly cut loose from their jobs. And without much hope of getting another. Right then and there I decided that I would never end up in their position, and never become solely dependent on one client for my financial security. I was thirty-seven at the time.

As I sat at home that night, sipping a drink and remembering the promises I'd made to myself, I was fifty-three—and in precisely the position I swore I'd never be in.

It was then that I realized that despite all I had struggled for and won over the years, I might have lost a far more important battle. But the high stakes in this fight wasn't power or even money.

It was me.

Suddenly Jack Hooper's words came back and slapped me in the face. Because "the Man" who was really gone was Robert Aime Maheu.

Chapter One

FROM ELM CITY TO ROMAINE STREET

A NUMBER OF MEMENTOS LINE THE WALLS OF MY STUDY IN LAS Vegas. There's a personal note from the late FBI Director J. Edgar Hoover, a photo of me with then Governors Reagan and Laxalt, even a tiny American flag that went to the moon on Apollo X. But I like to think that one thing says more about me than all the other pictures and plaques combined. It's a sign, far older than I am, painted on wood that reads ELM CITY BOTTLING. I doubt it's worth anything to anyone except me. Call it my personal "Rosebud." Elm City Bottling was the small carbonated-beverage company that my father ran from a barn behind his grocery store in Waterville, Maine.

Looking at that sign now, I marvel at the twists and turns my life has taken. To say they've been "unexpected" would be like saying that Howard Hughes was "well off." In fact, if anyone back then had told me even half the things I would do in my life, I would have told him he was out of his mind.

Or, as we say in Waterville, *"Il est plein de merde,"* if you'll pardon my French.

Waterville, about forty miles inland, is a little mill town on the Kennebec River best known as the home of the Hathaway shirt. I was born there in 1917. My parents, Ephrem and Christine Maheu, were full-blooded French-Canadians, and I grew up speaking as much French as English. I also grew up with a canoe oar in my hand, or at least that's how it seems looking back. I can't remember a time when I *wasn't* traveling around the Maine backwaters in an old bark canoe, light enough to lift up over my head as I ran from one stream to another. In fact, the first job I ever had was delivering newspapers by canoe when I was only nine years old.

Growing up I sometimes worked for my father. We weren't rich, but neither were we poor, and even during the Depression, my father never faltered as a provider, keeping me and my adopted sister Betty Ann fed, clothed, and sheltered from the pain and sorrow that was burning a wide swath across the country.

There's one story about my dad that captures him in a way nothing else can. Neither he nor my mother went to college, and they were determined that their children would, no matter what. As devout Catholics living in the Northeast, college for them meant Holy Cross, the finest Jesuit college in the area.

But Holy Cross was expensive, and I knew tuition would put a terrible strain on our finances. So when the principal of my high school told me that I had earned a partial scholarship to Holy Cross, I ran the two miles between Waterville High and my father's small store in a matter of minutes—I was that excited. I remember charging into the place barely able to breathe, let alone talk. After I caught my breath, I told him the good news.

I did not get the reaction I expected. My father looked at me coolly and said, "Let's go downstairs." "Going downstairs" meant lifting up a trapdoor and going down a ladder into the storage basement. What happened there is etched as vividly in my mind as if it occurred moments ago.

We picked up a couple of empty wood crates and sat between a barrel of molasses and a barrel of vinegar in silence. Then, finally, my father said, "Son, I'm going to ask you what may be the only favor I ever ask you in your life."

"What's that?" I asked.

"Turn the scholarship down."

I couldn't believe it. This scholarship meant thousands of dollars to us, and my dad was telling me to walk away from it.

"My formal education ended when I was eleven years old, the day I started to work in a cotton mill," he explained. "Since then I've worked for one purpose: to see that you and your sister are educated in a way I couldn't be. Please ... don't deprive me of that."

He had tears in his eyes. I couldn't help but be moved, and I agreed to let him do it his way and pay for my college education. But I had one proviso: that I come back home each vacation and work for him in his store. He looked at me and smiled in agreement.

Holy Cross is located in Worcester, Massachusetts, a tranquil college town in the center of the state. It's curious, but even though we were in the midst of a depression—*and* building toward war—my years at Holy Cross were idyllic. Oh, I had to work, all right, waiting on tables. But I never minded that. Most of my time was spent in study and discussion, two endeavors that I've always loved. I even found time to join the debating team, and to become its president. One of my closest friends on the team was a young fellow named Edward Bennett Williams. Years later, he would head his own powerful Washington law firm and become extremely influential in Washington. He would also change my life by opening the door to the man who would be my most important client—Howard Hughes.

In those days, Holy Cross was highly regimented. Dress code,

19

mandatory attendance at Mass, and strict curfews. Those things I didn't mind. There was one thing about Holy Cross, though, that I never liked: being separated from Yvette Doyon.

Yvette and I met when I was eleven and she was ten, and we've been in love ever since, through grade school, college, the FBI, the CIA, and my good and bad years with Howard Hughes. Yvette and I became engaged in 1940, the same year I was graduated from Holy Cross with a B.S. in economics.

We've stuck it out for over sixty-three years, fifty-one of them married, and I thank God every morning I wake up beside Yvette. It may not be fashionable to be that devoted a husband, especially today when relationships seem as disposable as diapers. But to tell you the truth, I could care less. I wouldn't trade Yvette for all the glamorous movie-star marriages in the world. I saw what that kind of marriage gave Hughes, and I know what my marriage gives me, and there's no comparison.

Soon after being graduated from college, I applied to, and was accepted by, Georgetown University's law school in Washington, D.C. I fell in love with Washington as soon as I arrived. What enchanted me even more than its charm and elegance was the almost palpable power that one feels there. The city that grew from the swamps of the Potomac is the nerve center of the nation, and if you're susceptible to power's intoxicating allure—which I must admit I was—Washington sweeps you off your feet.

I wasn't eligible for a scholarship at Georgetown, and the four years at Holy Cross was all my father could finance. So for me law school meant *night* school. I took a full-time job during the day with the Department of Agriculture.

It was a marginal job analyzing aerial photos to make sure farmers were growing the crops for which they were being subsidized. Though it wasn't something I wanted to spend the rest of my life doing, it paid all right; it didn't sap my brain, so I could still study at night; and—for a twenty-three-year-old wet-nose—it seemed like a lot of responsibility. I was perfectly content to maintain the status quo for the next three years, graduate from Georgetown, and then move on to what I intended to be my life's work: law.

Life, however, has an annoying habit of paying absolutely no attention to any of our plans.

A friend of mine from Holy Cross named Jack Delaney was attending school with me at night. During the day, Jack clerked for the FBI. One day he saw a memo stating that the FBI was looking for translators. The money was somewhat more than I was making, and since Jack knew I was fluent in French, he gave me an application.

I wasn't really interested. The extra money would have made a difference, but I was getting by without it, and, as I said before, I was happy. Jack, though, kept after me, until I finally went down to the Bureau and applied. I was given an examination that consisted of translating an article from French to English. This was easy for me, second nature really, and I finished it so fast the interviewer was amazed. Then, after we talked a bit he asked, "How would you like to be an agent?" As in FBI agent.

I thought he was kidding. I didn't know much about the Bureau, but I knew enough to realize that agents were supposed to be either CPAs or lawyers. I was neither, and was sure he was toying with me, maybe as a deliberate part of the interview process. "You know I can't be an FBI agent," I shot back. "I don't have the qualifications."

He looked at me and grinned, took out a sheet of paper from his desk, and shoved it in my direction.

"Just last week, it was decided that anyone with a college degree and fluency in a foreign language can take the same exam we give to prospective agents. You seem to have both."

I looked at the memo. I was eligible. But I still had to take the same test they gave to the more experienced applicants, and I didn't think I could pass.

"Take the lawyer's exam," the FBI man suggested. "All it does is give you sets of circumstances and then quotes statutes. What it comes down to is simple logic, and my guess is you can handle it."

He was right—I could, though I didn't believe it at the time. After taking the test, I forgot about the whole thing and happily went back to my routine of attending classes at night and poring over aerial photos during the day.

In a few days, however, I began to get a succession of worried phone calls from friends in Waterville and Worcester. It seemed that FBI agents were snooping around, asking questions about me. My friends thought I had gotten into trouble. I laughed it off, figuring the Bureau was doing the usual security check it performs before hiring a translator. But then, one morning around six o'clock, my landlady knocked on my door.

"Mr. Maheu," she said, obviously nervous, "there's a special-delivery letter here for you from the FBI."

Inside was a note from J. Edgar Hoover. I had been appointed a special agent of the Federal Bureau of Investigation, and was to report to the FBI training center.

I didn't know what to do. All my life, I had wanted to be a lawyer. Now I was being offered a job with the FBI. It was both thrilling and scary. The thrill won out.

I suppose it was the challenge. The unknown. In a pattern that would repeat itself throughout my life, I went for the excitement of uncertainty, and soon found myself in Quantico, Virginia, a quiet little village south of Washington on the banks of the Potomac.

Today, training for the FBI is a highly specialized affair. Even then, before the era of computers and high-tech forensics, it was supposed to take months. But in 1940, with a war brewing in Europe and the need for internal security growing in the U.S., the Bureau was desperate to get men in the field. To do it, it cut the training period to six weeks. Six weeks to turn a twenty-three-year-old with no graduate degree, no military experience, and no law

enforcement experience into an officer in the most elite investigative force in America. Looking back, it seems impossible. Somehow,
though, I made it, although I have to admit, I probably started my
career with the Bureau as the least-trained agent in its history.

My first assignment was in Phoenix. I had lived my entire life
in the corridor that runs from Nova Scotia to the Chesapeake Bay,
where rainfall is plentiful and winters are cold. That's how I
thought the whole country was—wet, green, and frozen in winter.
But Phoenix is located smack in the middle of the Sonoran Desert,
just a few hours' drive from the Mexican border, where you can
measure the rain in thimblefuls and the temperature average is
warm ... all year round.

In those days, new agents all seemed to dress the same: gray
flannel suit, wool overcoat, and snap-brimmed felt hat. That's how
I arrived in Phoenix—covered in wool from head to toe. People
stared at me like I was from outer space. For a moment I thought
that they had "made me," found out somehow that this G-man was
coming to town. I figured out what was really going on just about
the time the sweat soaked through my clothes. The wet-nose was
standing in the middle of a desert, dressed for the ice and snow.

Yes, I was naive, but I wised up pretty fast.

After finding myself a lighter-weight suit and reporting to the
special agent in charge, I was sent out on my first case. I was hoping for something worthy of Elliot Ness, a job tracking down bank
robbers or kidnappers, the sort of crooks who use "Kid" or
"Machine Gun" or "Pretty Boy" as a first name. What I got was the
file of a girl who wanted to be a stenographer at the FBI office in
Phoenix. I was supposed to canvass her neighbors and ask them
about her "background."

I drove to the girl's neighborhood. The first house I went to
was the one next to hers, and the moment I told the man inside
that I was with the Bureau, he went into absolute ecstasy. This man
was an FBI nut. He had read everything that had ever been writ-

ten about the Bureau and had been exchanging letters with Hoover for years, but I was the first *live* agent he'd ever met.

He dragged me inside and pulled out volumes of files containing his correspondence with Hoover, then proceeded to question me on life in the FBI. After enduring an hour of this, I finally turned the conversation around to the girl next door. The fellow had moved in only a week earlier. He didn't even know her!

I quickly made my excuses and headed out to my car, my admiring friend following me, still talking about the wonders of being a G-man. Suddenly I got a terrible feeling in the pit of my stomach. *I had locked myself out of my car.*

My admirer, though, wasn't the least concerned. He had read all about how FBI agents learned to pick locks during their training at Quantico. He hurried back into his house to get a paper clip, with which, he was sure, I could open my car door. He came back just as I was smashing the driver's-side window with the butt of my gun. I'd never seen anyone so disappointed. I drove off as quickly as I could, leaving him standing there, still clutching his paper clip in disbelief.

Soon after that I was sent to Bisbee, Arizona, to work with an older agent named Marvin Pash. Pash was a classic. He was a tough ex-cop who gave me a taste of the romantic, rough-and-tumble FBI life that I had dreamed about. He also taught me a thing or two about police work; how a little resourcefulness and a lot of guts can take the place of just about anything.

Bisbee, ten miles north of the Mexican border, was little more than a ghost town. In the 1880s, it had been a hell-bent boomtown that, along with nearby Tombstone, was one of the most illicit cities in America. God was an infrequent guest in Bisbee, and right and wrong were matters often adjudicated by a six-gun.

Though the saloons and whorehouses that once lined Bisbee's dusty streets had been boarded up for decades, there was still a touch of lawlessness about the place. It was, after all, a border town on one of the most open and unguarded frontiers in the world. The line separating the U.S. from Mexico is more visible on maps than in reality. It's a nebulous barrier that in truth doesn't separate anything. Often it seems to do just the opposite, serving as a magnet attracting some of the roughest, least desirable elements from both countries.

Not that any of them ever bothered Pash, who, I quickly realized, could handle anyone, or anything. One time we were sent from Bisbee to collect a prisoner who was wanted in the States, but was being held by the Mexican police in Nogales, Sonora—across the border from Nogales, Arizona. When we arrived there, the chief of police, who spoke no English, refused to give us the prisoner without an official document. I became nervous, because I knew it would take weeks, even months, to have all the extradition papers drawn up, and we were supposed to have this prisoner in Phoenix the following day. But Marvin—who spoke a fair amount of Spanish—wasn't concerned in the least. He smiled, shook the chief's hand, and assured him we'd be back in an hour or two, *with* the document.

We drove to Nogales, Arizona, and went into a five-and-dime store. There, Pash bought a facsimile of the Declaration of Independence, a box of crayons, and a ribbon. He wrote the prisoner's name at the top of the Declaration of Independence with a black crayon, melted a red crayon at the bottom to look like an official seal, tied it with the ribbon, and drove back over the border. The chief couldn't read English any better than he spoke it. Pash gave him the Declaration of Independence. The chief looked at it in grateful approval, gave us the prisoner, and U.S.-Mexican relations remained serene.

On another occasion, Pash and I were investigating a murder in Bisbee. The suspect was a vicious sort, and I don't mind saying that when we ran into some of his friends inside a bar, I was wary. Not Pash, however. He walked right up to the meanest-looking of the bunch and held up his FBI credentials. The guy was not impressed, and snatched the identification from Pash and tossed it across the room next to a jukebox. By this time, every single person in the bar was looking at us, and I was trying not to let my nervousness show. Without hesitating, Pash grabbed this slob by his shirt, picked him right up off the floor, dragged him over to the jukebox, and told him to pick up the ID and hand it back. The man did as he was told. After that, this so-called tough guy answered every question Pash asked. And so did everyone else in that bar.

Within a few months of joining the FBI, I started to earn enough money to support a family, so Yvette and I decided to get married. We also decided to take the leap because I was nearing the end of my first assignment, and we both figured that no matter where the Bureau sent me next, it *had* to be closer to our beloved Maine than Phoenix was. We were wrong. There *are* some places farther away from Maine than Phoenix. Seattle is one of them. When I was transferred there, I sent for Yvette, and we were married on July 27, 1941, along the water at Seattle, Washington, with a wedding party consisting of FBI men and wives.

Soon after, Pearl Harbor shattered whatever illusions the U.S. had about not getting involved in the world's problems, and we charged into war. The FBI was the primary line of defense against any breach in national security.

The most difficult part of this FBI work for me was rounding up Japanese-Americans and putting them into internment camps as part of the War Powers Act. At the time, the Pacific Rim was thought to be the region of the U.S. most vulnerable to attack, so Washington decided that the only way to tighten national security was to intern all the Japanese there. It didn't make sense to me then, and it makes even less sense to me now. Some of these people had sons fighting on our side in the war. Yet here we were, locking their families up in camps.

What infuriated me most was the way some of the area's voluntary police, who were assisting the Bureau in this operation, handled these people's religious possessions. All religious objects were supposed to be returned to the internees once they were released, and I took this very seriously. It was bad enough that we locked these people up; the least we could do was show respect for their religion. But one time I walked into a deputy marshal's house and saw a whole room loaded with Shinto and Buddhist treasures that he had stolen from the poor souls he had been arresting. If I could have had my way right then, *he* would have been behind bars, not the Japanese. After that, I made sure—on my watch, at least—that nothing like what this joker pulled happened again.

My distaste for the internment of Japanese-Americans did not mean that there weren't real concerns about national security and sedition in the Northwest at the start of the war. Numerous German, Italian, and Japanese nationals who were actively supporting the Axis cause were arrested, and many of them had overseas radios and transmitters that could potentially link them to foreign powers. Whether or not these people were part of a "Fifth Column," I can't say. But the fact that they posed a potentially serious security risk is indisputable.

Once, we made a series of raids that kept me up for over forty-eight hours. These arrests are probably unique in Bureau history, because I did something that's definitely not in the FBI guidebook when it comes to early-morning raids on suspected spy rings: I took my wife along.

Yvette was pregnant with our first son, Peter, and she hadn't been feeling all that great. Call me a nervous first-time father, but I was not about to leave her alone. I had rented a suite outside Port Angeles and made Yvette comfortable. Then I went to the Port Angeles police headquarters and began to coordinate the raids, which took place over a huge area.

The raids were slated to hit twenty-two different residences suspected of being storehouses for guns and ammunition. In order to make the operation a success, the raids needed to occur nearly simultaneously, as any lag time would open us up to the risk of exposure and the potential loss of our suspects. But because I was the only federal agent in the area, I had to be present to serve every search warrant.

I couldn't figure out how to be in two places at once, let alone twenty-two. My solution was to create the most intricate series of busts I've ever witnessed. At 5:00 A.M. in the morning, we had eighty-eight men—police officers, deputy sheriffs, military police, and a few volunteers—spread out across the city, four at each residence we were raiding. I would show up at each place just long enough to serve the warrant and then race off to the next bust.

In the midst of all this, I kept calling the suite in Port Angeles. Yvette was a trouper, and hung in there. She even had sandwiches waiting for me when I finally pulled in very late that night. I don't know what I would have done if she had gone into labor. Dropped everything and drove her to the hospital, most likely, and been drummed out of the Bureau, I guess, for doing it.

But Yvette didn't go into labor—not then, anyway—and I wasn't drummed out of the FBI. In fact, the raids went flawlessly and generated an enormous amount of positive press for the Bureau. The success of the operation raised my status within the organization; so much so that a year later I was called to Washington, D.C., and given a special assignment to go undercover, *indefinitely*, as part of a sting—code-named "Cocase"—aimed against a pair of Nazi spies traveling to New York City.

The prospect was daunting. For one thing, I had never previously worked undercover. On top of that, I hated the idea of leaving Yvette alone with our new son, Peter, who was then only a few months old.

Still, although it may be a cliché, this *was* war. The guys who really won it, of course, were on the beaches, and the price the rest of us paid will always pale by comparison. Yet anyone who lived through those times knows we all made sacrifices.

Dedicated or not, I still wanted a little time to say good-bye to Yvette, but I didn't get it. I couldn't even go back to Aberdeen, Washington, to help her pack. The FBI sent another agent, Charles Selfridge, to do that, so she and Peter could move in with my family in Maine while I worked undercover.

All I was able to do was talk to Yvette by phone from Washington and try to explain everything. She understood, and continued to understand throughout the whole time I was on that assignment. It wasn't easy. For over a year and a half, Yvette and I never set eyes on each other ... although most of the time we were no more than a day's drive apart. But that's how the Bureau wanted it. Nothing was allowed to compromise my cover. Yvette had a phone number she could call in case of an emergency, and any message would be relayed to me in a matter of minutes. We both felt like I had been drafted and sent off to some isolated corner of the world.

I reported to Assistant FBI Director E. J. Connolly. Connolly was the only person who had been given authority by J. Edgar Hoover to preempt any case he wanted in the entire FBI organization. A legend in the Bureau, Connolly was the man on whom the Efrem Zimbalist character was based in the TV series about the FBI.

"Cocase" revolved around two German spies who were about to start operating in the U.S. One was Dieudonné Costes, a famous French flying ace in the First World War, who had been drawn into the Nazi spy network after the Germans occupied Paris. Our French informants told us that the Nazis had seized some of Costes's relatives in Paris, then forced him to attend an espionage school they had in Hamburg, figuring that his notoriety as an aviator could gain him unique access into Washington's most important halls of power.

The other man was a German-trained technician named Jean-Paul Marie Cavaillez, whom Costes had met in Hamburg. An expert in clandestine radio transmission, Cavaillez, despite his French-sounding name, was Prussian to the bone.

The Bureau suspected that Costes was being sent to the States as a triple agent. A triple agent is the most difficult kind of spy to uncover, and potentially one of the most damaging in terms of security. Simply put, a triple agent is a spy who goes to the opposing side and offers himself up as a *double* agent—a spy who's been "turned" in his ideology but continues to go through the motions of serving his original masters, while actually passing them false information.

Where the triple agent differs from the double, however, is that this Napoleon of Duplicity is only *acting* as though he's been turned. In truth, his allegiance is always with his original masters, and once he's worked his way into the good graces of his new compatriots—gaining access, he hopes, to their most sensitive secrets—he will contact his old handlers, once again passing on *real* information to them.

Costes admitted to our contacts that he was being sent to the U.S. by Germany, and thereupon offered his services as a double agent. They, in turn, told him that when he arrived he had to be met by an FBI agent—namely me. What they *didn't* tell him was that we suspected him of being a double-crossing s.o.b., and that in addition to working with Costes, it would be my job to watch his every move.

Prior to that, though, I had to be trained in undercover work, which was still new to me. I was briefed on Costes and Cavaillez and lectured on the details of "tradecraft," which is spy jargon for the nuts-and-bolts work of espionage: letter drops, secret codes, disappearing ink, the whole bit.

I also had to develop a new identity. Although Costes could know I was in the FBI, it was critical to our plan that Cavaillez *not* know. The identity I was given was Robert A. Marchand, a successful French-Canadian black marketeer living in New York City. The name and nationality were picked because they resembled my own, making the cover easier to remember and maintain. Yet, even with the most careful planning, the unexpected is waiting to sneak up behind you and shout.

I had checked in at the Tatum Surf Club in Miami, confident in my new identity. I had no sooner gone to the bar where I was supposed to wait to make contact, when I felt a gruff slap on the back.

"Bob Maheu," I heard a voice boom. "What the hell are you doing here?"

It was an old classmate of mine from Holy Cross, excited at the opportunity of a reunion. I don't know which moved faster—my heart, sinking, or my feet, leaving. Fortunately, no harm was done.

Connolly and I eventually met Costes in Miami, when he arrived on a steamer with his Russian-born wife. We grilled him for two or three days, looking for a crack in his story, determined to find out if he was setting us up and planning to become a triple agent. But we came up with nothing. As far as we could tell, Costes was untrustworthy enough to double-cross the Germans, but trust-worthy enough to be true to us.

Not that there wasn't a price involved. Costes was a business-man, not a hero. He talked a lot about how the Germans had forced him into all this, but the truth was they *paid* him ... and so would we. Our plan was to make it look as though Costes had got-ten tight enough with U.S. officials to gain access to military secrets, giving him detailed knowledge of Allied operations. At that point, Costes would ask for Cavaillez, the expert radioman, to be sent over to transmit his information. Then, once we'd convinced the Germans that they had a reliable network in place, I would start to feed Cavaillez misleading information about the most important operation of the entire war: D day, the Allied invasion of Europe.

❖ ❖ ❖

All this seemed to go smoothly enough. Costes set up quarters at New York's Park Lane Hotel, with Costes and his glamorous wife making a splash as well-known refugees, while I established my identity as a shady trader from Quebec for whom wartime shortages meant profit, not poverty. Costes began sending the Germans communiqués cleared by U.S. and Allied sources through a series of mail drops in Lisbon and Portugal. All messages were written using invisible ink that was only revealed well inside Germany. Costes's messages included information about Allied troop movements, secrets that looked great but were actually harmless. Then, when the time seemed right, we told Costes to ask the Germans to send over Cavaillez.

He did, but they didn't, at least not right away.

The problem was Cavaillez. We got word from our European sources that Cavaillez's wife was about to have a baby, and he was starting to get cold feet about "covert ops"—operations that have a classified objective. The Germans wanted him to take off for the States, but he kept putting them off, saying he wanted to wait until after his baby was born.

This set off a small panic in Washington. The original date for the invasion—which would later be postponed—was getting closer and closer, and we needed Cavaillez here!

Connolly came up with a brilliant solution. We had just begun firebombing Germany's big industrial cities, and the effect on German morale was devastating. So we slipped information as to where and when the next firebomb attack would occur in one of Costes's communiqués ... making sure that it didn't reach his contacts until *after* the attack. At that point, of course, it wouldn't be information, it would be history. And not worth a damn.

The plan worked exactly as we hoped. The Germans got the communiqué just after the firebombing of Hamburg, and realized that if Cavaillez had been in America to send the information by radio, they would have gotten it in time to use it.

Within days, our reluctant spy, Jean-Paul Cavaillez, was on his way to New York. To our dismay, however, getting Cavaillez here was only half the battle. Once in New York the s.o.b. *stayed* reluctant, going for weeks without contacting Costes.

At first, we thought Cavaillez was just being cautious. After a while, however, we realized that his reluctance wasn't caution—he was taking a vacation!

Tall, athletic, and handsome, Cavaillez was a bit of a ladies' man, and was taking full advantage of his time away from war-torn Europe—and his wife. He went out with one woman after another, night after night. Finally, we decided that if the mountain wouldn't come to Costes, Costes would have to go mountaineering.

Cavaillez, if not a devout Catholic, was a practicing one. In fact, the only time he spent away from the ladies was at Sunday Mass. One morning at church, he was surprised to see Dieudonné Costes sitting only a few pews away. As much as Cavaillez might have liked to, he couldn't ignore him. The party was over. It was time to begin work.

Our first step was to help Cavaillez set up his radio so he could begin transmitting. As a black marketeer, it was my job to find the technical parts he needed and smooth the way in other areas like lodging, luxuries, income, whatever. None of this was hard, of course, because I was being given everything I needed by the FBI. But we couldn't let Cavaillez know that, so I had to go to great lengths to make it all *look* hard.

I set him up in a mansion on Long Island, which I claimed was the summer home of a rich industrialist I had worked with in the black market. Cavaillez loved it. The house was well out on the Island, on the shore, and gave him a straight, unobstructed shot for broadcasting to Germany. It made his job both easier and safer, as there appeared less likelihood that the U.S. authorities would pick up his signal.

We didn't want Cavaillez to get his radio together until we were ready for him, so I kept putting him off, making up stories about how I couldn't get hold of some of the critical parts. Throughout this time, Costes and I continued to send the Germans, via mail drop, verifiable but harmless communiqués about Allied troop movements, maintaining our credibility without hurting the war effort. We made it seem as though Costes was getting his information directly from the Pentagon, which—according to our setup—was questioning him about German fortifications in France. This allowed Costes and I to head down to Washington from time to time without Cavaillez, so we could be debriefed.

Suddenly, in late May of 1944, Connolly gave the word to provide Cavaillez with the last radio parts he needed. It was just before the Allied invasion of Europe. We had been laying the groundwork for this operation for over a year. Now, finally, it was time to *act*.

Once the radio was in place, we went straight for the jugular. The actual invasion was to occur on the beaches of Normandy, in the north of France right across the Channel from England. But the Bureau sent messages, using Cavaillez's radio, which claimed that the invasion was to take place in the *south* of France, on the Mediterranean.

In retrospect, this seems transparently false. With the 20/20 hindsight of history, the armchair tactician can easily see that England was the best place for the Allies to amass troops and that the Channel offered the shortest route to Europe—of course the invasion would take place in the north.

At the time, however, things were not so clear. The northern coast of France was heavily fortified, and—as was sadly proven by D day—an invading force there would pay a heavy cost in terms of lives. Added to that was the fact that the Allies had successfully invaded Italy, and a second southern invasion might easily join forces with the first, creating an imposing phalanx that could then push northward.

The Germans bought our story. It's impossible to say how many German troops were diverted south because of the Bureau's broadcasts. But it's known that the German high command expected the invasion to take place there, and it is certain that one critical aspect of D day's success was the fact that it took the Nazis by surprise.

Meanwhile, working undercover was becoming increasingly wearing. I was living a lie, plain and simple, twenty-four hours a day. Lying about my philosophy, my hopes, my dreams. Everything. And always worrying about slipping up. Even asleep I worried, afraid that if I shared a room, I might mumble something in the middle of the night that would give me away.

It drove me nuts. I was losing weight. My health started to go. The pressure was so bad, I literally lost my hair over it. When I started the operation I had as thick a mop as anyone; but when it ended, I was as bald as I am today.

What made things even worse was that I had gotten to *like* Cavaillez. That seems an odd thing to say about a Nazi, but Cavaillez didn't really go for the whole "Master Race" bit. More than anything, he was a German patriot. And, strange as it sounds, I found the fact that he truly believed in something—no matter what it was—refreshing. The clandestine world of double and triple agents is a landscape where lies are so complex that truth disappears, shrouded in a fog of vague motives and uncertain loyalties. It is a place without honor, without morality, without trust. It's an environment in which Costes thrived, precisely *because* he had no real loyalties. I could work with Costes, but I could never respect him. On the other hand, Cavaillez was someone with whom I could never work, but had to respect.

Cavaillez's arrest was scheduled for five in the morning, a few days after he had made his last radio transmission to Germany. We allowed him only one broadcast. Then the FBI took it away from him and sent the message indicating the invasion would be in southern France. Early morning is always the best time for a bust. People caught in their sleep are tentative, unaware, and usually harmless. Since Connolly wanted to maintain my cover, it was decided that I would stay away from the fireworks. My job was to take Cavaillez out the evening before and get him as drunk as I could, so that he would put up as little resistance as possible when the men from the Bureau showed up the next morning with handcuffs.

It was tough. I was glad to fight against Cavaillez's cause but I hated to deceive him personally. I felt even worse when, after a number of drinks, Cavaillez started to go on about how much he liked and trusted me. He even told me that at espionage school in Hamburg he had learned a technique to test someone's honesty. The test involved asking a series of personal and philosophical questions a number of times, varying the questions slightly each time, checking the subject's consistency. And that I had passed with flying colors. I had never wavered, he said, smiling and slapping me on the back. If only he knew, I thought.

A few days later, he did.

After Cavaillez was arrested, he refused to talk, so Connolly decided to break my cover and bring me in to question him. The interrogation took place in the FBI offices in New York. Cavaillez was sitting at a long table and smiled when he saw me walk in, glad to see what he thought was a friendly face. Then he frowned slightly, saddened by the thought that I must have been arrested, too. He greeted me warmly. I didn't say anything, just sat across from him and put my FBI credentials on the table between us. He looked at them for the longest time. Then he threw my I.D. card across the room and put his head in his hands.

"You and I are in a tough business," I said. "It would be easy for our positions to be reversed. The unfortunate thing, though, is that only one of us can be on the right side. I happen to think that's the side I'm on."

Suddenly, the Prussian in Cavaillez came out. He stood up, almost at attention. There were tears in his eyes. I thought, "Christ, get a grip." Then I realized that there were tears in my eyes as well. I stood up and shook his hand, then we sat back down. And from that point on Cavaillez talked.

I spent the rest of the war as a special assistant to E. J. Connolly. I was settling in for what I assumed would be a long and fruitful career with the Bureau. But once again, my plans and my life had nothing to do with each other. Only this time it wasn't an opportunity that changed everything—it was a near tragedy. Yvette was stricken, suddenly and violently, with tuberculosis.

The doctors felt it was important that once her sputum tested negative, she move out of New York and into a quieter, more restful environment, so she could fully recuperate. Everyone agreed the perfect place was Waterville, Maine, where we still had family. But the closest FBI office to Waterville was in Boston, which would have been an impossible commute for me, especially since I was still caring for Yvette.

The answer to our problem was supplied by J. Edgar Hoover himself. Hoover, aware of the situation, created an office right there in Waterville, with me as its only resident agent.

In later years, Hoover and I did have our differences, particularly after I recruited mob figures Johnny Rosselli and Sam Giancana for an extremely hush-hush CIA plot to assassinate Fidel Castro, his brother Raul, and his closest associate, Che Guevara. Hoover wanted to debrief me about what I might have learned concerning Johnny and Sam's "business ventures." I turned him down flat. The work we did on the CIA plot was classified, and unless the Company instructed me otherwise, I wasn't even going to admit it had happened, let alone blab about conversations that occurred in the course of it. Needless to say, my position did not please Hoover. In fact, he became extremely annoyed. But no matter what he did to me then, I felt indebted to him because of the way he'd helped me and my family when we needed it most.

Unfortunately, despite the best of intentions, life in Waterville was just plain dull. Considering my past experiences with the FBI, my days were void of excitement. Occasionally, I'd catch a draft dodger. That was about it. At one point, it was so bad that I called Ed Souci, who headed the FBI office in Boston, and pleaded for something to do.

Finally, I could no longer shake the idea that I was taking advantage of the Bureau. It ate at me until I finally decided to leave the FBI behind and enter private business.

This was the time when, according to some sources, I helped start up the CIA. I will say now, categorically, that I did *not* help to start up the CIA. I knew many of the men who did, but I was not working with them at the Agency's inception. I sure wish I had been, though. It would have saved me a hell of a lot of money.

Instead, I created Dairy Dream Farms, Inc.

My plan was to start up a canned-cream business with a new technology that I felt would revolutionize the industry. Despite an overwhelmingly positive reaction to the product from food distributors, the technology wasn't quite what I had hoped. A foul-up in the canning process caused the spoilage of nearly all our cream, ruining us overnight. I didn't just lose my shirt on Dairy Dream, I lost my shirt, a suit, and two pairs of pants. Not to mention my house, my life savings, and another hundred thou or so in loans. Simply put, Dairy Dream was a disaster. Everyone told me to declare bankruptcy. I knew it would have gotten me out of my debts, but my pride wouldn't let me do it. I was determined, no matter how long it took or what sacrifices I had to make, to pay everyone back.

J. Edgar Hoover came to my aid and recommended me for a

job as director of security and compliance at the Small Defense Plants Administration. When this agency became the Small Business Administration, I was promoted to special assistant to the administrator. Although I was making an excellent salary, we lived very frugally in an effort to repay my outstanding debts. Yvette and I figured out that—given the nature of government pay raises—we would finally pay back all we owed by the time we both hit seventy. For the next five years I toiled away, paying my debts bit by bit and dreaming of better things. Then, in 1954, those "better things" were made possible by a lucky game of craps.

I was at a party for ex-FBI agents. There were quite a few of us in Washington then, and we made a point of keeping in touch and having dinner together in one of the local hotels. Anyway, on this particular night we started playing craps, and for some reason I couldn't lose. Believe me, *I tried.* It's embarrassing when you're gambling with friends and you're the only one winning. The game went on and on. I wanted to go home, but you can't when everyone there owes you money. We finally stopped around two or three in the morning. By then, I had won $800 in cash, as well as a marker for $2,800 by the night's big loser, Jim McInerny, who was the assistant attorney general, in charge of the Criminal Division, for the Department of Justice.

I told Jim that I'd settle for ten cents on the dollar. His debt was just *too* big; this was supposed to have been a friendly game. But Jim wouldn't hear of it. "If the positions were reversed," he told me, "I'd insist that you pay me the entire amount. You better learn right now that gambling debts are one thing that you always pay. If you can't afford to pay, don't play," he insisted, and the next day he gave me the entire sum. That very same day I talked to Yvette, and together we decided that I should use this sudden windfall to start the business I had been dreaming of: a private consulting firm geared toward the solving of what might be termed "sensitive" problems.

And so, with $2,800 won in an illegal craps game from the nation's chief criminal prosecutor, Robert A. Maheu Associates was born. Almost immediately, I began working for the CIA. I must stress the *almost* because before the Agency would let me handle anything, it made a demand—I had to divest myself of any connection with the Kennedys. Even then, there was a deep animosity between the CIA and the Kennedy clan, something that went back to the early fifties and that revolved, at least at its inception, around Senator Joseph McCarthy. It wasn't the Kennedys who were fighting McCarthyism. It was the CIA, otherwise known as "the Company." Let me explain.

Shortly after I formed Maheu Associates, Jim O'Connell and Bob Cunningham, who had worked with me in the FBI and were now CIA agents, wanted me to perform "cut-out" operations for the Agency—i.e., those jobs with which the Company could not be officially connected.

At that time, however, I shared an office with Carmine Bellino, an ex-FBI agent who had created a very successful practice as both a CPA and an investigator. For years, Carmine had been a close associate of old Joe Kennedy, serving as both his personal accountant and private gumshoe. Now that the Kennedy boys were coming of age, Carmine began doing the same for them. And young Bobby—who fifteen years later would be thought of as a liberal White Knight—had started his career working as Joseph McCarthy's assistant counsel, outranked on McCarthy's staff only by the infamous Roy Cohn.

Because of Bobby, the CIA told me that if I were to work with the Agency, I would have to move away from Carmine and any possible Kennedy connection. I said I couldn't afford to move out. So the Company put me on a monthly retainer of $500, thereby becoming my first steady client and enabling me to move into an office of my own.

The CIA's dislike of McCarthy was admirable, but not without self-interest. To its credit, the Agency recognized he was evil and acted accordingly. But this was when McCarthy was going after the Department of State like a dog after a bone. State was run by John Foster Dulles. The CIA was run by his brother, Allen. Like much in politics, the CIA's ideological stand was built upon a very personal foundation.

In spite of the monthly retainer it was giving me, my first job for the CIA was not something it brought to me; instead, it was something I brought to it. The office I had rented with my $500 a month was a nondescript suite not far from the White House. I saw myself as a problem solver, someone who could handle business dilemmas the same way intelligence agencies deal with problems of national security. Much of my success was based on contacts within the FBI-CIA old-boy circuit, which I used for inside information in delicate or clandestine matters. My first project would put my talents to the test.

One day in 1954, a secretive Englishman appeared at my new offices. His name was L.E.P. Taylor, a London solicitor who was involved in a delicate situation concerning international businessmen, a foreign country, and secret negotiations.

Taylor had talked to Robert Gresham, another ex-FBI agent and an old friend of mine who was working for the U.S. Chamber of Commerce. Bob knew I needed work. He also knew that I was the perfect man for Taylor's needs. So he gave Taylor my name and a strong recommendation.

When Taylor called, I was in Boston. My secretary, Peggy O'Neil, excitedly left several messages at my hotel saying that an English attorney was chomping at the bit to see me, but that I was *not* to call him. We had to meet face to face, immediately.

I took the next plane to Washington. When I arrived at my office late that night, Peggy was still there. She called the mysterious Mr. Taylor at his hotel and he came around at once. He was quintessentially British—impeccably dressed, unfailingly polite, and unerringly competent. Taylor needed someone who could make sure the critical impact of his client's dilemma was brought to the attention of the American government.

Taylor, however, refused to identify his client, wanting to reach an agreement first. I would later learn it was Stavros Niarchos, the brother-in-law and bitter rival of Aristotle Onassis, a name unknown to most Americans in 1954 and only vaguely familiar to me.

"Mr. Onassis," Taylor said, "has signed a contract with the Saudi Arabian government, giving him exclusive rights to ship all the oil exported from the country. The contracts have been signed, ratified, and publicized." Then he asked if I thought I could find a way to deep-six the contract and make sure that no oil was ever shipped under the agreement. Frankly, I wasn't sure. But I told Taylor to give me a $500 retainer and I would let him know the next day whether or not I would take the case.

The implications of Onassis's contract, known as the "Jiddah Agreement," were enormous. After some checking, I learned that the Saudis were on the verge of becoming the world's largest oil producer, and their agreement with Onassis would effectively give him control of nearly 45 percent of all the oil reserves on earth. Unchecked, he could have gained an unprecedented amount of power and wealth, pulling off—as an individual—the very thing Saddam Hussein recently attempted when he invaded Kuwait.

The comparison between Onassis and Hussein is not as far-fetched as people might think. Onassis may not have possessed the full range of villainy Hussein is known for, but he certainly was the world's first "oil gangster," using bribery, intimidation, and suspect associations to gain control over global oil reserves.

Eventually, Onassis would become known as a jet-setter, a man whose fortune brought him into the world of music, culture, and Jacqueline Kennedy. But I saw a much darker side of Onassis, a rapaciousness and greed so destructive that Niarchos was willing to do anything to stop him.

I realized the only way I could pull off what Taylor wanted was to get the U.S. government behind me and make it a cut-out operation of the CIA. So the next morning I called Jim O'Connell, my contact at the Company, and went over the case with him. He was definitely intrigued. But he felt that before bringing in the Company, we should get strong backing elsewhere in government, preferably from the National Security Council.

When I told Taylor I would take the job, he gave me $6,000 in cash (a lot of money in those days) and a copy of the contract between Onassis and the Saudis. But he still wouldn't tell me who my client was, saying only that we would meet again in New York in ten days.

The first thing I did was hire a writer, a few researchers, and some ex-FBI agents to help me with the case. I wanted to know every detail about Onassis and the Saudis, and I wanted to be able to present our findings to the government in a way that was convincing.

We studied the contract and learned that Onassis's deal to ship all Saudi oil was not effective immediately. But as the ships currently carrying Saudi oil became obsolete, they would be replaced exclusively by Onassis. In time, everyone—even ARAMCO, the powerful consortium of American oil companies (Standard Oil of California, Mobil, Exxon, and Texaco)—would have to turn to Onassis to ship Saudi oil.

Onassis's reason for signing the agreement was obvious. The contract would mean a personal profit of $18 million at the end of the first year. In less than five years, his annual net profits would be in excess of $200 million. These figures may not seem that great in today's inflationary world, but in the 1950s they were staggering.

Yet the financial implications paled in comparison to Onassis's potential power. By regulating the chief source of energy in an oil-dependent world, Onassis would become one of the most powerful men alive, capable of bringing whole governments to their knees.

But why would the Saudis want to cut their own throats?

The answer was that the Saudi king had been conned. I was sure that someone in the Saudi hierarchy was making a very large personal profit off Onassis's contract; that Onassis had not made this sweetheart deal with the Saudis on his own. His help, I learned, had come from Spyridon Catapodis, another Greek dabbling in ships and oil. Catapodis, it turned out, was a key figure in negotiating with the Saudi ministers, including Sheikh Abdullah Al Suleiman Al Hamdan, the powerful finance minister. But eventually, Onassis cut Catapodis out of the deal, asking Dr. Hjalmar Schacht to take over negotiations with the Saudis. Schacht was an ex-Nazi who had worked with Hitler during the war as president of the German Reichsbank and who was eventually tried for war crimes at Nuremberg. After serving a jail sentence, Hjalmar began advising the Moslem world, which labeled him "the medicine man of high finance." He was the perfect combination of skill and corruption needed to serve Onassis well.

When it was time for me to meet again with Taylor, we were joined by Ambrose Capparis. Capparis—like Onassis—was Niarchos's brother-in-law. Niarchos, however, trusted Capparis.

From Capparis, I learned that Niarchos had decided to stop Onassis's deal with the Saudis at any cost. At that moment, it amounted to $20,000—the next advance on my fee, and again in cash. Much of that, of course, would go toward expenses. Even so, it was more than I had actually expected. We agreed that when I was ready to provide ideas to block the contract, I would fly to London and finally meet with Niarchos.

Four weeks later, John Gerrity—one of the researchers I had hired and a wonderfully talented writer—and I were ready to present our case to the National Security Council. We approached ex-FBI agent Scotty McLeod, who was Eisenhower's director of security and consular affairs at the State Department. McLeod was also a good friend of Richard Nixon, who, as vice president, was a main player on the National Security Council.

Scotty made a call, and a day or so later Gerrity and I found ourselves in Nixon's office, telling him about the Jiddah Agreement and doing our damnedest to make it clear how disastrous an impact the Onassis-Saudi deal might have on both the U.S. economy and its national security.

This was my first "mano-a-mano" with Richard Nixon. In the years that followed, our paths would cross again and again, via Hughes and, finally, through Watergate. While I always found Nixon to be cordial, I can't say I ever really warmed to him. His close friends—men like Scotty McLeod during the fifties and, years later, Dick Danner, who worked with me in Las Vegas and introduced Nixon to Bebe Rebozo—swore that in private he was as warm and friendly as any man you could ever meet. Away from his cronies, however, Nixon seemed stiff and awkward.

Nevertheless, I was impressed with how fast Nixon grasped the significance of the Onassis deal. The importance of oil is self-evident today; in those days, when oil was taken for granted, you had to have a degree of foresight to see it. Nixon had plenty. In my opinion, he was one of the brightest politicians of this century. He realized at once that there was no way we could let this agreement stand, and pledged his support, saying that he would bring it up at the next Security Council meeting.

Gerrity and I were thrilled. It was an emotion that would not last long, however, for as Nixon walked us to the door, he went over the top in his response. I would later learn it wasn't uncommon.

"If it turns out we have to kill the bastard," he said in hushed tones, "just don't do it on American soil."

When he closed the door, Gerrity and I stood there a moment, the wind suddenly knocked out of us.

"*Kill* the bastard?" we mouthed silently.

Neither one of us had even considered it. And, to be fair, I don't think Nixon really had, either. It was just something to say, something that sounded tough and showed his resolve. But it was,

45

to say the least, unwise. And it showed a lack of discretion that would haunt him throughout his career.

We prepared thirteen copies of our report and Nixon presented them to the National Security Council. The impact was immediate. The State Department denounced the agreement, with over a dozen other nations following suit. Shortly after that, my contacts at the CIA authorized me to tell Niarchos that from now on the Company would be clandestinely involved.

It was essential, though, that I work strictly as a cut-out, allowing the U.S. full deniability, because if our government was seen acting against the Saudis, ARAMCO might be thrown out of the country. All of which meant that if anything went wrong, I had no official standing ... and no protection. But I didn't mind. I was still only thirty-six years old and, as I said before, I've never been able to turn down anything that smacked of adventure. With the Company behind me, I hired a private detective to wiretap Onassis's telephones in New York City. Then John Gerrity and I flew off to London to meet with Stavros Niarchos.

Niarchos is a handsome man, with movie-star looks. His manners and dress were errorless, and he spoke English with only a slight accent. Our first "breakfast meeting" in his sumptuous suite at Claridge's in London went on all day long, through lunch, dinner, and beyond, as we went over the contract and our plans in minute detail.

Our primary efforts were directed at discrediting Onassis before the Saudi government. Toward that end, the most important discovery we made in our research was the confirmation of my suspicions: a high official in the Saudi government, a man close to King Saud himself, had accepted a million-dollar bribe from Onassis in exchange for the contract. Discreet contacts within the country suggested that the money had been deposited in a Swiss bank account by the official who accepted it. But we didn't have a clue as to who the official was.

As our "breakfast meeting" went into the night, Niarchos showed no sign of tiring. Finally, on the stroke of midnight, Niarchos clapped his hands and said, "All right. Let's all have a shot of brandy, go out on the terrace, relax, and then start talking again to make sure we haven't missed anything." And that's what we did, until four o'clock in the morning. This was my first time working with Greeks. I've loved them ever since. They are ambitious, tough-minded, industrious, and they do their homework.

Almost everything I did during the Onassis project I reported to the Company. There was always a CIA man who contacted me wherever I was, to kick back information to Washington and the National Security Council.

My staff of researchers and I devoured every bit of information we could about Saudi Arabia. In the course of our investigation into the area, we came across a book titled *Saudi Arabia* by a man named Karl Twitchell. His knowledge of the region made him a natural choice for our team. Twitchell was a mining engineer who had gone to Arabia in the early 1930s to help King Ibn Saud exploit mining properties. He became close friends with the old ruler, and helped set up the consortium that eventually became ARAMCO. Twitchell had a unique relationship with the Saudis, and I knew he could help us. Once Twitchell learned of the potential impact of Onassis's agreement, he quickly agreed, easily making his way back into the country.

The CIA had a telephone installed in my old wreck of an auto. This was thirty years before cellular technology, so I have no doubt that the phone was worth more than the car. I had car phones for another twenty years, but I never got used to them. They seem invasive, always ringing at the wrong time.

A perfect example was one Sunday in Washington, soon after Twitchell left for Arabia. Yvette and I were driving home from church when the telephone rang. It was Niarchos's brother-in-law Ambrose Capparis, calling from New York.

"Where the hell have you been?" he shouted over the phone.

"At Mass," I said. That changed his tone.

"Please, you have to go straight to the airport," he continued, politely now. "We have to leave for Athens immediately. Stavros just called. It's an emergency."

After racing home to quickly pack, Yvette and I discovered we had only a hundred dollars in cash between us. It was Sunday, decades before automatic teller machines, so there was no way to withdraw more. Finding cash in Europe wouldn't be much easier. To top it off, I also had no idea how long I would be gone. When I told Capparis on the plane how much cash I had, he took pity on me and fronted me a couple hundred more—pocket change, to the company I was keeping.

We rushed to meet Niarchos on his yacht, the *Creole*. But as we came on board, he stared at Capparis and me with surprise.

"What the hell are you two doing here?"

He had actually forgotten that he had sent for us!

The emergency, though, was real enough. Karl Twitchell's wife had suddenly taken ill and left Saudi Arabia for the States. In a few weeks, Twitchell would join her. It was imperative that I go to Saudi Arabia and attempt to have a meeting with the king while Twitchell was still there.

Since the U.S. government couldn't acknowledge my presence, it could do nothing to help get the appropriate papers. As a result, I spent two weeks in Athens trying to get a visa for Saudi Arabia, all the while attempting to run down documentation that might provide proof of the bribe. It wasn't long before there was little left of my $300, so Capparis gave me an extra $10,000, all in $100 bills.

Eventually, I gave up on getting a Saudi visa in Greece, and decided to go to Beirut, hoping it would be easier to get one there. I did have one problem in leaving Athens, however—or, rather, ten thousand of them. When I had arrived, I had only declared the $300, and I still had most of the $10,000 left.

At the American military commissary I purchased a jumbo

shaving cream tube, the kind used before aerosol cans. Then I emptied most of the cream from the tube and shoved rolled-up $100 bills into the little hole at the end, and packed the now extremely valuable tube in my shaving kit.

Fortunately, the customs officers in Athens didn't look hard at my toiletries. When I checked into my Beirut hotel, I started literally laundering my money. It took hours to get the ten grand out of the tube, wash it off, and then hang it around the room to dry.

In Beirut, I had to get some inoculations, and went to the American Hospital. When I arrived, I saw long lines of children waiting for treatment. I asked a doctor what was going on. It turned out that it cost twenty-five cents a shot to immunize the kids. Usually donations covered the costs, but in this instance donations had run out. And these kids would be left without immunization.

"How many of them are there?" I asked, meaning the kids.

"About two thousand, I suppose."

"Well, give them the shots," I said, and handed him $500 in cash. Very clean cash, I might add. I had never had that kind of money before, but I have to say that spending it this way felt even better than having it.

The gesture benefited me in other ways, too. At the hotel where I was staying, word spread about what I had done, and the workers there warmed to me. One of them heard that I was trying to get a visa for Saudi Arabia, and since I had helped his people, he decided to help me. He told me that a Saudi prince who might be able to pull strings for me dined at the hotel every evening at eight.

I met with my CIA contact in Beirut, and was given the okay to feel things out with the prince. That night, I struck up a conversation with the youthful aristocrat, and we immediately liked each other. He, too, had heard about my good deed at the hospital. A few days later, he personally took me to the Saudi embassy and made the necessary arrangements for my visa.

I landed in Saudi Arabia at five in the morning, and was

amazed to see a large crowd at the airport. In those days, there were so few flights in that country that the arrival or departure of a plane was something to go out and see. Even at that hour, the heat was oppressive. Swarms of flies crawled over people's faces, so many and so persistent that most didn't even bother to brush them away.

Real trouble came in customs. Air France had given me a gift on an earlier flight that I thought was perfume. It turned out to be a package of miniature bottles of booze. At the sight of the bottles, all hell broke loose. The weather isn't the only thing that's dry in Saudi Arabia. Possessing liquor is not only illegal, it's a mortal sin— absolutely forbidden by Islamic law. I was taken off to a little room and questioned by police, who were intent on throwing me in jail. But, thank God, before I arrived in Saudi Arabia, I had arranged for Karl Twitchell to meet me at the airport. With a few quick words, Twitchell explained everything and saved me from a quick trip to prison.

Saudi Arabia then was like something out of *Lawrence of Arabia*. My hotel was magnificent, with thick Oriental carpets covering all the floors. But I was appalled to see the Arab guests there spit on those beautiful rugs. Looking at all the wealth and splendor, it was easy to forget that they were barely a generation away from living in tents.

Twitchell immediately started to arrange a meeting for us with King Saud. With help from Onassis's ex-associate Catapodis and a private investigator whom Niarchos had hired in Europe, I had gathered enough documentation to prove that the bribed official was Ali Alireza. Alireza was the brother of the Saudi minister of commerce and a close friend of the finance minister, Sheikh Abdullah Al Suleiman Al Hamdan. According to Catapodis, all three men had conspired to put through the Onassis deal. We couldn't prove the case against all of them, but we felt we had Ali Alireza dead to rights.

My confidence was shaken a bit, though, when I saw King Saud in a parade that passed directly beneath my hotel window that afternoon. Standing arm in arm with Saud in an open limousine was none other than Ali Alireza—the very man I planned to say had sold the Saudis down the river for a cool million. I suddenly wasn't so sure King Saud would believe us. When the call for the meeting came from Twitchell, there was no time for further preparation or second-guessing. The good news was that we had been granted an appointment; the bad news was that it was with Sheikh Suleiman, the finance minister, rather than with the king himself. That worried me. If I was going to accuse the king's own ministers of graft, I wanted to at least be able to say it to his face.

Adding to my concerns was the fact that the U.S. ambassador to Saudi Arabia told Twitchell that after he introduced me, he was to stay out of the conversation. No one even vaguely connected to the United States could support my claims. I was to be all alone in my assertions. It felt damned lonely. If the Saudis believed me, I would be fine. But if they didn't—well, let's just say I was starting to wonder what sort of creature comforts there were in Saudi jails.

Suleiman's palace was on the outskirts of Jiddah, surrounded by nothing but desert. It was huge and ostentatious, the apotheosis of nouveau riche. Inside, we were greeted by King Saud's confidential assistant, who spoke perfect English. With him was Sheikh Suleiman. Both wore traditional robes. The four of us sat in a huge room together, Twitchell and I on a small settee, Suleiman and the king's assistant in ornate chairs.

Suleiman was tall and slender, with a strong, aquiline nose. The king's assistant was classically handsome, with dark penetrating eyes. We spent four hours together. Twitchell stayed out of the whole thing. He introduced me, then shut up, leaving me to either hang myself ... or save us all.

Throughout the meeting, the assistant kept stepping out of the room for a moment, always returning with some new questions.

51

Though I couldn't prove it, I was certain that the king was in another room eavesdropping. The way the meeting developed, I was glad he was. The more I talked about the payoffs, the more I became convinced that my fear about Suleiman was true. As I talked, he stared at me with eyes full of venom. I couldn't prove Suleiman was involved in the conspiracy, but—as with my feeling that the king was elsewhere in the palace—I sure as hell sensed it.

Fortunately, whoever the assistant kept talking to bought my arguments. What really did the trick was the documentation I presented regarding the million-dollar Swiss bank account. I showed it to Saud's assistant, who hurried off with it into the back room. While he was gone, Suleiman did little more than sit and stare.

A minute or so later, the assistant returned. "His Excellency is most grateful to you for having come here," he said. "He wants to think the situation over. I will be at your hotel tomorrow to tell you what action he plans to take."

While I still had no idea where I stood, I was relieved that King Saud's assistant, rather than his finance minister, would continue to play go-between. I didn't sleep at all that night, worrying about the king's decision. The fact that I *still* didn't have an exit visa didn't help ease my edginess. Without one, there was no getting out.

At noon the next day, Saud's assistant called. I met him in the lobby.

"His Excellency instructed me to thank you for your visit to our country, and to give you your exit visa," he said, handing it to me. "His Excellency also instructed me to tell you he would be pleased if this story about the payoff were to become known in the world press. But it must begin in a foreign country, neutral to both the United States and Saudi Arabia. It is important that this happen as soon as possible; though, of course, you are welcome to stay in our country as long as you like," he added, smiling slyly.

My only reply was, "When is the next plane out?"

I thought that breaking the story in Europe would be the easiest thing in the world. It wasn't. No news agency or magazine in

Europe would touch it. Onassis was known as a man who got back at those who crossed him, and no one in the media wanted to take that chance.

Just when I was starting to think we'd never get the damned story to the public, Niarchos called me from his yacht.

"I have a solution to your problem," he said.

He convinced the media the old-fashioned way—he bought them. Niarchos gave a "loan" of $75,000 to the publishers of an Athens newspaper on the condition that they print the story.

Once the bribe was made known, King Saud got out of the contract with Onassis without losing face. Onassis's dreams of an oil monopoly were dashed forever. Niarchos breathed a sigh of relief—as did ARAMCO, the U.S. government, and dozens of other countries reliant on Saudi oil.

Onassis didn't learn about the part I played in helping bring down his plans until long afterward, but I was pleased by his response when he did. Spyridon Catapodis, the man who had helped Onassis make the deal and then helped me break it, called to say that Onassis was so impressed with what I had done that he wanted to *hire* me. It was an easy offer to refuse, but it still made me smile. When your own enemies want you to work for them, you know you've done your job.

Later, Stavros Niarchos and I met for a victory dinner in Washington. It was quite a night, filled with laughter, good food, and a lot of Dom Pérignon champagne. After the wine had loosened us up a bit, Niarchos decided to teach me a lesson: "Bob, you're one of the most imaginative, gutsiest guys I know. But you're also the worst businessman I've ever met."

"What do you mean?" I asked.

"When I called you to Athens and convinced you to go to Saudi Arabia, I was prepared to offer you anything ... a half-a-million, a million—all you had to do was name it. But you never asked for an extra penny."

"Well," I ventured, "it's never too late."

"Yes, it is," he said, grinning. "If I gave it to you now, you'd never learn. But I'll tell you what—I don't like that little house you live in."

That took me off guard, because he had never been there. I had no idea he even knew where I lived.

"If you'll get a house that's, shall we say, commensurate with your talents, and if you'll buy a new Cadillac instead of driving that junker you use, I will give you a fifty-thousand-dollar bonus, at the rate of fifteen hundred a month. I can't give it to you all at once, because then you'd probably just bank it like a good American instead of spending it."

I bought a split-level in Sleepy Hollow, Virginia, where I added a swimming pool and a paddle tennis court. And, yes, I bought the Cadillac, a dark blue beauty with four doors.

Working with Niarchos, I had been introduced to a whole new world, where wealth is measured in millions and where power is judged not by the people, but by the *countries* you can influence. As rarefied as the air seemed with Niarchos, it was about to get even headier, as I started work for the man who would change my life forever ... Howard Hughes.

Chapter Two

WORKING FOR "THE MAN"

I DIDN'T EVEN KNOW WHO I WAS WORKING FOR AT FIRST.

Robert A. Maheu Associates was growing faster than I had ever expected. I was in the middle of a number of cases when I received a call from Seymour Mintz, a senior partner at Ed Williams's former Washington law firm, Hogan & Hartson.

Mintz, a tax attorney, had a client who needed some inside information regarding the CIA, and Ed Williams had told him about my contacts with the Company, so Mintz called.

Mintz probably told me even less than he'd told Ed. All he would say was that a nameless client needed information regarding an individual named Stuart Cramer and his relationship, or lack thereof, with the Agency. Cramer had been making claims that he was a CIA operative, and Mintz's client wanted to know if it was true.

I gave Jim O'Connell a call, and quickly learned that while Cramer might at one time have had a very tenuous connection to the CIA, he was certainly never an operative. The whole thing probably took me an afternoon, most of which was spent waiting for Jim to call me back.

I then called Mintz and told him what I had learned. He thanked me and paid me a fair, but by no means impressive, sum for my efforts. And that was it. I never gave the job a second thought, as it was easily forgotten among many more important projects.

What I didn't know was that the client Mintz was calling for was none other than Howard Hughes. Nor did I know then that this Cramer fellow I investigated was Jean Peters's first husband. At the time, Hughes was pursuing Jean. Though separated from Jean, Cramer had been edging his way back into her life, a move Hughes wanted to nip in the bud.

When it came to women, Howard Hughes was obsessive, and—I learned later—would go to any length to maintain his control over them. If you're wondering why Hughes would hire a man like Seymour Mintz, a tax attorney, to handle this sort of personal work, just remember ... to a man as rich as Hughes, nothing's more personal than taxes. A shift in his tax structure could mean as much in money earned or lost as all his other business efforts combined. So the men who handled Hughes's taxes were counted among his most intimate and trusted advisors.

Apparently, the information I provided about Cramer paid off, because a few months later Mintz called and offered me another job, this time identifying his client as Howard Hughes.

I have to admit that even though I had worked for and against some powerful men, I was impressed. At that time, no name carried the same aura of wealth and influence as Howard Hughes. Today, Howard is remembered for being the world's most famous recluse. But in the early and mid-fifties he was known as the "billionaire playboy," a mythic figure who ran airlines, designed and flew airplanes, made movies, swayed presidents, and wooed starlets, all at the same time. The truth was that he'd already begun to retreat into a self-imposed isolation, to fall prey to the neurotic obsessions that would plague him for the rest of his life. Back then, though, all I knew was the glamorous image of the man.

The job Mintz offered me was not my standard work. He wanted me to head up a surveillance team and keep watch on Ava

Gardner while she stayed at the Cal-Neva Lodge in Lake Tahoe. Ava was going through a tumultuous divorce from Frank Sinatra, whose despair over the breakup was so great that he'd reportedly attempted suicide. Ava had to stay in Nevada long enough to establish residence in order to receive her divorce. My job was to find out if any men visited her and what her relationship with them might be ... especially if one of those men was Sinatra.

What made this scenario classic Hughes was that at the same time, Howard was actually courting Jean Peters. His relationship with Ava Gardner was never very serious. She even later said publicly that she'd never really liked him. It didn't matter, though, how Ava felt; Howard was determined to keep tabs on her.

Howard never viewed relationships the way most people do. There were women he kept locked away as virtual prisoners inside Hollywood apartments, who he never even visited, watched day and night by small armies of bodyguards. Clearly, when it came to relationships, Howard was more interested in control than in romance.

In fact, it was control that mattered most to Howard in every relationship, business or personal. This proved true with Noah Dietrich, Howard's closest advisor for over thirty years, whom he fired unfairly during a petulant rage in 1957. And, thirteen years later, it would prove true again—with me.

Eavesdropping on Ava Gardner was not my idea of a good time. As my lawyer friends say, "I don't do divorces." Nor would I take on any of the jobs usually associated with "private eyes." The investigative work Robert A. Maheu Associates undertook was of far greater scope than merely finding out "who's sleeping with whom."

But this wasn't just anyone asking me to spy on Ava Gardner. And, as I said, I was impressed. So I made an exception. It was a mistake, for me and for Hughes. On the surface, it looked like an easy job. I had work keeping me in Washington, so I hired a private investigator in North Lake Tahoe who I thought was experienced enough to do the surveillance. But I was wrong.

It started off well enough. My P.I. set up a discreet round-the-clock surveillance of Ava, keeping me up-to-date on who she was seeing and what she was doing. I would then relay the information to Hughes's people in L.A. Unfortunately, my man made the stupidest damn error you could imagine. Sinatra had come to Tahoe to woo and coo, and talk Ava out of getting a divorce. He was successful enough to persuade her to go on a romantic little boat ride with him on the lake. Instead of waiting for them to return with the rented boat an hour or so later, my man impulsively rented one himself and went out after them!

Sinatra spotted the guy in no time and went nuts. He even brought in the police to find out who the P.I. was and what the hell he was doing. The whole thing hit the papers, creating a huge stink and bringing everything—even Hughes's name—out into the open.

I felt terrible. For someone who was supposed to be a whiz at dealing with sensitive matters, I had failed miserably, and I was sure I would never hear from Howard Hughes again. But I was wrong once more.

A couple of months later, I received another phone call from one of Howard's aides. Would I come out to California, he asked, and meet with some people in the Hughes organization? I was amazed. After the way I had fouled up the Ava Gardner investigation, I couldn't understand why Hughes would let his people even talk to me, let alone hire me.

Years later, I asked him. The reason was revealing, and it proved I wasn't the only source Hughes had for inside information on the intelligence community. Through individuals he wouldn't name, Hughes had somehow learned about my work with the CIA and my record as an FBI agent, as well as very specific details concerning my work with my fledgling company. My successes in those international arenas, Howard said, were impressive enough for him to forgive my sloppy efforts on the banks of Lake Tahoe. And now, according to the aide, Howard wanted me in California to deal with a particularly vexing problem. Blackmail.

It was early 1955. In the years that followed, I got to know L.A. nearly as well as my hometown of Waterville, Maine. But that winter, L.A. was still new to me. And intriguing. The first time I had headed west during winter was when I was a rookie FBI agent, and the change in weather shocked the hell out of me. This time I looked forward to letting the sunny western skies thaw me out of my Washington deep freeze. And, trite as it sounds, I also looked forward to my first visit to Hollywood.

In 1955, L.A. looked nothing like it does today. It was a place with its own charm and illusion, still the magical hub of the entertainment industry. The Hughes headquarters at 7000 Romaine Street was smack in the middle of it all, within walking distance of the famous street corner of Hollywood and Vine.

7000 Romaine was a huge and imposing Art Deco fortress, with the jagged lines and sharp edges associated with pre-WWII modernism. It didn't just look like a fortress, it *was* a fortress, guarded as heavily as any government building by legions of security people, whose diligence was fueled by the never-ending energy of Hughes's paranoia—and the paranoia of his aides, whom I was about to meet.

In L.A., the aide wanted me to see Bill Gay, who oversaw Hughes's personal staff and with whom I was told I'd be working. I was happy to do so. But I had certain demands. For one thing, I wanted a suite at a first-class hotel. Also, ever since that victory dinner I had had with Stavros Niarchos, I had driven new Cadillacs, and I wanted one waiting for me in L.A. when I arrived.

What I was doing was making a point. I was, as I said, thrilled to work for Hughes. But I was not impressed with the kind of work

I was doing for him. I was not just another P.I., and if Howard wanted me, he was going to have to treat me as something more than one.

And he did. I got the suite, the Cadillac, and a per diem. All three of which were the beginning of my problems with Bill Gay. It was an unwritten law that if you worked for Hughes, you were kept on a very short leash in terms of salary and expenses. If you had to stay at a hotel on business, it should be in a room, not a suite; and if you were renting a car, it should be a Chevrolet, not a Cadillac.

I made it clear right from the start that Hughes's unwritten law did not apply to me. I was a free agent, not one of his employees. And I kept things that way. Early on, I realized that it would be personally and financially advantageous to me if I stayed outside the Hughes corporate structure. Instead, I remained the sole owner of Robert A. Maheu Associates, and throughout my tenure with Hughes, it was the services of my company that he hired on an independent contracting basis, not just me.

These arrangements did not please Bill Gay. And the jealousy that I sensed from him—even in our very first encounter—would eventually lead to disaster for all of us. Especially Howard.

I didn't see Bill Gay when I arrived in Los Angeles. Instead, I was greeted at the airport by one of his aides. The aide apologized. It seemed Gay had been tied up in a two-hour meeting, and the aide had been instructed to take me to lunch in the meantime. I was annoyed. If I had been told straight off that an aide would meet me, it would have been fine. But I wasn't. I was told that Gay would meet me, and I sensed that this absence was something of a slight. But I didn't want to overreact, so I let it pass.

After lunch, the aide drove me back to 7000 Romaine, where Gay kept his offices. As we pulled up, the aide turned to me with a condescending air.

"Mr. Maheu," he said, "if you're going to get along with Bill Gay, I had better tell you right now that he and most of us around him belong to the Mormon Church. And I have to tell you ... I noticed that you had some wine with your lunch today. I suggest you not drink in the presence of Mr. Gay. He won't approve."

For a moment I just looked at him. He probably thought I was about to thank him. I wasn't. I was trying to calm myself so I wouldn't tell this jerk to go nonstop to hell and quit the job right then and there.

"Well, I happen to be Roman Catholic," I finally said, "and I noticed at lunch today that you ate meat. It's Friday. But I'll tell you what—I won't tell you when and where you can eat meat, if you don't try to tell me when and where I can drink a glass of wine."

Things went downhill from there. Instead of my being brought inside 7000 Romaine to meet Bill Gay in his office, he came outside to meet me. On the street. That's when I realized these people didn't do business the way I was used to doing business.

Bill Gay was a complex man. Though I didn't know it at the time, he was frustrated in his work. He had started off with the Hughes empire in the late forties as little more than a "go-for," running errands for Howard and Howard's secretary, Nadine Henley. Nadine took a liking to Bill, and helped him move up the corporate ladder. In Hughes's eyes, though, Bill always remained an errand boy, having to grab power instead of being invested with it.

In the end, of course, he grabbed it all. But the effort took a toll on Gay that was evident even then. Tall, rail-thin, and sallow, with blondish hair, Bill Gay had an almost visible air of hunger about him. Knowing now the Machiavellian morass in which I was soon to be caught, it's easy to say that I should have had the foresight of Shakespeare's Julius Caesar, who, when looking at the treacherous Cassius, observed:

Yond Cassius has a lean and hungry look;
He thinks too much: such men are dangerous.

61

Not that Caesar's foresight did him much good either, of course. At least the knives that ended up in my back were figurative.

The truth is I actually liked Bill Gay on first sight, even though he had a rather weak handshake, which is not something I admire in a man. But he was urbane, polite, and, even out on the sidewalk of Romaine Street, friendly. He also had a peculiar neediness about him, a vulnerability to which one couldn't help but respond.

One incident that illustrates this neediness occurred a few years later, right after I had taken office space in the Kirkeby Building on Wilshire Boulevard in the Westwood area of Los Angeles. It was about midday, and Gay suddenly walked into my office. He almost had tears in his eyes. And in his hand he held a box containing a beautiful mink stole.

Gay had ordered the stole through a friend of his at Hughes's request. The stole was to be a gift for Jean Peters. But the furrier had made a mistake. Instead of calling Gay at the office, the furrier had called Gay's house directly, and spoken to his wife, asking her where the stole was to be delivered. Gay's wife went into absolute ecstasy. It would either soon be her birthday or their wedding anniversary, and she was certain that the stole was a gift from her loving and thoughtful husband.

Bill Gay had driven across town from 7000 Romaine Street to ask for my advice. If he told his wife the truth, he said, she'd be crushed. I thought the solution was simple. Give the stole he had to his wife, and order another for Hughes. That's when Gay got to the real crux of the problem. The stole cost about $1,800. Hughes underpaid Gay miserably, and he was already being forced to live beyond his means. There was no way he could afford it.

So I lent him the money. All of it. It was a lot, but he seemed so damn needy that I was glad to help. And, as I had made sure I was well paid by Hughes, I could afford it. But there's another detail to this story that reveals much about the other side of Bill Gay, the one shrouded by politesse and vulnerability: he never paid me back.

Gay made a great show of being a devout Mormon. Eventually, his clique within the Hughes organization became known as the "Mormon Mafia." I never called them that, as I thought it smacked of religious prejudice, which I abhor. But it was true that Gay worked a little too hard at surrounding himself with supporting players who shared his own religious beliefs. He actually used to brag that 95 percent of the people who worked for him were Mormons.

I think that's bad business policy. It's like the old saying: if two people agree on everything, one is unnecessary. You can't build an effective organization without a clear view of the big picture. And you'll never see that big picture if the world you create is closed and parochial.

It also bothered me that Gay made such a public display of his Mormonism. Not that I'm antireligious. Outside of the time I spent in Saudi Arabia, I probably haven't missed Sunday Mass for over sixty years. And I have great respect for the Mormon Church. But I believe religion is a personal matter, and I've always had a little trouble with anyone who plays the zealot. It's easy to give lip service to religious values. Living them, however, is another thing altogether.

The assignment Gay spoke with me about on Romaine Street made it vividly clear just how easy it is to feign religious devotion. Hughes, according to Gay, was being blackmailed, and the blackmailer, believe it or not, was a minister. He was a man of some standing in the L.A. community, and had found out that one of his young female parishioners had had an affair with Howard.

Apparently either the girl, or a friend of the girl's, had confessed about the affair, looking for advice. Well, instead of saving the poor girl's soul, this so-called "man of God" decided to turn a tidy profit, and threatened to release what he knew to the press unless he was sufficiently compensated.

One might wonder why Hughes—a man infamous for his affairs—would give even a second thought to such a threat. But in spite of the headlong way Howard pursued women, he had an almost pathological fear of his relationships becoming public. On top of that, Howard was still wooing Jean Peters, who was then in the process of divorcing first husband Stuart Cramer. Hughes knew that Jean would be furious if she heard what this minister had to say, and would most likely dump him.

My assignment was to meet with the minister and see to it that he kept quiet. If that meant paying off the s.o.b., so be it. All that mattered to Hughes was keeping his story out of the press.

He wasn't asking for much, just a few thousand dollars, but I had learned back in the FBI that the worst thing you can do with a blackmailer is pay him. It simply never stops there. Eventually, the blackmailer will want more money; and, having figured out an easy way to get it, he'll always come back.

The toughest question, of course, is how to neutralize a blackmailer without paying him off. In this instance, I thought the key might lay in the fact that he was something of a public figure. Blackmailers, like many criminals, tend to have sleazy pasts—often sleazier than those of the people they're blackmailing. The difference is that the blackmailers usually have nothing to lose. This man had a lot to lose, so I decided to do a little research.

I went to Peter Pitchess, an ex-FBI agent and a friend. Since leaving the Bureau, Pete had become an undersheriff of L.A. County, and would soon be elected to a long and illustrious tenure as sheriff. I asked Pete if the minister had any kind of record, and I hit the jackpot. Not only did our blackmailer have a record, he had a record as a pederast! He'd been charged, though never convicted, with molesting young boys. I couldn't wait for my tête-à-tête with the blackmailer now. This was a meeting I thought I might even enjoy.

The preacher came to my room at the Beverly Wilshire Hotel. Physically, he was unimpressive, soft, even a bit effeminate, and he was sweating visibly, probably from nerves. Looking at him was unpleasant, like watching snails being prepared for escargot: the fat, spineless things are cured in salt, oozing what must be half their body weights in fluids.

The preacher asked for his money, and I told him that under no circumstances would Hughes make payments to him or any other blackmailer. Then I told him what I had found out about his own sexual escapades, threatening to take what I knew to the *Los Angeles Times*. The sweat began to pour from his body. Obviously, if such information were made public, his days of leading a congregation to the glory of the Lord would come rapidly to an end.

The preacher pleaded with me not to go to *The Times*.

"Okay," I said. "You keep your mouth shut, and I'll keep mine shut."

Not surprisingly, he agreed. The affair was kept out of the press, and Hughes eventually married Jean Peters. When I started working for Hughes, however, their relationship was still in its early stages, and Howard's determination to hold on to Jean outweighed all his other concerns, even those fueled by his phobias.

I had heard from Gay that Hughes was pleased with my handling of the case. I try not to take compliments too seriously. The truth is it's easier to say something nice than to make a necessary criticism. But in this instance, I soon knew they weren't lying, for only a month or so later I got a call asking me to take on another blackmail case. And once again the request came from Hughes's own people at 7000 Romaine.

This blackmailer lived in New York, so I didn't have to fly across the country to meet with him. Unfortunately, though, the tactic I'd used in the previous case wouldn't work this time. This blackmailer was no public figure. He was just a petty thief who found out about a young starlet Hughes was "keeping" in one of the many Hollywood bungalows he rented specifically for that purpose. The blackmailer wanted $2,000 in exchange for his silence. Otherwise, he would take his story to the papers.

My instructions were the same as before: the money was nothing; I could pay it if I felt it necessary. But my attitude toward extortionists remained the same: they're scum, and I'd rather do anything than let them profit from their villainy.

I rented a room in Manhattan's old Commodore Hotel, on 42nd Street near Grand Central Station, and had the blackmailer meet me there. I was waiting when he knocked. I let him in, took an accommodating tone, asked him to sit down, then poured us both a drink. He was not a very subtle criminal. When I asked him what he intended to do if we didn't pay, he readily told me everything, revealing his entire plan for blackmail.

"Well," I replied, "it's obvious you have us over a barrel."

Whereupon I got out a roll and peeled off twenty $100 bills. Grinning, he took the money and, satisfied that the deal was done, got up to leave the room. Abruptly, I grabbed the s.o.b. by his wrist and twisted it to force him back down on the couch.

"Before you leave," I told him, "I'd like to play you a little music."

I walked over to a dresser, opened a drawer, and pulled out a wire recorder, the kind they had before magnetic tape. I played back a recording of our entire conversation, a conversation in which he'd readily implicated himself as a blackmailer.

"What I have in my hands is enough to put you in jail for years," I said. "You see, I've convinced Mr. Hughes that bastards like you don't deserve to walk the streets. And—in spite of the publicity—he's given me authority to go straight to the district attorney with this tape."

The blackmailer started to tremble. "Can we strike a deal?" he asked.

I asked him what sort of a deal. Again, he didn't possess an ounce of subtlety. Instead of getting me to define the terms, he outlined them himself, implicating himself even more.

I listened to him dig his own grave, then said, "Sure. We can strike a deal."

"How about we split the two thousand?" he asked.

"No, I want it all back."

Now he started pleading. "If I give you the money, will you give me the recording?" he whined.

I told him I would. I took the wire recording off the machine. He stood up and we made a simultaneous exchange: the money for the wire.

Again, he started to leave. And again, I grabbed his wrist. "Not yet," I said, and sat him back down.

I opened another drawer, and took out another wire recorder.

"Now I want you to hear some more music," I told him. "This recording has our whole conversation on it. From the beginning right up to now."

I played it back to him. The entire conversation.

He was really worried. He knew I had him. "What are you going to do with this one?" he asked.

"This one," I said, "I'm going to keep."

"Is there any price—"

I cut him off before he could finish. "No price. Except one. You keep your mouth shut. It's that simple. And it's your choice to make." Then I told him he could go, and he practically ran out.

A few minutes later, I used the hotel phone to call Bill Gay at 7000 Romaine and inform him that the case had been dealt with successfully.

"Thank God," he said. "Mr. Hughes has been waiting for your

report. We have instructions from him that you are to dictate exactly what happened, not leaving anything out." So I dictated the story to Gay, who said, "Stay there. Hughes wants to read this report before you check out of the hotel."

It all seemed pretty odd to me, but I used the excuse to take a breather. About a half hour later, the phone rang and I picked it up.

"Hello, Bob! This is Howard. Goddamn, that was great! Tell me about it, will you, blow by blow?"

It was Howard Hughes. The invisible legend was calling to tell me that he loved the way I'd handled the blackmailer so much, he wanted me to tell him the whole story myself, from beginning to end. As I talked, he interjected questions and comments in a voice higher and squeakier than what I had imagined, laughing the whole time, sounding like a little boy.

"Now, tell me again," he said when I was finished. "Just to make sure you haven't forgotten anything."

By the time I hung up, Howard had made me repeat the story three times, enjoying each telling as if he were hearing it for the first time. Afterward, I felt strangely happy and sad. I was happy to have at last spoken to Howard Hughes himself, instead of to an endless assortment of assistants. I was even happier that he liked my work and didn't hesitate to tell me. Yet, there was something else—a much stronger sadness that clouded my enthusiasm. I sensed that Hughes was somehow living vicariously through my stories. I had no idea yet of the degree of his isolation. He was one of the richest and most powerful men in the world, yet he seemed one of the poorest—desperate for any real-life adventures that I could give him, having receded into a shell that allowed him far too few of his own.

It was a feeling I had again and again. Over the years, Howard and I talked innumerable times, and often the conversation was exactly like this first one—my telling Howard about some exploit, or court appearance, or social event, and Howard having me repeat the story over and over, sucking all the life he could out of my activities.

I had crossed over some invisible line with that first call from Hughes. No longer was I an outsider. From that point on, I was Howard's man.

At the same time, Robert A. Maheu Associates continued working with other clients. I shuttled back and forth between Los Angeles and Washington constantly, a grueling commute. And I also continued working with Scotty McLeod, then head of security for the State Department, who would recommend potential clients to my firm.

It was Scotty who had contacted me about a visit President Sukarno of Indonesia was about to make to the U.S. It's easy to underestimate the importance Indonesia played then in international relations. Indonesia is the fifth most populated nation in the world, and at that time was a tremendous force in a region where the balance of power was in constant flux. We had just fought the Korean War over Communist expansion in Southeast Asia and were only five or six years away from starting another war. It was Sukarno who countered the newly created Southeast Asia Treaty Organization (SEATO) by organizing a conference of "nonaligned" underdeveloped nations, presenting us with what seemed a very fickle ally.

So when Sukarno visited Washington and then made a tour of the U.S., the State Department was determined to please him. And pleasing Sukarno meant one thing: supplying him with women. Many women. A new one, in fact, each and every night.

But Scotty McLeod was concerned about the potential problems for the United States if our government supplied a foreign leader with prostitutes. It was, to everyone, a distasteful necessity.

Yet, putting aside the inherent moral dilemma over what amounts to pimping for one's country, there remained serious questions about security.

What, for instance, would be the consequences if one of the girls went public? Stories of the State Department pimping for Sukarno was not something President Eisenhower wanted to read in the *New York Times.* In addition to the embarrassment, a leak of this story could have a devastating effect on the U.S.'s relationship with Sukarno, throwing him even further into the Soviet camp.

And what if one of the girls turned out to be a Soviet plant? Again, the potential for disaster would be enormous. She, or an associate of hers, might somehow take pictures of the encounter or make a tape recording, using the scandal to blackmail either Sukarno, the U.S. government, or both.

Doing security checks on the girls was a touchy but necessary affair. Local authorities, such as the various police departments, had to be contacted. And although the State Department had taken on the job of surreptitiously selecting the girls for Sukarno, under no circumstance could it be officially involved. So Scotty had turned to the CIA for the security checks, and it—in order to assure complete deniability—had turned to me.

As the junket moved across the country, a man from the State Department and I traveled a day or so ahead of Sukarno and his entourage. When we arrived in town, the State Department's man, who was really just an underling, did the research necessary to pick out a selection of girls from which Sukarno could choose. Then I would go into action, meeting with the local police and checking the women out.

My questions ran the gamut, from finding out about the women's prior records to determining their political affiliations. We had to know who their associates were, who their pimps might be, who picked them up, who dropped them off—every detail of their lives was potentially germane. Only after every aspect of these girls checked out would they be among those offered to Sukarno.

There's a rather moving footnote to this story. Just prior to the Sukarno trip, the fellow whose job it was to actually solicit the women came home unexpectedly from work one afternoon to find his wife in bed with another man. Needless to say, it hit him pretty hard. He and his wife patched things up, but even so, the last thing the poor guy wanted to do after that was leave town and deal with a bunch of hookers. Frankly, the whole thing repulsed us both.

Basically, I believed in my part of the operation. If our government felt the only way to stay on good terms with a foreign power was to keep its head of state supplied with girls, I wanted to be sure that at least they weren't security risks. But I would have greatly preferred it if we had found better ways to maintain our relationships.

In reality, it didn't work anyway. For while Sukarno may have left the States satisfied sexually, he was frustrated in every other regard. Sukarno was looking for support from us, especially in arms sales. But the Eisenhower administration didn't approve of the way he was handling things back home, particularly the Communists he had been appointing to his cabinet. So it sent Sukarno away empty-handed, causing him to shift his hopes toward the Soviet Union.

It was nearly a year after Sukarno's visit to the States when I received a call from Colonel Sheffield Edwards, head of the CIA's Office of Security. He sounded a bit nervous, and wanted to know if he could stop by the house for a drink on his way home. Even as I said yes, I knew something was boiling.

At the time, I was living in Falls Church, Virginia. Our meeting place was our recreation room. It was a large area designed for entertaining, with a nautical motif—a bar made from half of a real lifeboat, lamps made from driftwood, and an entire wall of cooking facilities for lobster dinners and clambakes. Most important, it offered us total privacy.

Sheff went over a little background with me. In the past few months, Sukarno's relationship with the U.S. had continued to deteriorate. At the same time, the incipient alliance he had formed with the Soviets seemed to be maturing. Sukarno had initially only tolerated a Communist presence within Indonesia. Now, it appeared to be blossoming into out-and-out support. Interestingly, all these changes had followed a trip Sukarno had made to the Soviet Union.

Sheff got out an envelope and proceeded to show me pictures of a living room and a bedroom that were actually inside the Kremlin. These were private quarters, made available only to Soviet leaders and to visiting dignitaries. Sheff never said how he got the pictures. But clearly, we had intelligence sources buried deep within the Soviet bureaucracy.

Then Sheff told me the story of Sukarno and a blond. While visiting the Soviets, Sukarno had been treated the same as here— supplied with a constant flow of women. But the Soviets had gone us one better: one of the women they supplied Sukarno was an agent in the KGB.

The woman's cover was that of a stewardess aboard the Soviet plane Sukarno used while in the Soviet Union. It's possible he thought she was an actual conquest. And it's certain he didn't realize she was in the KGB. Sukarno fell pretty hard for the girl, and she visited him on a number of occasions in Indonesia.

Sheff showed me her picture. It was easy to see the attraction. She was a knockout. Whether or not she was actually the cause of Sukarno's increasing closeness to the Soviet Union was, of course, questionable. No one doubted, however, that she had exerted some sort of influence over him; and it was undeniable that she was what's known among spies as a "honey trap," a sexual enticement planted to gather intelligence.

Sheff felt that by exposing the liaison, the Company could either drive a wedge between Sukarno and the Soviets or humiliate him before his own people and weaken his base of power. I had to agree. The Soviets sure as hell weren't playing by the rules, and neither could we.

The CIA's informants told the Company that Sukarno and the blond had spent at least one night together inside the bedroom pictured in the photos. Sheff wanted me to use the Hollywood contacts I had made through my work with Hughes to produce a film that looked as if it had been taken by the Soviets themselves as Sukarno and the blond had made love in the bedroom. It was never in any way intended to be a "porno" movie. All the CIA wanted was a surveillance camera view of a man who seemed to be Sukarno caught on the verge of the act with a woman who seemed to be the Soviet agent.

Sheff knew who my contacts were in L.A., and the people the Company asked me to work with were Bing Crosby and his brother Larry. The reason was simple: the Company liked Bing and Larry's politics and, after doing a security check on them, felt they could be trusted completely.

I had actually become friendly with Larry and Bing years earlier, not through Hughes, but through my old business, Dairy Dream. Larry was running Bing's foundation at the time, and I was hoping Bing could do for Dairy Dream what he had previously done for Minute Maid orange juice. Unfortunately, Dairy Dream did a belly flop before Bing got a chance to help it. But Larry and I hit it off when we met, and often I would have lunch or dinner with him and his wife, Mary, when I visited Los Angeles. Months later, Larry invited me to the Bing Crosby Pro/Am Golf Tournament at Pebble Beach. And there I met Der Bingle himself. As a dyed-in-the-wool New Englander, I found those clambakes that followed the tournaments among the few times in California that I ever felt truly at home.

A day or so after I talked to Sheff, I flew out to L.A. That night I took Larry Crosby to dinner and told him what I needed and why. He absolutely loved it.

"Bing will eat this up," he said, laughing and shaking his head.

He was right. In fact, many years later, only about two months before Bing died, I ran into him at St. John's Hospital in Santa Monica. Even then, he talked fondly about making the film and our little adventure together. And it was an adventure.

Bing and Larry found a small studio in Hollywood and made it up to look just like the pictures I showed them of the rooms inside the Kremlin. They got hold of a camera for me, but because we didn't want to cut too many people in on the operation, Larry taught me how to use it. It wasn't that hard really. I threw a magazine of film into the camera, turned on a light, and flipped a switch. Fortunately for me, this wasn't to be an award-winning film, just surveillance footage, and there's nothing worse than the camera work in surveillance films.

The real problem was the cast. We looked over some of the local "talent," the sort of actors and actresses who had done the kind of low-rent work that would make our PG project look like a walk in the park. But no one was really right, either for Sukarno or the blond.

Finally I turned to Hal Marlowe, the undersheriff of Los Angeles County and assistant to Sheriff Pete Pitchess. I showed Hal pictures of both the blond and Sukarno, and he came up with some wonderful suggestions. He supplied me with the name of a girl who was perfect for the blond. She was not, strictly speaking, an actress. She was an informant. Pete got her to do a favor for us, making it clear that she was to keep her mouth shut about it. I don't think the poor girl ever did figure out what the hell we were doing or why.

After I discussed the Sukarno role with Hal, he reminded me of his old roommate, a Hispanic-looking man named Chuck Kayes who was working for me in Tucson. While he didn't really look that much like Sukarno, by the time Bing Crosby's makeup artist was done with him, you would've sworn the man was the Indonesian president.

The actual shooting took place in the middle of the night, with only me, Hal Marlowe, and the "actors" there. The whole thing lasted less than five minutes. Some reports claim the film showed the actors in flagrante delicto, and others have even said we put the actor in a Sukarno mask. It's all so much bull. They were never actually in bed together, and there was certainly nothing that even approximated pornography. By today's standards, it would be tame indeed.

In the end, though, the Company decided not to use it—at least not the whole thing. It wasn't a classic, that's for sure, and the fear was that if the film was seen in its entirety, it might become clear that our Sukarno wasn't legit. Instead, just a few stills from the movie were leaked in Indonesia and elsewhere. Even so, they had their effect. They started showing up here and there, both in Asia and Europe, and eventually Sukarno had to stop seeing the blond. By the late fifties, his close ties to the Soviets had diminished considerably. Sukarno's power at home diminished as well. There was dissension and even a revolt, which some people trace back to a lack of confidence caused by the scandals surrounding Sukarno's rumored affair with a Soviet spy.

Sukarno's position in Indonesia, though always powerful, was never quite the same. And I don't think it's stretching things too much to say that, in its own way, my little film marked the beginning of his end.

Years later, I actually traveled to Indonesia. I was doing consulting work which required that I first stop in Hong Kong and again in Singapore along the way. I had not shaved and the air was very muggy. After several hours, I was in the air again, feeling very grubby.

I was handed a declarations form as we were making our final approach into the airport in Jakarta. Among the items on the form was a line to declare any exposed film in your possession. I had to laugh, since the government had initially started to control the import and export of film after the photographs of President Sukarno and his Russian blond were made public.

As I walked through customs, I was still remembering the story. When I arrived at the window marked IMMIGRATION, I must have been smiling. The young lady smiled back and in flawless English asked to see my passport.

After examining the document, she said, "Mr. Maheu, you have a big problem."

My mind began to race. Although Sukarno had been dead for many years at this point, I realized that he might still have some loyal servants. This girl, for all I knew, was the daughter of one of them.

I cleared my throat and asked, "And what problem might that be?" I did my best not to look guilty, though I knew it wasn't working.

"You only have three more months left before your passport expires," she answered. When I nodded in agreement, she continued, "Unless your passport is good for a full six months, you have to have a visa to enter Indonesia. It's the law." With that she shook her head, turned, and disappeared into a side room, taking my passport with her.

I could feel the sweat beginning to pour beneath my open shirt. Suddenly the hall felt very small and warm. After several minutes, she reemerged and signaled for me to follow her.

Entering the huge room, I saw people seated behind ten or twelve desks. As I was shown to an empty chair, all of the people suddenly got up and left the room. I rubbed my unshaven face and tried to look unconcerned. Shortly, an official walked into the room and shut the door. He took his time looking me over before speaking.

"Mr. Maheu, you have a big problem," he said when he finally spoke.

"What can I do to correct it?" I asked, trying to play on his sympathy.

"You can leave the country," he replied. "Go back to Hong Kong and get a visa. Or," he offered, "you can go back to the United States and get another passport."

The man turned silent once again, waiting for a reply. I thought perhaps I was being set up, that a payoff was about to be suggested. Holding my own, I politely informed the man that I couldn't leave his country.

"What do you mean, you can't?" he snapped, his eyes suddenly taking on the intensity of a challenged beast.

"Just look at me," I said, drawing attention to my travel-weary body. "Can't you tell I'm dying?" I asked him. "I'm a very sick man. I have to rest. Perhaps you have a hospital where I might go. Maybe I could sleep on the floor here. I must rest."

The man clearly was convinced that what I was saying was true. The very thought of an American dying in his office seemed more than he could handle.

"I called my doctor just before I left Hong Kong and he told me that he'd allow me to make this trip only if I went to bed immediately," I added, determined to keep him off guard. "You're not trying to kill me, are you?" I asked sincerely.

When he responded that he wouldn't be trying to kill someone he didn't even know, I realized that the official had no idea about my background and wasn't looking to set me up. As I let my head fall loosely to one side, I apologized for causing him so much trouble and offered to pay a fine for my offense. Suddenly a large smile crossed his face.

"How much of a fine do you think you should pay?" he queried.

I reached into my pocket and pulled out a new $100 bill as I heard my lips say, "Even though I'm going to die, if I should recover, I promise I'll never come into your country again unless I'm healthy and have a visa."

As the man took the money and stamped my passport, I

couldn't imagine what he was thinking about the crazy American before him. I was just thankful he didn't know the real story. Or President Sukarno, for that matter.

Looking back, as successful as the Sukarno caper turned out, there was another "covert op" I ran around the same time that worked even better. This operation, though, wasn't for the CIA. It was for Howard Hughes.

Chapter Three

THE NIXON POLL, POLITICS, AND POWER

IN 1956, HOWARD HUGHES HAD A GOAL. HE WANTED RICHARD NIXON to remain as Dwight Eisenhower's running mate in the 1956 presidential election. It wasn't that he thought Nixon was doing such a good job. It was more that he felt the vice president was malleable, and Hughes wanted to see him stay in the White House.

A lot can be said about Richard Nixon's political career, good and bad, but I doubt anyone would ever claim that he was the most popular vice president in the history of the nation. Nixon back then might best be compared with Dan Quayle today. He was young, was viewed as having limited experience, and was considered far more conservative than the man he served under. And, as there is with Quayle, there was considerable talk about dumping Nixon from the ticket for the second term.

As the Republican National Convention drew closer, the movement to dump Nixon picked up steam. It was spearheaded by Harold Stassen, a moderate Minnesota Republican who was then the party's fair-haired boy, and Eisenhower's special assistant on disarmament. The president was doing little—if anything—to bring the movement to a halt. That was where I came in.

As the Republicans prepared for the upcoming convention at

the Cow Palace in San Francisco, Stassen started making noises about a "poll" he claimed to have conducted on Nixon's popularity, the results of which he said he'd announce at a press conference. Though not yet the perennial and quixotic presidential candidate he later became, Harold Stassen had already made a few runs at the White House and failed. This time he was making a run at Nixon, and almost dealt him a devastating hand.

When it came time for the press conference, Stassen announced that he was supporting Massachusetts Governor Christian A. Herter for vice president. His poll results showed Nixon would detract 6 percent or more from the overall popular vote if Eisenhower made the mistake of choosing him a second time as his running mate. When the reporters pushed Stassen for the source of his information, he said it was secret. When they pushed him to release the complete results, Stassen said he would, but "at a later date."

The poll rolled like a tidal wave over Washington, and Stassen soaked up the publicity. But not everyone was impressed or convinced, and one day, I received a call from a group of leading Republicans in D.C. who wanted to make me Nixon's savior. These guys weren't heavy-hitting politicians, just a group of people who were philosophically closer to Nixon than they were to Stassen—or even Eisenhower—and truly believed that one day Nixon would go on to become president.

I knew, however, that if I took on the project, it was going to need a bankroll. And Howard Hughes had the bank. I talked it over with Hughes to see if he'd like to participate. "By all means" was the answer.

A day or so after Stassen's announcement about the poll, Harold made another announcement. He decided to open up Washington headquarters for his own vice-presidential candidate, without even waiting for a convention vote. Eisenhower, in the meantime, was absolutely silent, leaving Nixon to swing in the wind.

My best bet in fighting Stassen was to find out first if his poll was legitimate. My gut suspicion was that it wasn't. I had a man working for me then who was a very imaginative undercover operative, so I gave him the assignment of becoming a volunteer at Stassen's new headquarters in Washington. He quickly found out that Stassen didn't even *have* a poll when he'd called the press conference. He was picking the numbers out of the air, figuring that would be enough. Remember, this was back in the dark ages of political polling, less than eight years after the infamous polls that predicted Dewey over Truman in a landslide. The whole science of polling was shady at best, and something no one really knew much about.

But when the media started pushing hard for the facts, Stassen had to start polling people to get himself off the hook. My undercover man, being the good volunteer that he was, wound up getting a set of keys to Stassen headquarters. After a discreet search, he turned up information indicating that the poll Stassen was going to conduct wouldn't exactly be unbiased—it was going to be heavily stacked against Nixon.

Stassen planned to release the full results at a press conference during the convention. That didn't give us much time. So, Robert A. Maheu Associates quickly put together a second poll—a nonsecret poll, set to begin the day after Stassen finished his. This one would be more recent, conducted exclusively by former FBI agents in one major city and one country town in every state. Staunch Republican William Loeb, who published New Hampshire's *Manchester Union* newspaper, agreed to print the results. When we were ready, I flew off to New York and met Bill at the airport, the new poll results now in my hands.

While Stassen was getting prepared for his show, I got on another plane, flew all night, and arrived in San Francisco on the morning that the convention was set to open. Meantime, my volunteer continued to work side by side with Stassen, following his every move.

The moment we found out that Stassen had called his press conference for 11:00 A.M., we persuaded Nixon supporter Senator Styles Bridges to book the same room for a press announcement immediately following Stassen's. Harold had no idea that we were calling his bluff.

Stassen went in front of the press and gave the complete results of his poll, which conveniently backed up his earlier claims. When he was finished and left the room, all the media were still in place. Moments later, Senator Bridges walked up to the same podium and announced that he had his own *nonsecret* and independent Nixon poll. These results showed Nixon wouldn't hurt the ticket at all—in fact, just the opposite. Stassen's bubble burst and the campaign to dump Richard Nixon died at that very moment.

Hughes was so happy that he asked me to cancel a reunion with my family in Florida and fly to Los Angeles. He wanted me there for a week or more. As it turned out, there wasn't anything special he needed me to do. I got the feeling that he only wanted me in L.A. to keep me from being anywhere else. It was the old business of control.

Maintaining Nixon in the vice presidency made a lot of Republicans happy, too. One exception might have been Eisenhower. I never saw any evidence that Ike was definitely disappointed, but there were hints that he and Nixon didn't get along. Eisenhower was an amiable man, liked by the people and by both political parties. He had a way with the public—Ike talked to waiters, chauffeurs, the common man. He was fond of them. There's never been much evidence that Nixon liked people. He used them. As a matter of fact, I saw him the day after we defeated the Stassen threat and, despite the fact that he knew what we had managed to accomplish, he never even said thank you.

It turned out, he would use me again only months later. In those days, I had a favorite table at La Salle du Bois, a restaurant around the corner from my office. I would get so many calls and have so many meetings there that I finally had my own phone put in. Well, Richard Nixon took a fancy to the same table and used it when he stopped by for lunch.

One day I was going over the bill from the restaurant telephone and noticed a lot of strange numbers. I knew that I hadn't made those calls. When I checked, they all turned out to be Richard Nixon's. He was ringing up quite a tab—and I was picking it up. Eventually, I had the phone pulled out. It was easier than collecting long-distance charges from the vice president of the United States.

Although the fight with Stassen played out in my favor, there was another time that I got involved in trying to save Nixon's neck that didn't work out half as well. Just before the 1960 Nixon-Kennedy presidential election, Hughes called and said there were two reporters digging into a loan he had made to Donald Nixon, Richard's younger, ne'er-do-well brother. If it ever came out in public, the loan could cause Richard Nixon tremendous embarrassment, and possibly the election.

On Howard's orders, I flew to Hollywood immediately. Waiting at the Bel Air Hotel was the loan file, which had been sealed for years. It was bigger than I had expected. The original loan was for $205,000, which the Hughes Tool Company had lent Donald Nixon in 1956 and $40,000 of which was going to pay off an earlier bank loan, with the remainder going directly to Donald. Of all the documents inside the file, however, the most interesting was a quit claim deed signed by Nixon's mother, Hannah. The deed meant that if Donald defaulted, Hannah pledged all of her personal property as repayment.

The moment I found the quit claim deed in the files, I was elated. It indicated that Donald Nixon had every intent to repay the loan, and helped to remove a blanket of suspicion that cloaked the transaction. Still, I had two problems. The first was that the deed had never been officially recorded. Undoubtedly, Hughes considered it too unimportant. Getting Hughes on the telephone, I suggested that we disclose that the reason the deed hadn't been recorded was to save Mrs. Nixon any undue embarrassment. Howard, of course, was not above embarrassing anyone, and it took some work to finally convince him of my logic. With that accomplished, I turned my attention to problem number two. Since the deed remained unrecorded, I needed to prove that it was genuine, and not something that had sprung from the mind of Maheu when he'd been pushed into a corner. I approached a reputable document examiner and asked him to authenticate the age of the deed. In a matter of days, he confirmed in writing that it was over three years old. It was all I needed to put my plan into action.

Meanwhile, the reporters were continuing to dig for what they believed was a scoop. I finally showed them the document, begging for it to be kept off the record, suggesting that this poor lady was willing to give up her worldly possessions to save her stupid son Don. I went for the sympathy angle. If they printed the story, Hughes would be forced to take all this woman's assets. Fortunately, those were the days when you could count on the press to have a heart, and they printed not a word.

The entire episode died down, or so I thought, until the day I received a call from Bob King. Bob had worked as the administrative assistant to Nixon during his vice-presidential years, and was now one of my business partners. He was currently traveling with Nixon and his entourage on the campaign trail.

"You're not going to like what you're about to hear," he warned me over the telephone. "I just attended a conference, and the group has decided that they're going to break the Don Nixon loan story via a correspondent who's a friend of theirs." The writer's name was Peter Edson and he had a syndicated column in about 175 papers around the country.

Nixon naively believed that he could control the "spin" on the story, if he was the one to release it. I begged Bob to try and get the committee to reconsider, but we lost the battle. The best I could do now was plead for them to tell the entire truth. They didn't. The story broke and my secretary read it to me over the phone ... after suggesting that I get a brandy. It was a hodgepodge account of the transaction. To call it unbelievable was being kind. I counted many outright lies in the story that people had told Edson.

Nixon, of course, wound up losing the election. Bobby Kennedy, calling Nixon's lack of honesty a stupid mistake, later said that the loan cover-up was the main reason JFK won.

Nixon's ability to bend the truth to his own form would haunt him throughout his entire political career. It hit a peak years later during Watergate. At the time, I told Yvette, "This has to be the loneliest man in the world." By then, Nixon didn't have any old friends, just presidential pals who were testifying against him. Every last bridge had been burned.

Eventually, playing politics became a big part of my job, but 1956 was my baptism by fire. That year, right around the same time as the convention, Hughes was having some problems in Culver City, the site of the Hughes Aircraft Company. He owned a lot of land all over Los Angeles County, but he was particularly concerned about Culver City and who controlled it. Hughes was convinced that the majority of members sitting on the City Council came from "Communist-infected" groups. And because they were "Reds," all of their decisions were rigged against the big-money guys—Hughes among them.

He was fiercely protective when it came to land. But unlike other tycoons, Hughes wasn't interested in development. He was totally against it, and never gave an inch—literally. County officials learned their lesson when they wanted to widen the road that ran next to the old Hughes Aircraft strip. It was only a matter of two feet. But when I tried to convince Hughes that it would be a good public relations move to work out a satisfactory deal with the county, he blew his stack.

"Bob, do you have a ruler handy?" he asked over the phone. Once I found one, Hughes ordered me to block off a square inch and give it a good look. Hughes then said, "You see how big that is? Now listen to me carefully. I don't want to give up one goddamn square inch to the Church, to the Vatican, or to God."

And if he wouldn't sacrifice something that small to anyone on heaven or earth, he certainly wasn't forking over two feet to the county. Hughes had a lot more than two feet at stake in Culver City and the County of Los Angeles. And he wasn't about to let that raw land be manipulated by left-wing politicians. My assignment was to investigate the Council members and find dirt about any of their connections or any groups they may have belonged to over the years.

The idea didn't sit well with me. I warned him it could backfire. People still had powder burns from the blast of McCarthyism, and they might accuse him of persecuting innocent people. I tried to convince Hughes that the best way to change the City Council would be to get some prominent people together, pick some good candidates, and beat the incumbents at the polls. Hughes was flabbergasted that I thought this could work, but he gave me a shot anyway.

I started going to the public meetings about land problems and noticed that there was no coordination between the special-interest groups. Through an old FBI contact, I got together with a local newspaper publisher and we came up with a list of prominent area citizens. I already had a list of landowners who had problems similar to those of Hughes.

My next step was to invite about twenty of them to the Bel Air Hotel for cocktails and dinner. After wining and dining them, I explained that we all had mutual interests but weren't working together. I told them that I thought it would be mutually beneficial for us to form a group called the Better Business Association of Culver City. That way, if there was a problem with the Council, we'd tackle it as a united front. And, if at any time a member disagreed, he could peel off and side against us with the understanding that he would be welcomed back after the issue was settled. Lo and behold, everyone shook hands and the association was born. That night, we picked our own political candidates.

We got them elected, too; and it impressed the hell out of Hughes. Not only was it easier than his idea, it was also less expensive and didn't open him up to a lot of liberal criticism. Some people might have called it a political fix; I like to think of it as "conditioning the atmosphere." Whatever it was, it placed me in a new realm with Hughes. I wasn't just an investigator anymore. I was now Hughes's official troubleshooter, and trouble, it seemed, was everywhere.

There was a void within the Hughes organization created by the firing of Howard's top commander, Noah Dietrich.

Dietrich was with Hughes for thirty-two years. He was a brilliant businessman, quick to get to the point and efficient as hell. As I learned more about him over time, it was obvious that he was the one person responsible for Hughes's financial success. He successfully ran the Hughes Tool Company, which provided the foundation for Hughes Aircraft and the money to support Hughes's eccentric ways. Besides his business savvy, Dietrich was truly dedicated to his boss.

Hughes was the playboy and Dietrich was the man who delivered him net profits as high as $55 million annually. Hughes had been dangling the promise of stock options under Dietrich's nose for a long time, and finally, in 1957, during Hughes's most needy time, Dietrich tried to collect. The demand didn't work—Hughes refused and Dietrich was fired.

Others may have had a hand in the end of Dietrich's era. Some of his aides had already started staking their own claims on the empire and thought Dietrich was getting too strong. Bill Gay used to brag that he'd pushed Hughes to get rid of him. He did the same thing with Frank Waters, Hughes's lobbying activist for state and national issues. Bill Gay didn't read Machiavelli ... he wrote it.

The end for Dietrich came in May, 1957. After firing Dietrich over the telephone, Hughes called Bill Gay and gave him instructions to change the locks in the Romaine building that night. Dietrich had to get a court order just to remove his personal things. He later had to go back to court to sue for his severance pay. He got it, but it wasn't enough payment for a lifetime of dedication.

While I was aware of what was happening, none of this seemed particularly relevant to me—not even when I was summoned by Hughes to the Bahamas late in 1957. He had gone to the islands to investigate Nassau's real estate potential. I received a call to fly in and help out. It was there that I first heard Howard's plan. He wanted me to become his next public persona—the one who would protect him from the rest of the world.

The whole time he was talking, it never dawned on me that what had happened to Dietrich might happen to me. I was absolutely convinced that I would never allow anyone to take over my life. Hughes, after all, was still just a client, I told myself. But years later, after my own head went on the chopping block, I received a wire from Dietrich. In effect, it said, "I told you so."

Yet, at the time, I hadn't the advantage of hindsight. I was too busy working with another big client. Dave McDonald, president of the United Steel Workers of America, had hired me to help the union with an image problem. The union didn't want to be seen as a bunch of left-wing radicals or thugs—a reputation that had harmed many of the old CIO-affiliated unions—and it didn't want to be linked with organized crime, a problem that had been plaguing the Teamsters.

Even though I never really corrected its image problem, the Steel Workers job was important to me. For one thing, I was very fond of McDonald, a handsome, charismatic man who was a pleasure to work with. For another thing, it was quite lucrative. The $100,000-a-year the union was paying me was far more than I was getting from Hughes at that time. Working with the Steel Workers and other meaningful and lucrative clients, including the CIA, brought me nearly as close to the power center of the nation as working with Hughes did.

Now, however, the urgent call from Hughes had to take precedence over everything else. He had been in the Bahamas for quite some time and had taken up residence at the Emerald Beach Hotel. I was given a suite on the floor below his quarters. The first time we talked on the phone, Hughes wanted me to buy the local communications company, all the available beachfront properties, the airport—virtually anything that was up for grabs. Hughes had made up his mind to make every investment he could—and to wind up owning the entire place. And he was determined that I would handle every transaction.

It was over the phone that Hughes officially revealed that he had handpicked me to become his alter ego. Looking at me more as troubleshooter than businessman, he often said that he had never seen anyone who could cut his way out of the jungle without any scars as well as I could. He wanted me to be his only spokesman to the outside world. Basically, when people talked to me, it would be the same as talking to Hughes—and everyone at every level of business and government would know this. Hughes hoped this would keep him from being called as a witness in any civil case, regulatory hearing, or congressional investigation. In fact, he hoped never to have to appear in public again.

The news came as quite a shock. It must have been even more surprising to Bill Gay, who had anticipated running Howard's show himself. Yet, once I was aboard, Gay welcomed me with open arms. He saw me as an additional tool in his quest to take over the empire.

Howard had become so reclusive that using me to do his public bidding seemed to him to be the ideal solution—the answer to
his neurosis. What he didn't anticipate is that it would make him
more vulnerable, more open to manipulation by others, and eventually cause his downfall.

The strangest part about the arrangement, of course, was that I
still hadn't actually met the man. And as I said, I never would. I did
come close, however.

I had been expecting a call from Hughes one day in the
Bahamas, but was told he had gone out. I went to the hotel lobby
to buy a newspaper, and had no sooner sat down on the couch
when, all of a sudden, there was a commotion. Hughes had come
in with his entourage.

I didn't know it at first. Then I recognized someone in the
group; otherwise I would have probably just looked the other way.
Hughes was giving his aides hell because the elevator door wasn't
open by the time he got there. He had only had to wait about two
or three seconds, but the man was furious.

I didn't really see Howard's face as they passed, but the
moment he shrieked at his aides I recognized the voice that had
called me countless times.

I stood up and stared over at the elevator. Howard was a tall
man, quite thin, and I could see him clearly from the back, standing out from those around him, his hair lank and longish (though
by no means shoulder-length at this point), his posture a bit
stooped, gesturing and shouting orders. After a moment the elevator doors opened ... then he was gone.

At that point in 1957, I still didn't know that my sighting was
anything special. I knew that Howard was a bit antisocial, and that
he made himself almost inaccessible. But I didn't realize yet that
no one outside the inner sanctum ever saw Hughes face to face. It
just didn't seem possible.

That I still hadn't met Howard personally didn't really surprise

me. After all, I was an independent consultant—not an employee—despite the fact that Howard would have been delighted to
add me to his weekly payroll. As I've made clear, he was less than a
generous employer, with most of his top executives at Hughes Tool
earning under $40,000 a year.

So when Hughes made me the offer of becoming his alter ego,
I suggested we keep the same arrangements as before. I figured
that if his top executives ever found out I was making more than
they were, it would have caused major problems. Also, I felt that if
I stayed independent, I could play both sides of the fence, which
would work out best both for me and for Howard. That way, if I
had to use certain people in and outside of the Hughes organization to get this or that job done, Howard could always say, "Well,
hell, that damned Bob Maheu ..." as if he had no idea what I
was up to—ultimate deniability. I would soon become Howard's
fall guy.

The more time I spent in the Bahamas, the clearer things
became. Hughes wanted a place where he could be king. California was growing in spite of him. There, he was just another big fish
in a very big pond. But here, he could be the one in charge of
everything.

Over the next six weeks, I enlisted the help of some locals to
work out the property deals. The group that called the shots in the
Bahamas in those days was called the Bay Street Boys. The head
honcho was Sir Stafford Sands, a very well qualified and respected
lawyer. Hughes had his tool company send me a $25,000 retainer
for Sands. But after I met with him and his partners, Sands said he
wouldn't take the check until he could meet Hughes face to face.

When I told Howard his condition, he didn't seem to have a
problem with the request. He told me to take Sands to my hotel
suite and call him when we got there. Sands got on the phone with
Hughes and they talked ... and talked. Finally, Sands said, "Okay,
Howard. That's how you want it done, right? You want Bob to give

91

me the check, is that it?" When he hung up, Sands took the retainer without another word about any meeting.

We went back to Sands's office to get the papers. His partners couldn't wait for a report on Hughes. "Did you see him?" they asked. Sands said, "Oh sure," knowing damn well that I wasn't going to expose the bluff. It wasn't the first or last time anybody lied about having seen Howard Hughes. Years later, while sitting on a witness stand, I summed it all up: "Those who say they see him, don't. And those who see him, don't say."

A month and a half into the trip, I had to head for New York because of a previous commitment. Yvette and I had plans to meet Johnny Mitchell and his wife, Aileen, two of our dear friends. Mitchell was a Houston oil tycoon, and Yvette had met them during a trip to Sarasota. I told Hughes I had to go. He wasn't happy.

"Well, you have a major decision to make," he said. "You know, we've already made plans that you're going to be my replacement in the world. You're going to be my one and only spokesman. And now you're going to leave me."

I didn't back down. I promised to come back in a few days, but added, "If that will irrevocably disrupt our relationship, then you'll have to make that decision. I have no choice." We went back and forth for a while. Then I left.

Hughes had me intercepted at the airport. He kept me on the phone until the final boarding call. I wasn't going to miss the flight, so I hung up without telling him where I could be reached in New York. I arrived later that night at the Pierre Hotel. And I said to Yvette, "I think I just kissed a big client good-bye." Early the next morning, the phone rang. It was Hughes. He had tracked me down by having his men find out the "in" hotels and call each one, asking for Bob Maheu. This time, there was no argument—just another assignment.

He wanted me to—as always—drop everything and head for Washington. Hughes was very afraid that the government was seriously lagging in its evaluation of above-ground nuclear testing. I was supposed to check the accuracy and timeliness of the fallout statistics. If there was a problem, I should tell the government that Hughes would foot the bill to implement a system that would bring the statistics up-to-date and keep them current. None of it made sense to me, but I agreed to leave the next morning.

Yvette and I had lunch and dinner with the Mitchells. In the meantime, I made a few calls. To my amazement, the fallout figures were running sixty to ninety days behind. What was even more shocking is that no one seemed to care. I went to Washington and made the offer, but the government said it would update the information at no cost to Hughes. He never did tell me how he knew something was wrong.

Hughes had a very severe nuclear paranoia, and this time, it was valid. Not long after the inquiry, Senator Chet Hollifield of California called for a hearing by a joint committee overseeing nuclear affairs. The results showed that the statistics were running way behind the actual fallout—maybe even more than the government had admitted.

Meanwhile, back in the Bahamas, things were not going as planned. A major crisis was brewing. Political unrest in the region was escalating. The black locals had had a bellyful of being pushed around by the Bay Street Boys. Castro's revolution was going on in Cuba, and there was talk of a general strike in the Bahamas.

I had told Hughes to get out of there at the time the strike rumors had first started flying. He wouldn't listen, so I had some ex-FBI agents from Miami go to Nassau to see how serious the rumors were. One of the investigators came up with information that if the strike did hit, all air transportation to and from Nassau would be cut off. Cab drivers planned to park their cars on the runway so no plane could take off or land. Hughes would be isolated.

I was in New York when I received the news, and I called Hughes. His love affair with the Bahamas had already started to sour. One of his main complaints was the communications system. Hughes spent a lifetime on the phone, and the connections from the Bahamas were poor at best, forcing him to repeat things constantly. The fact that the island was now facing violence was the last straw, and Hughes made immediate plans to leave. The TWA jet that had been kept sitting on the airport runway for weeks was finally prepped and Hughes flew it back himself, without a copilot, nonstop to Los Angeles near the end of November, 1957.

With Howard back in the country, I heard from him with ever-increasing frequency. Getting in deeper with Hughes meant being at his disposal—anytime, anywhere, anyhow. I was still living in Washington, but spent a lot of time commuting between coasts. It was a tough schedule to juggle. I had a lot of other clients who paid me better retainers than Hughes did at the time. Fortunately, it wasn't exactly economy-class travel. I started staying at the Beverly Hills Hotel, and then moved to the Bel Air.

High-class hotels, four-star restaurants, and Hollywood parties. There were dinners at Perrino's, Chasen's, Larue's, and the Coconut Grove. I was on a first-name basis with the town's heavy hitters—politicians, film executives, and Hollywood legends. Like good champagne, it can go right to your head. It went to mine.

The only person who probably had more Hollywood connections than Hughes was his attorney, Greg Bautzer. Bautzer was a partner in one of the town's most powerful law firms. A flawlessly dressed, articulate man, Bautzer was a powerhouse. He had contacts for everything. Eating with him in a restaurant was an event. It didn't matter where we went—Bautzer knew everybody who walked in. And with the ladies, he had a reputation that rivaled Hughes's.

Bautzer didn't need to throw Hughes's name around town to get what he wanted. But he did have this insatiable need to tell people that he had just talked to Howard, or just had lunch with him. It wasn't true, but nobody knew it. Years later, during the Las

Vegas era when Howard was holed away on the ninth floor of the Desert Inn and nobody but his personal aides saw him, Bautzer told William Randolph Hearst, Jr. that he and Howard had just had lunch. People say hell hath no fury like a woman scorned. They ought to listen to a publisher scorned sometime. Hearst called me, absolutely furious. He had been after me for months to see or talk to Howard, and I had been stonewalling him. Then in walked Bautzer—a mere lawyer, from Hearst's point of view—with his claim. Hearst called me every name in the book, demanding to know why Bautzer could see Howard but he couldn't. It didn't matter that I denied it was true. Nothing I said changed his mind.

Bautzer had not meant to cause trouble. He considered Hughes to be a true friend and was one of his greatest champions. To some degree, though, the relationship meant power, and Bautzer used it like everyone else around Hughes did.

The power Greg wielded, both through his connection to Howard and in his own right, often proved useful to me. In fact, it even helped me prevent an international scandal. I got a call at my Washington office one afternoon in the late fifties from the CIA. The Company had been called regarding Jordan's King Hussein, a real playboy back then. It knew about my connections to Howard and in L.A. generally and wanted me to help throw the king a party at a private Hollywood home with a guest list that included famous celebrities. It seemed like such a simple thing to do.

Bautzer and his wife, the actress Dana Wynter, had a beautiful home just above the Bel Air Hotel. He graciously agreed to host the bash. The CIA graciously agreed to pick up the tab. Everything went off without a hitch. It was a star-studded gala, and much to his delight, King Hussein met a young actress by the name of Susan Cabot. She wasn't a major celebrity—one of the biggest parts she had played was a desert temptress in the lackluster "B" movie *Flame of Araby*, opposite Jeff Chandler and Maureen

O'Hara. Now that Arabian fantasy was being reenacted in the hills of Bel Air.

Hussein must have been infatuated with Cabot because the next thing I knew she had been invited to Jordan as his guest, but it wasn't to be a match made in heaven. Suddenly, there was a frantic call from CIA agent Sheff Edwards telling me we had to get Susan out of Jordan immediately. It turned out that the Arab king's lovely new playmate was Jewish! Apparently nobody knew this little detail before, and now it threatened to cause an international incident. Not that anybody was really concerned about her safety; the CIA just didn't want to cause the king any embarrassment and have him blame it on the U.S. I would never want to stand in the way of true love, but this was a potential powder keg. I immediately called Bautzer.

"Don't you have some client who has a big movie part opening up?" I asked. "You must get her the hell out of there."

Greg took charge and managed to slip Susan quietly out of the Middle East, though I don't know how he did it, and I don't know if Susan ever got that part. It pays to know the right people, especially when you're dealing with Arab kings and Jewish princesses.

Although I continued to live the high life in Los Angeles, the man footing my bill didn't allow his other employees such luxury.

On one occasion while I was staying at the Bel Air Hotel, enjoying a suite, and driving my usual Cadillac convertible, Hughes's secretary, Nadine Henley, called and said, "Honey, we really have a problem. Raymond Holliday, the executive vice president of Hughes Tool Company, is coming into town. He wants to stay at the Bel Air. And you know, he only drives Chevys and he always has a room." She thought there might be a problem if he saw me with a better setup than he had.

"I don't have a problem," I told Nadine. "He has a problem." I wouldn't give up the suite or the Cadillac. I wasn't an employee—I was a free agent.

It wouldn't be long before that freedom began to slip. I was making more and more trips west and spending less and less time in Washington. Eventually, I closed up the Washington office entirely. In retrospect, it was the biggest mistake of my life. I had a lot of clients (the United Steel Workers of America and Westinghouse, among them) who were paying me good retainers. But the world of power is an incredible seducer.

Hughes first decided he wanted me to move to Los Angeles in the beginning of 1959. I agreed to come for the summer, only if Hughes would provide a house, a maid, and two Cadillacs. Howard didn't balk at any part of my request.

That spring, I brought Yvette with me so that Virginia Tremaine, the woman who handled Hughes's real estate problems, could show us some rental properties. We had no sooner checked into the Bel Air Hotel when the phone rang. Virginia had lined up some places for us to see the next morning. The first property we checked out was located in Beverly Hills. It was a house Grace Kelly used to rent before she became a princess. The second place was on Saltair Avenue in the prestigious Brentwood section of Los Angeles, right next door to General Omar Bradley. It was perfect—complete with a gorgeous backyard, a huge swimming pool, outdoor barbecue pits, and a guest house. Mrs. Tremaine told us Hughes had already made arrangements for a maid to move in. Apparently, Hughes was very serious about keeping us happy. And he did, as long as I kept producing miracles. But he seemed to expect them with increasing frequency.

With Howard, everything was always an emergency, like the day in the late fifties that I received a call concerning his flying boat. Hughes called it *Hercules*, but the world knew it as the *Spruce Goose*, a name he despised. Then, as now, it's the world's largest plane—five stories high and some two hundred tons. Its life began in 1942 when Nazi submarines were making mincemeat out of America's naval fleet, sinking ships faster than they could be manufactured. Master shipbuilder Henry J. Kaiser thought the answer to the continuing destruction were giant "flying boats" so large that they could ferry men and supplies through the sky over the ocean where "no submarines could shoot them down." Kaiser talked the government into supporting his ideas, and Howard Hughes into building a prototype. It was a joint venture under the control of a government agency known as the Reconstruction Finance Corporation (RFC).

Mismanagement and an impossible production timetable threw the flying boat well behind schedule. This began the first of many serious government inquiries into Howard's business practices. These inquiries by the Special Senate Committee Investigating the National Defense Program brought Hughes to Washington to testify on his own behalf, and it would be the last time Hughes allowed himself to face such public hostility.

Chief among the committee's complaints was that the *Hercules* had never flown. It was to be Hughes's finest hour, when on November 1, 1947, he gathered press and crew at Terminal Island in Long Beach. Taxiing the *Hercules* through the choppy waters of Long Beach Harbor, Hughes would make history by flying the huge craft seventy feet above the water for a distance of one mile. The Senate hearings would come to an end within three weeks.

The *Hercules* would never fly again. Though officially the plane was owned by the U.S. government, it remained hangared in Long Beach, and always held a special place in Hughes's heart. So it came as little surprise when I got a call one afternoon, Howard's voice raised in nervous anxiety.

"Bob, at five P.M. Washington time, my whole deal with the government is going down the drain. The government is going to pick up the flying boat in Long Beach and have it destroyed. I've had people working on stalling them for two years and they won't give me any more extensions," he said. This would have been the most devastating thing ever to happen to Hughes. And he wanted me to stop it.

In typical Hughes fashion, he told me to drop everything and see if I could put the government off until I could go there and handle things personally. He didn't care how much it cost. I hurried Howard off the phone. After he hung up, I stared at the receiver. I had exactly an hour and a half to pull off another miracle.

My mind raced for an answer, until I remembered a friend of mine named Len De Lissio, a former FBI agent and chief of security for the General Services Administration. The GSA had taken over management of the flying boat project from the RFC. I got Len on the phone. "I'm going to talk very fast. Do you trust me?" I said to Len. He did. I asked Len to pave the way for me with Max Medley, the GSA controller, because I needed something immediately. Len put me on hold and made the call. A moment later, I was cross-connected with Max Medley. Unfortunately, Medley didn't have the same kind of faith in my integrity.

Medley had been pushed around pretty hard by Hughes's people in the past and wasn't in any mood to negotiate. I tried the humble approach, telling him that I had just gotten on the job and didn't deserve his criticism. When that failed, I played up my old government ties, hoping Medley would feel some kind of camaraderie. When he still didn't bite, I got desperate and told him to check my references. Medley took me up on that challenge, and I waited nervously for him to call back. It turned out that he checked with a couple of his close friends, Tommy Webb and Francis Flanagan, who just happened to be ex-FBI agents, and they said that I could be trusted. When Medley called back, he told me to be at his office at 10:00 A.M. on Monday. It was a temporary reprieve.

I took the next plane out and showed up at Medley's office. I didn't hear the good news I had hoped for. Medley had called in John Russell, who had been working on the project. Russell said nobody in the government gave a damn about Hughes's flying boat. It was nothing but a headache, it was just gathering dust, and they wanted it off the books. Finally, one of them said, "Why don't you just buy the goddamn thing." Why not indeed?

Right then and there, we settled on a $50,000 price tag. I couldn't wait to call Hughes, and he was in ecstasy. Unfortunately, his tax people weren't. They said the title had to stay in the government's name, otherwise Hughes would have to shell out over a million a year in undeductible expenses just to keep the *Spruce Goose* in Long Beach. The thrill of victory faded. How was I going to persuade the government to keep the title but not tell it why?

Sometime that night, I hit upon the crazy idea that perhaps we could rent the plane from the government, promising to continue to absorb all costs involved in upkeep. So instead of hammering out a purchase deal, I found myself convincing the government to rent Hughes the *Spruce Goose* for $9,600 a year.

The arrangement continued until 1979. At that time, the government definitely wanted out—there was talk of putting a piece of the wing in the Smithsonian, talk of complete destruction, and even talk about selling bits of it as souvenirs. Finally, the *Spruce Goose* was sold to the Aero Club of Southern California, which then worked out a lease deal with the Wrather Corporation. Today, of course, it's a major tourist attraction in Long Beach, California, where hundreds of thousands of visitors have marveled at Howard Hughes's vision. The Man would have been very pleased.

Airplanes and flying played an important role in Hughes's life, both before the *Spruce Goose* and after, so it's hardly surprising that as I became increasingly involved with Howard, I would get drawn into that arena as well. It would culminate with my entering the biggest battleground of all: Hughes's fight with TWA.

It was no wonder Hughes and TWA became adversaries. Hughes had begun investing in TWA stock in 1939. Back then it was called Transcontinental and Western Airlines, and Howard would eventually end up with 78 percent of the stock. He ran that airline as his own private company, with complete disregard for the ten thousand or so minority stockholders.

It was Hughes who hired, and fired, the company's president. And while he never attended a single board meeting, he alone determined the topics to be covered. He approved every advertisement, okayed the color of the planes' interiors, and even designed the red flying dart that is to this day the airline's symbol. Make no mistake, it was Hughes's pride and joy. At one point, he nearly ran it into the ground.

The problem came in the mid-fifties when jet planes were about to make their appearance in U.S. commercial aviation. After years of bumpy propellor-driven flights, the airline industry was on the verge of being able to offer smooth, fast service on the sleek wings of jet-powered aircraft. Yet as promising as the future seemed, the expense of converting entire fleets to jet power sent a ripple of anxiety throughout the industry, a ripple no one felt more strongly than Howard Hughes.

Long considered a leader in airplane design, Hughes was expected by many to pilot TWA into the forefront of jet aviation. This was not to happen. Despite the pressure on Hughes, he declined to purchase several jets proposed to TWA by leading British manufacturers. Claiming that the jets were either too slow or unreliable, Hughes continued to investigate alternates, and in doing so lost valuable time to the competition.

In October, 1955, Pan American World Airways, TWA's leading rival on international routes, became the first American carrier to order jet planes, giving it an advantage in transatlantic routes. A few weeks later, American Airlines, TWA's major domestic competitor, placed its order, insuring that it would have the first jets flying from coast to coast.

After some attempts at having his own planes designed for TWA, and months of negotiations, Hughes finally jumped into the ring. In February, 1956, Hughes placed an order for $185 million worth of Boeing's new 707s. To that he added another $126 million in orders for Convair's new 880s, plus some $90 million in jet engines from Pratt & Whitney Aircraft. Totaling over $401 million, it was easily the largest order in aviation at the time.

Yet, even as TWA was writing a new chapter in its history, its foundation was beginning to crumble. Just a month before Hughes placed his jet-plane order, longtime TWA President Ralph Damon was stricken by a heart attack and died. And after eight years of unbroken profits, TWA lost $2.3 million in 1956, placing it in a vulnerable position to finance such a large purchase.

The call reluctantly went out to find financing outside the company, with the negotiations handled by Hughes's Houston attorney, Raymond Cook. It was not to be an easy job. What none of us really realized at the time was that Howard, then living at a bungalow at the Beverly Hills Hotel, had already begun to exhibit the kind of weird behavior that would dominate his later life. It meant nothing for Howard to take a new plane out of service and keep it for days at his personal disposal, losing hundreds of thousands of dollars in potential passenger revenue in the process. And whenever I traveled on the airline, Hughes invariably would call just minutes before departure time. It was always a long conversation and no matter how hard I tried telling him that the plane was being held for me, I was never able to get Howard off the phone quickly.

"Don't worry about it, Bob," he would reply. "I've told them they can't take off without you."

One time, he held up the plane with a two-hour conversation. I pleaded with him to hang up, figuring that when I did get on board, the other passengers would be set to kill me. The word got out that the flight was being held up by Howard Hughes, but this was of little consolation to people eager to begin the thirteen-hour flight and trying to make connections. Instead of getting special treatment because of my ties with Hughes, I was treated like Public Enemy Number One.

Such actions weren't lost on TWA's new president, Carter Burgess. After less than a year on the job, he decided he couldn't take it any longer, and suddenly resigned. It would be seven months before Hughes appointed a replacement—ex-Pentagon official Charles S. Thomas, a hard-nosed executive who was once President Eisenhower's secretary of the Navy.

After much negotiating on the part of Cook and others for more than a year, a deal was finalized for a loan from investment bankers Dillon, Read & Company in February, 1959, only thirty days before the first Boeing 707 was set to leave the assembly line. The company would arrange for $165 million to be loaned to Howard, but only if he agreed not to change TWA's management. If he meddled, Hughes would have to place his airline stock in a ten-year voting trust, with Dillon, Read electing the majority of trustees. It would have effectively ended his control of the company and there was no way Howard was going to agree, no matter how much he needed cash.

Meanwhile, Hughes and Thomas were at loggerheads practically from the word go. Like Burgess before him, Thomas didn't hang around to take much abuse. In July, 1960, he resigned to take over the administration of the huge Irvine Ranch development in Orange County, California. Though the Thomas skirmish was over, the war continued.

In late 1960, Howard made another one of his "drop-every-thing calls." He wanted me to check out other sources of generating cash. Hughes had a feeling that the other major airlines were working out better deals with the banks and the insurance companies for their jet financing than he was. Hughes put me to work on an assignment researching other airlines' loans and interest rates. Eventually, I wrote a sixty-page report condensing my findings. I included interviews with presidents or loan officers of some thirty banks around the country, plus information I had learned from research done through insurance companies and investment houses. It turned out that Hughes was right—he wasn't being offered the same kind of deals, even though he was matching the financing almost dollar for dollar. All things considered, Hughes should have been given a better interest rate, not a worse one.

However, when Hughes tried to get the same deal as the other airlines, he was stonewalled. The East Coast financial institutions seemed to be out to get him. Although Hughes Tool Company was still turning a huge profit, the patents were running out and competition was heating up. They had Hughes over the proverbial barrel.

He finally capitulated, although he knew that the rate of interest was unreasonable in comparison to that charged the other airlines. The banks were ready for him, declaring that they had decided to add a 22 percent prepayment penalty. Hughes was more furious than I'd ever seen him before. He ordered me to find out the highest prepayment penalty ever included in a conventional financial transaction in excess of $50 million. When I reported back to him that we couldn't find any such loan with a penalty of more than one year's interest, he decided to go elsewhere for his money.

He asked a friend who was a top executive at Bank of America in San Francisco to form a syndicate of West Coast banks and insurance companies to finance the loan. Several days later, the friend called me and asked me to meet him for lunch at the Jonathan Club. At our meeting he announced solemnly, "We have to bail out of the deal. We cannot withstand the pressure from the East Coast."

Backed against the wall, Howard decided to accept the Dillon, Read plan late in November. With ex-TWA president Thomas no longer in place, the bankers now insisted that Hughes place his TWA stock in trust *immediately*. Seemingly trapped, Howard agreed; and on December 15, 1960, Howard Hughes lost control of TWA.

Yet, while all seemed to have gone against him, Howard was not quite out of fight. Before the year was out, he unexpectedly moved his entourage—Jean Peters included—from the Beverly Hills Hotel to a rented house in Rancho Santa Fe, a hundred miles south of Los Angeles. The move seemed to renew his spirit.

The following month, he slapped back at TWA from afar. The airline hadn't counted on the strength of Howard's friendships within the board membership. When the new management called the first meeting of the trustees, Hughes stopped his contingent from attending, thereby squelching a quorum.

TWA's management, led by its newly appointed president, Charles C. Tillinghast, Jr., cried foul. What hit the fan fell to earth on June 30, 1961, when TWA slapped Hughes with a $105 million lawsuit, setting off one of the longest and most expensive legal battles in America's history.

Representing the airlines was an attorney named John Sonnett, a partner in the Wall Street law firm of Cahill, Gordon, Reindel & Ohl. When Howard realized that he was in for a protracted legal joust, he decided to be represented by a prestigious Wall Street firm as well. We pursued a number of firms, trying to find one that would take the case, but in each instance we were told that it would represent a conflict of interest. Finally, a loudmouthed Wall Street attorney named Chester C. Davis agreed to leave his partnership in a Wall Street firm and handle Hughes's defense personally. Ironically, since Hughes owned 78 percent of TWA, he found himself in the extraordinary position of footing most of the plaintiff's costs, as well as the entire cost of his own defense.

In the meantime, John Sonnett had assigned a young lawyer named Frederick P. Furth to personally serve Howard Hughes with a subpoena to testify in the case. Furth in turn hired an ex-FBI agent turned private eye named Alfred E. Leckey to uncover his prey. It didn't take Hughes long to learn that process servers were stalking his whereabouts. His next phone call was to me.

He wanted me to throw my old friend Leckey off the track. By this time, Hughes was living in a house in Bel Air, having moved out of his rented Rancho Santa Fe digs due to faulty plumbing. While he remained in his darkened bedroom surrounded by his aides, I began to stage a subterfuge truly worthy of Hollywood.

Working with Mike Conrad, Howard's security chief at the time, I hired a tall, lanky actor to impersonate Hughes. I had the performer make appearances in restaurants and nightclubs in Reno and Lake Tahoe. One weekend, he was in San Francisco; the next, San Diego. Hughes was spotted in a New York elevator, in a Beverly Hills drugstore, and at a secluded Mexican resort. Each step of the way the press followed, and so did the process servers.

We even went so far as to have a photo released showing our fake Hughes in shirtsleeves busily going over papers on a patio at a hotel in Squaw Valley. The process servers were frustrated as hell, and so was Leckey. At one point, he had ten men on staff tracking down my phony leads.

While I had men following Leckey, at one point he started to tail me personally, foolishly thinking that I might lead him to Hughes. The surveillance teams began tripping over one another like something out of a Keystone comedy. One day when I spotted Leckey in the rearview mirror of my car, I pulled over to the side of the road and confronted him directly.

"Look," I began. "Your job is to find Howard Hughes. You're not going to do that by tailing me. It's a waste of your time and energy," I said. "Since Hughes owns seventy-eight percent of TWA, and since TWA is paying your salary, that means Mr. Hughes is footing seventy-eight percent of your bill. I'm going to see that you do a good job. So, go after him, not after me, because I'm just not going to lead you to him."

The case would drag on for almost three years, and over that time much of my work was directed toward the litigation. The legal fees alone ended up costing nearly $20 million. During that entire period, Hughes steadfastly refused to come out of hiding and testify in court, and they never were able to serve him.

TWA finally won the case by default. The news sent Hughes into an extreme emotional depression. Equally depressing was the judgment levied against him. Howard had told me that Davis guaranteed him that the maximum judgment, should he lose the case, would not be more than $5 million. The estimates were way off. Asserting that Hughes deliberately and willfully defied the court's order to appear, Judge Charles M. Metzner threw the book at the richest man in the United States. When the final cost was determined at a separate hearing, the actual judgment amounted to $145,448,141.01.

Though Chester Davis continued to appeal the case, it was much more serious than anyone had thought. Hughes became obsessed, unable to talk or think about anything else. And while he would eventually end up making money on the deal, through his sale of TWA stock, he couldn't know that at the time. And in reality, Hughes never did see the end of the litigation—it wasn't actually settled until recently.

Even though the TWA action never left his mind for long, it occasionally made way for Hughes's eternal wanderlust and his vision of a private kingdom. With the failure of the Bahamas still a fresh memory, Hughes no longer had plans for an island in the Atlantic. Instead, he set his sights on an island in the desert. A place called Las Vegas.

Chapter Four

TARGET: FIDEL CASTRO

"GOT ANY PLANS FOR THE WEEKEND?" THOSE FEW WORDS SIGNALED my introduction to the town that would eventually come to define my entire life and career: Las Vegas.

It seemed a simple enough question. But this was the spring of 1959, a time when Las Vegas was nothing like it is now. The man asking the question was Hughes's West Coast attorney, Greg Bautzer, a man who knew everyone in Las Vegas, as he did in Hollywood. Bautzer had called the first weekend I was in Los Angeles as I was attempting to find a rental home to use for the summer. My wife and I had just gotten back to the Bel Air Hotel after agreeing to take the home on Saltair Road in Brentwood when Bauzter phoned.

"Bob, how would you and your wife like to go to Las Vegas at my expense, with a bundle of cash?"

I had to admit it sounded good. It seemed that Bautzer had a little job for me. One of his major clients had been trying for six weeks to serve a subpoena on Beldon Kettleman, owner of the El Rancho Hotel. Kettleman was inside the hotel, but none of the men trying to serve papers could get past security. Bautzer said that he had convinced his clients that I had the imagination to pull it off.

Since I have always been tempted by jobs that are supposed to be "impossible," and I liked the idea of an all-expenses-paid vacation in Las Vegas, I took Greg up on his challenge.

Although within a few years I would be making Las Vegas my full-time home, in 1959 I was pretty much ignorant of it. I knew it was a gambling town, and I'd certainly heard the rumors about Bugsy Siegel and the creation of "The Strip" in 1947 with the construction of the Flamingo Hotel and Casino. And while the Mafia was said to still control things, the names of the owners and the gamblers and the reputed mobsters meant nothing to me yet.

Bautzer dropped off an envelope for me at the Bel Air filled with about three grand in cash and a copy of the subpoena. I was on my own from there. Even so, it seemed like a walk in the park—until Yvette and I tried to get a room.

From L.A., I called the El Rancho to reserve a room. I figured that I might as well get a foot inside the door before I tried to serve Kettleman. Good idea, but unfortunately there was no room at the inn. Same story at the Flamingo, and the Desert Inn, and every other hotel in town. I started to get a little desperate. Time was ticking away, and already the job wasn't going well. Fortunately, I had one more option—my old friend Edward Bennett Williams, who had his own connections in town.

When Ed heard my problem, he told me to sit still. Ten minutes later, a man called back and asked what I needed in Las Vegas. I told him a room at the El Rancho, and he said it was a done deed. Moreover, the stranger said he would drop by to meet me the next night at nine o'clock sharp at the bell captain's desk.

"I'll be wearing a dark suit and I have gray hair," he said. "And my name is Johnny."

The next day we drove to Las Vegas. At the El Rancho, they rolled out the red carpet. Yvette and I were given a beautiful bungalow, filled with flowers and fruit. And they told us everything was on the house. I was impressed. Johnny must be some kind of miracle worker, I figured.

Bautzer had told us before we left that Kettleman was notorious for bugging the rooms and bungalows at the El Rancho. My wife and I decided to play it safe. If we needed to talk about anything important, we did it outside. Kettleman would get nothing but idle chitchat from us.

Right after dinner, I decided to get a little action at the craps table. I got pretty lucky—lucky enough to later buy my wife a bracelet she spotted in the gift shop. Just before 9:00 P.M., I headed for the bell captain's desk. Standing there was a man who looked like money—good-looking, expensive suit, shined shoes ... the works. As I approached him, he gave me the once-over and said, "My name is Johnny Rosselli." The name meant nothing to me then, but it would soon. Introductions out of the way, Rosselli became expansive and told me that I should meet the owner.

"He's playing it quite cozy these days, because they're trying to drop a paper on him," Rosselli confided to me. He continued, laughing, "They think they can get to him. It's a big joke. They'll never do it." He laughed again.

The idea of the cat-and-mouse game seemed to appeal to him. Of course, Rosselli obviously had no idea that I was the one who was trying to get Kettleman, and I sure as hell didn't enlighten him.

Rosselli motioned me to follow him, and we walked over to a well-hidden corner, set apart from the rest of the casino. Sitting right there at a table was Beldon Kettleman, having a drink with Zsa Zsa Gabor. Johnny pushed me forward and introduced me, making a big show of it. Kettleman stood up and shook my hand. And all the while the subpoena was burning a hole inside my pocket. It was right at that moment that I made the decision. There was no way I could serve the paper. I couldn't care less about Kettleman—but I did care about my friendship with Ed Williams. If I served Kettleman after that introduction, I would piss off this "Johnny" fellow something fierce. And while that didn't bother me much, I was worried about what it would do to Ed's relationship with Johnny. I started wishing I hadn't bought that bracelet for my wife, because I could have used my winnings at craps to pay back Bautzer. It was too late at that point, though, so I decided to forget about Kettleman, Bautzer, and the subpoena, and just have a nice weekend—all the while planning to do some fast talking once I returned to L.A.

When I did, I called Bautzer and told him I would have to return my fee. When I explained why, he couldn't stop laughing.

"Do you know who Johnny Rosselli is?" he asked, obviously enjoying my confusion. "It's a damn good thing you didn't serve that," Greg went on, still chuckling. "If you had, you'd never have left Las Vegas," he said, suddenly quite serious. Bautzer told me to keep the money. The laugh, he said, was worth every penny.

I later learned that Johnny Rosselli had emigrated to the U.S. from Sicily as a child, and—according to most reports—joined the mob back in the twenties, as a member of Longy Zwillman's gang in New Jersey. He then moved onward and upward to Chicago and Al Capone. Rosselli's special talents included labor racketeering and extortion. When Capone was nailed for income tax evasion in '31, Rosselli became the mob's man in Hollywood and wound up serving four years in prison for trying to extort money from movie companies. He also ran the syndicate's casino in Havana and eventually became one of its top men in Las Vegas.

A few nights after I flew back to L.A., Bautzer saw Rosselli at Perrino's in Los Angeles and told him the story. Rosselli got such a kick out of it that he gave Bautzer his home phone number and told him to tell me to call the next time I was in town. When Greg told me, I couldn't help feeling a little odd—one of the most powerful mob figures in the country wanted to take me to lunch.

Rosselli and I wound up sharing a lot of lunches. We built a solid friendship over the years—so solid, in fact, that my children took to calling him "Uncle Johnny." I suppose I should have known from the start that it would eventually go sour. To save his own skin years later, he opened his mouth once too often about one of the biggest secret operations in U.S. history. It was an operation that I brought Johnny into, and which many have tried to link to the assassination of President Kennedy.

In 1959, the CIA decided that Fidel Castro had to go. From the beginning, the Agency had kept a close eye on Castro and his revolution. When President Juan Batista fled Cuba on January 1, 1959, Castro took control and immediately started going back on his promises. There were no open elections, no civil liberties, no spreading of power. He was in bed with the Communists, and in concert with Moscow. Even so, the CIA felt that Fidel Castro played by his own rules and that he had a deep-seated hatred for America which made him extremely dangerous.

Castro started pushing his weight around with subversion and other activities in places like the Dominican Republic, Panama, and Nicaragua. From the looks of things, he was out to undermine American interests in the Caribbean and Central America. His direct line to the Kremlin gave him all the military muscle he needed. It became crystal clear in Washington that he had to be eliminated, one way or another.

Plans for the Bay of Pigs invasion were drawn up during President Eisenhower's last year in office. It became the CIA's boldest operation to date. Yet, things were not to go as planned. Through no fault of the CIA, the invasion nearly set off World War III. President Kennedy literally cried. And the Company was hung out to dry by the White House and a congressional commission some sixteen years later.

In the winter of 1959–60, however, the CIA still thought it could pull off the invasion. But it thought the odds might be better if the plan went one step further—the murder of Fidel Castro. All the Company needed was someone to do the dirty work for it. Professional killers. A gangland-style hit.

It was then that the CIA conceived the notion to let the mobsters do it themselves. They'd had a grudge against Castro ever since he'd forced them out of the Havana casinos. It was even rumored that Meyer Lansky had put a million-dollar bounty on Castro's head. CIA Director Allen Dulles passed the ball to his deputy director, Richard Bissell. Bissell handed off to the CIA security chief, Colonel Sheffield Edwards. And then I received the call.

When my family and I lived in Virginia, we used to throw big Maine-style clambakes. Barrels of fresh lobsters, buckets of steamers, and plenty of booze. These parties became legend, and one of the most famous was one I threw for Scotty McLeod, the ex-FBI agent who had been picked by President Eisenhower to clean up the State Department. Unfortunately, he never had the chance to complete his assignment. There had also been some bad publicity about Scotty's use of polygraph tests inside the State Department. Having second thoughts, Eisenhower decided Scotty was too hot to handle at close range, so he made him ambassador to Ireland.

To bid Scotty bon voyage, I threw a farewell clambake and invited two of my CIA contacts, Jim O'Connell and Sheff Edwards. John Murray, chief of the Air Force's intelligence unit, was there as well, along with Hal Marlowe, undersheriff of Los Angeles County. On the day of the event, one more name was added to the guest list: Johnny Rosselli was in town, and I invited him over.

It was quite a bash. The liquor was flowing. Murray took over the piano. McLeod backed him up on drums. By the time Marlowe arrived, things were rolling.

Just as the clambake started to peak, Yvette told me I had a telephone call. I was in the middle of cooking the lobsters, and I couldn't simply walk away (all those who cook lobsters *know* that timing is everything). So as Styles Bridges, the senator from New Hampshire, walked by, I grabbed him and put him in charge of the pots.

This creep on the phone turned out to be some lobbyist calling about an upcoming Senate bill that I was interested in. He told me there was only one man in the world who could help me. And only he knew this man intimately. In fact, he said he "owned" the man. Curious now, I asked just who we were talking about. He claimed it was Senator Styles Bridges. I immediately told the creep no deal, but I didn't tell him that Bridges was downstairs right that minute tending to my "animals."

Back at the party, I told Styles about the call. I have never seen a man so angry in my life, and Styles later roasted that lobbyist. That jerk had messed with the wrong clambake.

Meanwhile, in another part of my backyard, the CIA was rubbing elbows with the Mafia. Sheff Edwards had cornered Rosselli for a little chat. I don't know what was said, but it must have been interesting. And though I know that the Castro situation wasn't discussed then, that meeting planted the seed that would eventually turn me into a link between the Feds and the mob.

Soon after the clambake, Edwards and the CIA checked out Rosselli to determine just how far his connections ran. They independently learned that Johnny had access to the highest levels of the Mafia. And that's when the Company came to me, to see if I could get Johnny interested in the Cuban situation.

Though I'm no saint, I am a religious man, and I knew that the CIA was talking about murder. O'Connell and Edwards contended that it was a war—a just war. They said it was necessary to protect the country. They used the analogy of World War II: if we had known the exact bunker that Hitler was in during the war, we wouldn't have hesitated to kill the bastard. The CIA felt exactly the same way about Castro. If Fidel, his brother Raul, and Che Guevara were assassinated, thousands of lives might be saved.

But in my mind, justified or not, I would still have blood on my hands. I had to think about it. The deal carried a pretty big price tag. I kept thinking about my family. What kind of danger would it put them in? If anything went wrong, I was the fall guy, caught between protecting the government and protecting the mob, two armed camps that could crush me like a bug. That night I locked myself in the rec room, turned on my favorite music—an album by the 101 Strings—and wrestled with the choice. At some point, I decided to go ahead as the Company asked and try to recruit Johnny Rosselli. If it saved even one American life, I decided, it was worthwhile.

I flew out to L.A., and Johnny and I met at the Brown Derby restaurant in August, 1960. When Johnny arrived, he was his usual dapper self, from manicured nails to gleaming shoes. He strutted to the booth, a man sure of his power and his place. I waited until coffee to broach the subject. When I presented Rosselli with the proposition, I made it clear that anything we talked about was strictly confidential. Nobody could know the details—not even the rest of the U.S. government. This was a "cut-out" operation, and the Agency must have total deniability.

Rosselli's first response was laughter. "Me? You want *me* to get involved with Uncle Sam? The Feds are tailing me wherever I go. They go to my shirtmaker to see if I'm buying things with cash. They go to my tailor to see if I'm using cash there. They're always trying to get something on me. Bob, are you sure you're talking to the right guy?"

When I finally convinced Rosselli that I was serious, *very* serious, he sat staring at me, tapping his fingers nervously on the table. I didn't want to pull any punches with the man, so I was totally upfront about the conditions of the deal.

"It's up to you to pick whom you want, but it's got to be set up so that Uncle Sam isn't involved—ever. If anyone connects you with the U.S. government, I will deny it," I told him. "If you say

Bob Maheu brought you into this, that I was your contact man, I'll say you're off your rocker, you're lying, you're trying to save your hide. I'll swear by everything holy that I don't know what in hell you're talking about."

Furthermore, I wanted it clearly understood that this was a one-shot deal. "I won't ever do business with you again," I emphasized, to assure him that I had absolutely no intention of getting into bed with the Mafia. Yet, I wanted him to feel comfortable with the arrangement and to know that he could trust me completely. "I won't ever reveal the content of any private conversations I may overhear while I'm in your company," I stated. "It's none of my business or anyone else's." He stared back at me in silence.

Surrounding us at the Brown Derby were the usual stars, producers, and agents who make Hollywood a town of fantasy. Yet, nothing they were discussing could have come close to the incredible plot I had laid on the table for Johnny. Not even in the movies would people believe that the United States government and organized crime were holding hands to remove a dictator from power.

Rosselli hesitated at first, but then agreed. Many people have speculated that Johnny was looking for an eventual deal with the government, or some sort of big payoff. The truth, as corny as it may sound, is that down deep he thought it was his "patriotic" duty.

Understand that the world was quite different then. The Cold War was raging. Only months before, Francis Gary Powers had been shot down while flying his U-2 reconnaissance plane over the Soviet Union. The relationship between Washington and Moscow was at an all-time low, with Soviet Premier Khrushchev going so far as to openly call President Eisenhower a liar on several occasions.

Once the decision was made, it didn't take Rosselli long to put his plan into motion. On October 11, 1960, we took off for what would be the first of many trips to Miami. We booked ourselves into the Kenilworth Hotel, selected because Arthur Godfrey did his TV show from there. In Miami, Johnny introduced me to two men who would help us—"Sam Gold" and "Joe." Sam was Johnny's backup man; Joe would be our direct contact in Cuba. These weren't ordinary mob lackeys. Johnny didn't bother to tell me that "Sam" was Sam Giancana, his boss within the Mafia and the chief of its gigantic Chicago operation. Or that "Joe" was Santos Trafficante, former syndicate chief in Havana, and the most powerful Mafia man in the South.

I later learned that Johnny didn't just need a little help from these men, he needed their okay. Trafficante was necessary to get Castro because he had the connections inside Cuba, and Giancana was necessary to get Trafficante, because Trafficante had the stature of a "Godfather," and only a man of equal stature—like Giancana—could approach him for help. Johnny couldn't do it on his own. Both were among the ten most powerful Mafia members—a fact I learned only after seeing their pictures in a magazine soon after meeting them.

Sam Giancana was a proud and charismatic man. Though small in stature, he was in top physical shape and had a dynamic style. It was also odd that such a tough individual was so sentimental. He got tears in his eyes whenever he heard the song "You're Nobody Till Somebody Loves You." It meant something special. He said, "Someday I'll explain it to you," but he never did. Watching Giancana in Miami made me understand the curious appeal mobsters have in American culture. I've seen all sorts of men in all sorts of situations—presidents, sheikhs, you name it. But never have I seen anyone with the almost palpable sense of power possessed by a Mafia don. When Sam Giancana walked through the lobby of the Fontainebleau Hotel, where he was staying, it was like a king passing. People just made way.

In November, 1960, Nixon lost the presidential election to Kennedy. While all the rest of America was preparing for the holidays, Kennedy was preparing for the White House, and Howard Hughes was preparing to make him feel welcome. Admittedly, Howard was playing catch-up. He was so certain that Nixon would win the election that he hadn't properly covered his bases with the Kennedy campaign. With the election results, Hughes suddenly became a Kennedy man—this despite the fact that he never really liked the Kennedy family. It was my impression that this dislike dated back to his Hollywood days, when Hughes supposedly had a confrontation with Joe Kennedy. Regardless, Howard wanted to make a sizable contribution to the Kennedy inaugural, and he wanted everyone in Washington to know it. He instructed me that no expense was to be spared.

Kennedy's people had planned a spectacular gala at the Washington Armory, with Frank Sinatra leading the entertainment. I gave prominent Washington attorneys Gillis Long and Bob Collier carte blanche to come up with ideas to make a big impression on Howard's behalf in the Kennedy camp. They managed to get a number of choice seats at the swearing-in ceremony, as well as two adjoining suites in a hotel overlooking the inaugural parade where we planned to serve an all-day buffet for our guests. Plans for the inaugural ball called for the dance to take place in six or seven different locations, so great was the demand for tickets. Long and Collier made arrangements for a half-dozen new limousines to be on call to transport our guests. Additionally, they booked hospitality suites at each of the hotels where the dances would take place, knowing that the invitees would become impatient waiting for President and Mrs. Kennedy to make an appearance at each location.

Just when everything seemed to be in place, Frank Sinatra placed a call to Greg Bautzer asking whether Hughes wanted to donate a TWA jet to carry entertainers and VIPs from Los Angeles to Washington and back. The gesture would have cost Howard $40,000, an insignificant amount as far as he was concerned.

Unfortunately, it was illegal for an airline to make a political contribution of a chartered flight. The Democratic National Committee suggested that Hughes buy four $10,000 box seats at the gala. The committee could then legally use the money to charter the jet. Hughes immediately accepted the idea, arranged for the airplane, and assigned me to drop everything and accompany the stars to Washington.

Luckily, the CIA gave me time off from my delicate mission. It wasn't my idea of fun, but it actually turned out to be quite enjoyable. No sooner had we become airborne than Milton Berle took over. He had us all in stitches from lift-off to touchdown, helped by a performance in flight by the Nelson Riddle Orchestra.

Despite all the planning, Mother Nature threw us a curve. An enormous blizzard on the day of the inauguration kept all of our guests prisoner in their hotel, and all of our box seats remained empty. With traffic at a total standstill, by the time I arrived at La Salle du Bois, where my wife and I were hosting a pre-gala dinner, I was just in time to pick up the tab. The fact that all this hoopla could be plotted in the shadow of the planned assassination of Fidel Castro illustrated the bizarre world in which I found myself operating at the time.

Once the inauguration was behind me, I traveled back to Miami and eventually set up our headquarters at the Fontainebleau, with Sam placing us in a five-room suite on the top floor with a kitchen and a dining room. The minute I walked in, Giancana said, "Okay, smart-ass. You've been bragging about your cooking. This is going to be an opportunity for you to either satisfy my taste ... or I'm going to throw your butt out of the goddamned window."

He took me into the kitchen, showed me the special kettles he had ordered, and gave me a pad of paper. He told me to write down whatever I needed to feed him and Rosselli for three days. We weren't going to eat outside the suite. I'll never forget that Sam

119

requested spareribs. I only had to ask one question: how he liked them. That night, we feasted on champagne and gray beluga caviar that Giancana had flown in every day from a gourmet shop in New York. Then we tackled the spareribs. Giancana filled himself to the gills. He said it was the biggest meal he'd ever had in his life. I didn't sail out any windows.

In addition to a certain style, both Giancana and Rosselli had an innate distaste for the young Mafia punks who tried to act tough around them—the sort who seem to be constantly auditioning for the latest Hollywood shoot-'em-up. One time, we were all sitting by the pool when a good-looking man walked up and immediately started talking tough. Without even looking at the punk, Giancana grabbed his necktie and yanked him close. Sam stared right into the kid's eyes and said, "I eat little boys like you for breakfast. Get your ass out of here before I get hungry!"

As tough as the man could be in public, he was almost childlike at times in private. Each day, he would get a call from the front desk, alerting him that his daily delivery of caviar had arrived. And every day, upon hearing the news, he would get just as excited as the day before. He would run from room to room in his shorts shouting, "It's on its way!" Then he'd make this mad dash to the refrigerator and take out all the ingredients he had prepared in advance—the chopped white and yolk of a hard-boiled egg, finely chopped white and green onion, plus sour cream. Only then would he pick up the phone to alert room service to deliver his favorite snack. Seeing him like that made it hard to imagine that here was a man who had been arrested over fifty times by his mid-twenties.

He also had nerves like I've never seen. We would be eating dinner at the hotel, and some man would walk into the restaurant with a beautiful woman. Sam would reach right over and pat her on the rear as she passed. And her boyfriend or husband wouldn't say a word, because nobody told Giancana what he could or couldn't touch. And nobody touched what was his, especially Phyllis McGuire.

Professionally, she was one of the singing McGuire Sisters; privately, she was Giancana's mistress. More important, she was his true love. During one of our meetings in Miami, Rosselli told me that Giancana wanted to take off for Las Vegas immediately. I told him no, and so did the CIA. It seemed that Giancana was upset about Phyllis. He had heard that she had been dating the comedian Dan Rowan while he and partner Dick Martin were appearing at the Desert Inn. Since Sam couldn't go in person, I agreed to at least arrange for a tail to be put on Rowan.

I also called up Sheff and asked if the CIA could authorize placing a sensitive microphone on the wall of the room adjoining Rowan's suite at his hotel. Since it wouldn't penetrate the wall, it would not be breaking and entering, and would therefore be legal. The bug would simply pick up conversations from Rowan's bedroom. Sheff told me that the Agency wouldn't take part in such a bug, but would pay up to a thousand dollars if I wanted to hire someone to do the job.

The man I called was Ed DuBois, the same Miami private eye who had checked on the situation in the Bahamas for me. He sent one of his operatives to Las Vegas. Unfortunately, the man put an illegal tap on Rowan's phone and was caught. Just why he thought tapping Rowan's phone would help determine details about his love life, I'll never understand.

Rosselli had to call Tom Foley, a Las Vegas attorney, to bail the man out of jail. When Giancana heard about it, he thought it was hilarious. He started laughing and didn't stop for what seemed all afternoon. The CIA wasn't laughing, though: these gangland helpers were getting to be a nuisance. Furthermore, the man was interrogated by the FBI before being released and said I hired him.

One day soon after this fiasco, two FBI agents called on me, and read me a formal statement of my legal rights. It was obvious a criminal investigation had begun, and the potential for my arrest, along with Giancana's and Rosselli's, certainly existed. I turned to Sheff Edwards for help, and got his permission to refer the FBI to him, which I did.

While this controversy swirled around us, we continued to try to plan the Cuban operation. It didn't help when I noticed that people were beginning to tail us. They were FBI agents, now very interested in our every move. One night at dinner, I noticed one agent following Rosselli into the bathroom. When Rosselli came back to the table, I went to the men's room and cornered the operative. I put him in the kitchen, went back into the dining room, and picked up another FBI agent who was spying on us from a table across the room. I escorted him to the kitchen, too, and made the introductions. Both agents were pretty angry that I had embarrassed them. Of course, neither man had any idea about our mission with the CIA, and they certainly didn't hear about it from me. It was just further proof of what you always hear: one branch of the government doesn't know what another is doing. I knew my phone was tapped, too, so I tried to make things easy on the government. I'd purposely call the CIA from my hotel room rather than from a pay phone. That way the FBI could listen in, and save both agencies some extra work.

The big problem was keeping the surveillance a secret from Rosselli and Giancana. I was in a horrible position. Let's face it, they weren't neophytes. I presumed both could spot a tail a mile away. My credibility was on the line. As it turned out, I was lucky. Neither man suspected anything.

The FBI was even more of a problem after the fact. Particularly Hoover. He sent a couple of agents over to my house to "debrief" me. They didn't care about Castro. Hoover wanted to know about any conversations I overheard while around Giancana. I tried to explain to the agents that I had a promise to keep with

Rosselli and Giancana: never to reveal anything. It was naturally very difficult for them to understand how an ex-FBI agent like myself who was still very loyal to Hoover would not at least tell them something about what I may have heard. I felt then as I still do—my word is my bond and no one can break it—so I held my ground.

Despite the rumor that my relationship with Hoover hit the skids at this point, I did receive a communication from him years later which indicated that I was still on his "favored list." I think Hoover received a bad rap about his leadership of the Bureau. Sure, he was tough, but you need that kind of regimentation in law enforcement. There are rules, and you can't get too soft. When I was an agent, I was never asked to do anything I hadn't been told about in training, and I never took an assignment that I didn't believe Hoover would have taken on himself, so I have nothing but respect for the man.

In any case, as I mentioned, the CIA wanted a gangland-style hit. Castro would be gunned down by a Cuban assassin hired by Giancana and Rosselli. But Sam said it was too dangerous, and too tough to recruit the gunman. He came up with the idea of poison. Something neat and clean, that eliminated the need for an ambush. The CIA technicians started to work on a pill that could be slipped into Castro's drink. What they finally developed was a colorless, round, gelatinlike capsule the size of a pea, which released botulism into any liquid.

Eventually I passed an envelope containing the tiny pills to Giancana and Rosselli, who were in charge of delivering the capsules to our Cuban contact. As far as I know, the delivery was made, but perhaps the Cubans involved got cold feet. Castro never drank his Mickey.

Meantime, Washington was getting nervous. Officials there thought Castro might know about the plans for the Bay of Pigs invasion. He was beginning to get big arms shipments from the

Soviets. In February, 1960, Castro signed a trade agreement with Moscow, and then cut more deals with East Germany and Poland. When Soviet weapons started hitting the Havana docks, the Kremlin issued a statement. Nikita Khrushchev said the Soviet military was willing to support the Cuban people with rocket weapons. The more time that passed, the more likely that Castro would have the Russian missiles armed and ready. The U.S. had no choice—it had to act immediately.

I knew we were getting close to action when the CIA told me that a car would pull up in front of the Fontainebleau and the driver would get out, leaving the keys for me in an envelope at the front desk. I was to pick up the automobile and drive it to an empty lot in Hollywood, Florida. After I left it in a certain place, another car would pick me up and I would be taken back to the Fontainebleau. Only later did I learn that in the trunk of that car was supposed to have been a high-powered transmitter that was going to be heading to Cuba that night. The CIA later informed me that during the failed invasion and for a day afterward, the only operative communication that we were getting out of Cuba was via that transmitter.

The Bay of Pigs plan would likely have worked if President Kennedy hadn't interfered once it started. The plan called for a U-2 spy plane to fly over Cuba and identify the Russian missiles. Then, a high-altitude precision bombing raid would follow and destroy the hardware. Finally, our boats would pull in, under adequate air cover. The entire thing was declared a militaristic project—meaning nobody should change the orders in the last forty-eight hours. But somebody did. I never identified him at the subsequent Senate hearings, but according to my CIA contacts who were in a position to know, it was Adlai Stevenson. He'd been able to persuade Kennedy to call off the massive air attack. Inadequate air cover was substituted, and without every angle of the mission at full velocity, there was no way it could work. Every military person who was consulted on the invasion confirmed that to be true, yet Kennedy allowed it to proceed anyway.

If we weren't going through with all aspects of the invasion, we had a responsibility as a nation to intercept those boats and bring those men home. But we didn't. Instead, the government let those young men land on the beach and be destroyed. I call that murder.

One of my CIA contacts alerted me to the fact that the precision bombing raid and adequate air cover were being pulled out of the plan the day before the invasion. I couldn't believe it, and tried to reach President Kennedy through Dave McDonald, the president of the United Steel Workers of America. I found Dave at his home in Palm Springs, and told him that it was imperative I talk with the president concerning a matter of great national security. In the past, Dave was able to pick up the phone and speak with the president within a matter of minutes. This time it didn't happen, and I never reached Kennedy. It's been something that's gnawed at me ever since.

Washington tried to deal with the defeat. Everybody on the Hill was making excuses. I was one of the few people who kept his mouth shut. And it stayed shut for years. Some people appreciated that—like Sam Giancana. I never saw him after the Bay of Pigs disaster. But years later, while I was walking through the Desert Inn in Las Vegas, an associate of Giancana walked up to me and said, "Our friend Sam asked me to tell you how grateful he was about your silence after the affair. He'll never forget it."

After my well-publicized split from the Hughes organization, Giancana got in touch with me again, this time through a somewhat more famous intermediary. I was working at my office when someone rang my doorbell at home. Phyllis McGuire was standing outside when my son Peter opened the door. She told him that she'd just heard from Sam, who was then living in Mexico. "He wanted to know if you needed any help," she continued. When Pete relayed that to me, I was touched. I know they say there's no honor among thieves, but you have to admit that's amazing loyalty.

Johnny Rosselli didn't have the same kind of style. He was always getting involved in some scam or other. In fact, in the late sixties, Johnny was caught in a card-cheating scam at the Friars Club in Los Angeles. The men behind it were ripping off their friends. Rosselli was convicted of swindling Friars Club members like Milton Berle, Zeppo Marx, and Phil Silvers out of $400,000. After the trial, Johnny's lawyer called me. He said that he had a statement for me to sign. It talked about Johnny's role in the Castro situation. Perhaps they thought that the judge might go easy on Johnny because of his patriotism.

When I acted completely ignorant, the lawyer was dumbfounded, but I said there wasn't any other position I could take. When Johnny subsequently called and invited me to dinner, I stupidly said yes. As we were sitting at Perrino's, he never once mentioned the little chat I had had with his lawyer. But he had something else to ask. He wanted to know if Howard Hughes would help pick up the legal tab for the Friars Club trial.

I said "Johnny, that's not fair shakes. I mean, Hughes wasn't even involved. Why the hell should you have the audacity to even ask?"

We never ate our dinner. Johnny started raising his voice, saying stuff like "you've got plenty" and "you guys owe me."

Next, I started raising my voice. Then I walked out. It was the last time I ever saw Johnny Rosselli.

Even after Rosselli went public with his information shortly before his death, I chose to keep quiet. At one point I was going to be a government witness in a case of hidden ownership at the Frontier Hotel. Despite the fact that the case predated Hughes's purchase of the hotel, the government thought I might be helpful. I called John Mitchell, who was attorney general at the time. Rather than go before a grand jury, I arranged for Mitchell to take my testimony. I'd been in front of a grand jury before, and it can very easily get out of hand. By this time, Rosselli had been telling his side of the Castro thing and I was denying it. My deal with Mitchell had nothing to do with the fear of being questioned under oath; I was afraid the press would be waiting for me in Los Angeles, making me fair game for unrelated questions. So I flew directly to Washington, first meeting with Mitchell alone. He then brought in one of his top assistants and I told both of them the entire Castro story and assured them that I intended to keep my word and maintain the secrecy of that mission. Mitchell appreciated my position and arranged for my testimony to be given in private that very day.

My silence finally did end in 1975. To understand why, you have to understand what was going on in Washington at the time. In 1974, Nixon was exposed in the Watergate scandal. The White House wasn't a place of trust anymore. Gerald Ford took the oath of office and had a big cleanup job ahead of him. Until then, the government had been ambivalent toward intelligence—as long as the CIA didn't embarrass the president and kept up the old idea of "plausible deniability," nobody rocked the boat. But after Watergate, things changed.

Ford was the first to order a detailed investigation of the Agency's "skeletons," which were labeled internally as "the family jewels." The White House was going to distance itself publicly from the CIA and its troubles, while at the same time trying to protect the Company from total disclosure. Ford knew that if everything was disclosed, the CIA would have been left helpless. So rather than let Congress do the investigating, he formed the standard "blue-ribbon" panel to check allegations that the Agency had overstepped its bounds. The commission would then recommend ways to make sure the abuses wouldn't happen again, without destroying the CIA in the process.

Nelson Rockefeller chaired the commission, and the results confirmed Ford's fears about the assassination plots, but Congress still wasn't satisfied that Rockefeller had gotten all the answers. So both the Senate and House formed their own select committees and demanded to know everything. The House committee was chaired by liberal Democrat Otis Pike. Fellow Democrat Frank Church led the Senate crusade.

The walls were about to come tumbling down. A top official at the CIA called me one day and said, "I'm sorry, Bob, but we've decided we're gonna let the laundry hang out." The CIA was going to testify before the Church Committee and tell the truth about the Castro incident. Then I got a call from Jim O'Connell. He'd been called as a witness and was going to let it air, including my participation. To this day, I think exposing our mission was a big mistake.

As I expected, I was subpoenaed. Before I flew to Washington, I received a tip that Bill Gay and Chester Davis had a source on the committee's staff. They had a plan to have that source feed bits and pieces of my testimony to the press to make it sound more incriminating than it was. Their sole purpose was to discredit me in order to increase their own stature with Hughes. The moment I heard that, I called a friend who worked in the White House press corps. I asked him to let everybody know that I'd hold a press conference at the completion of my testimony. I figured that this might stop Gay and Davis from trying to crucify me.

On the way into the hearing, I stopped off in the pressroom. About a hundred reporters from all over the world were waiting around for something to happen. We were having some miserable weather, so I said, "It's a rainy day. Don't go outside and hide with your cameras. Keep in touch with the committee. They'll give you advance notice of when my testimony is finished. I guarantee you I'll come back here and let you have me as long as you need me." They gave me a standing ovation.

A lot of my testimony before the committee was off the record. I also pleaded the Fifth Amendment so they'd give me immunity. I didn't do it to protect myself from prosecution; I did it so that one day, I could explain to my grandchildren that the same government that had once made me take a vow of secrecy was now forcing me to talk. When I told the committee members this, they were floored. It was a twist these people had never heard before.

By the time I talked, the CIA had already exposed the whole story. But I think I rattled some cages. I said something like: "Senator, I find it difficult to understand all the time and money that is being spent to determine if our country plotted to murder a foreign leader—a murder that never took place—when there is no evidence that any time and money is being spent to turn the spotlight on the murders that in fact did take place." I tell you, everybody jumped out of their seats.

"Are you saying that murders *actually* took place?" Church asked.

I said yes, but my explanation wasn't what he was expecting. The murders I meant were the boys killed during the botched Bay of Pigs invasion.

"After the mission became a militaristic one and after no necessary element should have been changed, a former senator was able to impose his thinking on the then-president," I said. "As a consequence, the air raid was called off completely and the proposed cover was substituted with junk planes out of a foreign country. I have no problem with those decisions. But simultaneously with those decisions, we as a nation inherited the obligation to call off the invasion. Instead we continued the mission and as our volunteers attempted to land or actually did land on the beaches, they were destroyed by the Russian hardware that we should have destroyed according to the plan. And that, gentlemen, is *murder.*"

Interestingly enough, none of the above testimony was ever included in the published report. When I was finished testifying, I kept my promise to the press. Before answering all their questions, I gave them a brief statement: "I just finished telling the committee members and staff that all of us have an obligation to future generations. We cannot destroy our cathedrals just because the stained-glass windows might need repair." Presidents come and go, but the agencies that serve them—be it the FBI, the CIA, the IRS, or any other—continue far beyond any one administration. For the government of the United States to try and save face at the expense of its agencies was no more acceptable then than now.

Thirty years later, the CIA is still taking the rap for the Bay of Pigs. It was basically Kennedy and Stevenson's fiasco. That's why Kennedy hung so tough during the missile crisis a short time later. He was trying to make up for what he'd done.

Ironically, it was only during that investigation by the Church Committee that I learned how close I came to actually being arrested for the wiretap I had arranged on behalf of Giancana years earlier. During the congressional investigation, I learned that conversations about the incident were being traded among the FBI, the CIA, the attorney general, and President Kennedy. And that on April 10, 1962, J. Edgar Hoover had sent a memo to Assistant Attorney General Herbert Miller regarding my prosecution. According to Hoover, he had spoken to Sheff Edwards and Edwards was "firmly convinced that prosecution of Maheu undoubtedly would lead to exposure of [the] most sensitive information relating to the abortive Cuban invasion of April, 1961, and would result in [the] most damaging embarrassment to the U.S. government." As a result, Edwards staunchly objected to any prosecution. Hoover must have believed him, for there was none.

About a year after the Church Committee started digging into CIA files, a report came out that included a long list of alleged assassination plots. The results weren't exactly solid. Church and his panel could prove the plot against Castro, but couldn't definitely link the CIA to the deaths of people like General Rene Schneider in Chile or President Rafael Trujillo of the Dominican Republic. The committee also couldn't say for sure whether the plots were authorized by the White House or other senior officials. What the report did say is that the CIA didn't act on its own. The worst thing the committee could say was that maybe the Company "misunderstood" presidential instructions.

What's kind of interesting is that the Church Committee didn't rule out assassination as an option in certain cases. Frank Church qualified it by using the same Hitler analogy that O'Connell had used at our first meeting. But Church did say that Latin and black leaders of small countries didn't pose the same kind of threat to the U.S.

I'm one of the last people left who knows what really went on during the operation to assassinate Fidel Castro. A lot of the people involved died pretty suddenly. Maybe just a coincidence ... maybe not. Rosselli was hit in 1976. He had served some prison time and was finally out, but was suffering from a bad case of emphysema. Somebody wanted to pay him back for something. They got him aboard a yacht and a hit man appeared out of nowhere, plugging his nose and mouth. Period. He was pretty weak, so it didn't take long for him to suffocate. Then, they decided to cut him into pieces. They stuck his foot in his mouth, wrapped his legs around his head, and then sank him in a steel drum. I'm not sure how I want to go, but I am certain that I want my body to be in one piece when I do.

The Mob had taken out Sam Giancana with seven shots from a .22 handgun in the basement of his house more than a year earlier. Some time before, Giancana had been hauled in by the Feds to testify about the Mob. They gave him immunity, but he wouldn't talk. And that meant a mandatory prison sentence of one year plus one day. He served it, but it killed him. Not literally, of course, but part of the man just died. The moment he was released, Sam went to Mexico. He was going to spend the rest of his life there. No way was he going back to the joint.

Nick Gage, a former writer with the *New York Times,* has a

theory about why Giancana was finally hit. I think it's probably true. Nick had an informant inside the Mob. According to the information the writer received, Sam had to die because the Mafia couldn't afford to let him talk again. And someone high up in the Mob decided to assure himself that Sam *wouldn't*.

If you think about that theory for a moment, it scans pretty well. Just as the Mob feared, Sam wound up being arrested and brought back to Chicago. He was about to be called before a grand jury in Chicago and asked about organized crime. In addition, it was right around the time of the Church Committee hearings. He was about to be given immunity again, and immunity means that you *cannot* refuse to answer questions. The Mob knew the odds were Sam wouldn't keep his mouth shut this time. So it silenced him for good.

I know what all the conspiracy buffs think—that the Mob was scared Sam would reveal something incriminating about the Kennedy assassination. I believe it had nothing to do with that. What spooked the Mob was the fact that the Feds were going to ask Sam about the Mafia connection to the Castro hits. They'd use it as an excuse to get Sam talking. And, since he had immunity, once he started talking, he would leave the door wide open for bigger questions about underworld operations across the board.

There are a lot of people who think the Kennedy assassination is directly tied to the attempted assassination of Castro. Some say that Kennedy tried to get to Castro but that Castro got to him first. Others pin the assassination on the Mob and Bobby Kennedy's all-out efforts to destroy organized crime. Well-connected Washington columnist Jack Anderson thinks it's both—that the Mafia killed Kennedy at the instigation of Castro.

Anderson has been trying for nearly twenty years to get the government to admit the Castro-Mafia conspiracy, but frankly, I don't buy it. While Jack is a friend of mine, I nevertheless have a problem with the people supplying him with his information.

Some of them seem to believe every word that Johnny Rosselli ever said. One thing is certain. After the Castro plot, Johnny did shoot his mouth off a lot—usually so he could get something from somebody. Anderson says he never caught Johnny in a lie. Rosselli's attorneys said he may have been a hardened criminal, but he always told the truth. All I know is that Rosselli used a lot of people for his own advantage—there's no way to know how far he'd go. And neither he nor Sam Giancana ever talked about Kennedy while I was around.

The official conclusion of the Warren Commission was that Lee Harvey Oswald acted alone. Unfortunately, the Warren Commission was just plain sloppy. Its people didn't follow through on leads. If it had been done right the first time, there wouldn't be so many question marks. And it might have stopped people from trying to fill in the gaps with their own ideas.

It's just my opinion, but I think that the commission would have come up with the same conclusion even if it had conducted the investigation properly. I'm not sold on the "second gun" theory. From what I know, Oswald did act alone. And Jack Ruby killed him out of anger. Just because the man worked for the Mob and probably had ties to Rosselli doesn't mean he didn't feel strongly about Kennedy, as evidenced by Rosselli's own feelings when asked to take a stand against Cuba.

Word has it that Castro was saddened by the news that Kennedy died. Apparently he was with a French journalist at the time, talking about how he'd like to live peacefully with the U.S. When the assassination news reached him, he reportedly said, "*Es una mala noticia*"—this is bad news.

The CIA dropped its plans to kill Castro after Kennedy's death. The government opted to support Roland Cubela, an ambitious Company contact who was close to Castro. Cubela was planning to mount a coup and unite the Cuban exiles. But in 1964, he asked for a sniper's rifle. The CIA had to say no. President Johnson had just passed down the word that the White House wasn't backing any more assassinations.

There's one thing that I say for sure about the Bay of Pigs and the plot to assassinate Fidel Castro: I wish to God I'd never been involved in it. It was the right choice at the time ... but the wrong choice looking back. Jack Anderson and I and everyone else can sit around all day and come up with theories about what happened. Problem is—we'll never know for sure. The truth is buried in a lot of graves.

Chapter Five

GIVING IN

IT WAS 1961 WHEN HUGHES FINALLY HOOKED ME. LINE AND SINKER.

Up to that point, I had held my ground rather well. The East Coast was my home—where my family lived, where my business operated. If he wanted my services, I would hop on a plane. But he wanted more, and frankly, the commute was wearing me out.

Just before my children had to register for school, Hughes handed me a deal. I would move permanently to Los Angeles and open an office there. Hughes would let me keep Robert A. Maheu Associates alive in Washington, but when it came to my time, Hughes wanted an exclusive. In return, he would provide me with a house for one year—the same kind of arrangement we had for the past three summers—and a very bright future.

Now, I had always been a free agent. I'd vowed never to let anybody take over my life, but it must have been the right offer at the right time. I know my ego played a big part in my decision. After all, the world's richest man had just personally summoned me to do his bidding. It was bait too attractive to pass up. More than just a sweet business deal, it also gave me the chance to do something I had always wanted to do: buy my family a home where we could spend the rest of our lives together.

I made the move to Los Angeles on September 21, 1961. My children and one of my nieces, Judi Doyon, came out with me, and

Yvette flew out a short time later. As promised, Hughes rented us a place. It was a beautifully furnished home in Brentwood and cost $1,500 a month—an enormous amount for rent in those days. During the first year, we bought a place in Pacific Palisades. It needed work, but this was the kind of house we had been dreaming about—a six-bedroom Spanish mansion.

Funny thing about dreams—good ones can become nightmares in a hot minute.

The remodeling was supposed to be finished by the time our Brentwood lease was up. In reality, it wasn't even close to being completed, so I extended the lease in Brentwood for another six months. That half year sped by, with still no end in sight on the Palisades remodeling. The people who owned the Brentwood house wouldn't give me another extension. They had been traveling the world for a year and wanted their house back.

So we packed up and headed to a beach house I had kept for years in Santa Monica. It was a garden house on Pacific Coast Highway, in between two parking lots, with five bedrooms and a pool. It was perfect for visiting dignitaries from Washington and other contacts, but it wasn't the place to try to raise a family. We really had no choice, however, and remained there for another four months.

When we finally did move into our new home in Pacific Palisades, I had spent over $100,000 for renovations. Yet, I felt it was worth it. I remember standing outside with Yvette. I turned to her and said, "Honey, take a good look at it, because this is where we're going to spend the rest of our lives." How foolish I was. We would end up packing again in 1967.

For the time we were there, however, we made the most of our new house, and our new social status. I joined the California Yacht Club, the Navy League, the Silver Dollar Club, and the Balboa Bay Club in Newport Beach, where I rented a penthouse for entertaining. I was already a member of the Jonathan Club and the

California Yacht Club. I also bought a thirty-four-foot motor sailor, the *Alouette*, which slept six. I kept it moored in Newport and entertained guests on Hughes's behalf. Eventually, I donated the *Alouette* to charity, and bought a larger yacht—a fifty-seven-foot Sports Fisherman that we named the *Alouette Too*. The luxury of the yacht represented Hughes's image well.

Thanks to my sons, I became active in the Boy Scouts. I was appointed to the Los Angeles District Attorney's Advisory Council, and I was asked to become a director of the American Foundation for Ecumenical Research and an officer of the American Cancer Society. At home, we had formal dinner parties once a month. When the weather was good, we would have outside tent parties. Life was one big guest list.

These parties were work, though. They helped place us among the A-list, both politically and socially, in order to establish necessary contacts. And it wasn't as if Yvette and I sat back and put our feet up. There weren't a lot of servants running around. We didn't even have a live-in maid. Frankly, I can't figure people who buy these enormous houses and then can't take care of them themselves. I'd saddle myself with a whole bunch of people and then end up worrying about them all. It's not the money—it's the complications. Even if I hit the jackpot tomorrow, it wouldn't matter. I've never minded pushing up my sleeves—doing the cooking or rinsing the dishes. Ordering somebody around just isn't my style.

Hughes was the exact opposite. Control was important to him, and he directed everybody who worked for him. He owned his women as well—particularly the legendary group of starlets he kept "on call." They were always young girls, innocents really, who wanted a career in show business, and for some reason Hughes liked to keep them around. Their names aren't really important. When one left, two would take her place.

I remember one particular Friday night. I was getting ready to leave for Washington when Howard called. I couldn't believe what

I was hearing. He started to talk about the Miss Universe pageant, which was being held down in Long Beach. Hughes wanted me to hightail it down there and meet eight of the contestants. I guess he had been sent some pictures and had handpicked these girls. Anyway, he said, "Go sign them up to a movie contract." Just like that.

So I went down there to follow his instructions. My first challenge was getting past the chaperones. It wasn't easy. I only had forty-eight hours before the gals would be parading on stage, and then jumping on planes to head home. But I gave them the line about Hughes wanting them to act—and seven of them signed.

Problem number two was figuring out what to do with them. We wound up getting each of them a little apartment in Beverly Hills. Hughes never touched them; hell, he never even saw them. But he put them under surveillance. They weren't allowed to go anywhere or do anything, just sit around and wait. Before long, these lovelies had had just about enough of that. One by one, they started to drift off. Except Miss Norway.

For some reason, Hughes wanted her around. He had never even been in the same room with her, but that didn't matter. After a few more months, however, even Miss Norway got antsy. She was a young girl and wanted to go home. Hughes tried to keep her by making more promises about a contract. But finally, the Norwegian embassy came to her rescue, demanding the girl be sent back to Norway. The whole thing was crazy. I finally told Howard flat out that he had to let her go. We were facing an international incident here. His Scandinavian doll finally got shipped home.

As for Howard, he went out and found himself yet another pet. Her name was Yvonne, and she was the last of the young women in Hughes's life. She was your basic starlet—no great screen star, just an attractive package. In other stories about Hughes, there's often been talk about somebody named "Miss Riverside." That was Yvonne. And Hughes became obsessed beyond reason.

I don't think he ever slept with her—I don't think he ever slept with any of them. But Hughes wanted to make sure that nobody else did either. Setting her up in a little house in the Hollywood Hills, he threw a tight web of security around her. He barely even called her on the phone, yet Hughes knew her every move, and he made sure she didn't move much. But keeping Yvonne celibate wasn't easy. She had quite an appetite for gentlemen, and not even Howard Hughes was going to keep that bed cold. She started having an affair with a half-assed L.A. hood who was a tough ex-marine. The guy even moved in with her. That added insult to injury, since Hughes was paying her rent.

This hood knew I was keeping track of Yvonne and that I was an ex-F.B.I. agent, so he went out and bought himself a gun. Since he didn't know how to use it, he went with Yvonne to a firing range in the vicinity of Long Beach. He wasn't too bright. While he was doing some target shooting, a bullet failed to fire. He looked down the barrel to see what had happened—and it was a delayed reaction. He got hit in the head.

Ironically, when Hughes heard that Yvonne's lover was dead, he thought I did it, even though I wasn't anywhere near the place. He wanted to know if the incident could be traced back to me. I told Hughes I had nothing to do with it, but I could tell he didn't buy it. Hughes always thought I was this tough guy; you know, ex-FBI agent, good with a gun. He was fascinated by that aura. But, I'm no killer. So when he thought I had the stuff to kill Yvonne's lover, at first I was totally amazed. Then I got a little scared. I called my friend Hal Marlowe, the Los Angeles County under-sheriff. Even though it was out of his jurisdiction, I asked him to make sure there was a ballistics check. The test would show the trajectory of the bullet and prove it came from the gun in the dead guy's hand. A little insurance policy, just in case somebody else thought the way Hughes did.

What Hughes knew but Marlowe didn't was the fact that I did have one run-in with this fellow at Yvonne's place. I had to go there and get some jewelry Hughes had given her and now wanted back. The Hollywood Hills are steep, with houses built right on the mountainside. I had to huff and puff up about two hundred steps that led to this hideaway. When I get to the top, there was this thug holding his new .45 on me. He started asking me what I wanted.

I'll never forget: I looked at him, right down the barrel of his gun, and said, "Don't try scaring me with a firearm. I can take it away from you and shove it down your throat." It must have been the right answer, because I ended up with the jewelry.

By this time, we were all rather fed up with being on Hughes's starlet patrol. And this thing with Yvonne showed it was time to do something. Hughes's Hollywood attorney Greg Bautzer and I called Howard and pleaded with him to stop. At the time, Hughes had been married to Jean Peters for three years; she knew all about the girls stashed in various places around Hollywood, and it wasn't helping his connubial bliss. We were very blunt. If Hughes didn't want a divorce or more bad publicity, the girls had to go. And they did—every last one.

Hughes's mind had more than enough to occupy it without the girls anyway. California was growing every day. It was becoming a big pond with a bunch of new fish. Hughes started feeling small; his voice wasn't quite as loud as it once was. The California tax people were on his back. Being a man with perpetual wanderlust anyway, Hughes decided the time was right for a move someplace where he could be big again—all by himself. Having learned his lesson in the Bahamas, this time he decided to stay closer to home.

His first idea was Tucson, Arizona. In the late fifties, Hughes decided he wanted to move his helicopter operation, a division of Hughes Tool Company, from Culver City to Tucson. He was aware that Douglas Aircraft was on the verge of abandoning three large hangars that it was leasing from the Tucson Airport Authority—hangars totaling one million square feet. Hughes wanted to acquire the lease on the buildings without his name becoming involved before the fact. He was afraid it would drive up the price tag. It had happened before. People heard the name Hughes and immediately saw dollar signs.

We used Gillis Long to get the hangar. Long had been counsel to the Small Business Administration in Washington, and he would go on to become a Louisiana congressman. Long was able to handle the negotiations with the Tucson Airport Authority. Hughes got his hangars, and eventually we had to tell authorities that he was the tenant. But by then, the ink on the lease agreement was already dry.

With the hangars secured, Hughes began to seriously think about moving his entire operation to Arizona. He even had me start to rent houses in the area, both for himself and for some of his chief executives. I'd look over a place and send him a description. If Hughes liked it, he'd call and say, "Okay. I want that one. Rent it and get the people out of it right away." I ended up renting about four houses, including a cottage at the Arizona Inn. Hughes wanted security around them twenty-four hours a day, so we came up with the idea of having my private company provide the guards. Hughes liked to describe it as an opportunity for me to supplement my income, but basically it was just a way for him to keep his other executives from finding how much I made every year. Keep in mind that I had a much sweeter deal with Hughes than anybody else, and if the figures ever leaked out, he was in for one hell of an uprising.

Some folks in Tucson just weren't interested in renting a house. It was buy it or no deal. Now there was this beautiful house in the foothills with which Hughes was truly enchanted. The owner was a woman named Ruth. She was in her mid-thirties, a former bar girl who'd married a rich older man. Just her luck, he died a short time later. Hughes wanted to rent the house, but Ruth insisted on selling it. So Hughes told me, "Why don't you just take Ruth out for dinner. Buy her a few drinks. With your line of chatter, I'm sure you can convince her." Basically, he wanted me to get her drunk.

Ruth had no idea that it was Hughes who wanted her place. I picked a restaurant where I was sure nobody would recognize me. But the moment we walked in, I spotted the chief of police and the head of the Tucson Airport Authority sitting together having dinner. I tried to ignore them and proceed with my mission.

I got Ruth drunk, all right, but she wasn't giving an inch. In fact, she started to get downright hostile. I was trying my best to quiet her down, but Ruth got louder and louder. Suddenly she started to bellow, "You know what's wrong with you, Bob? You don't recognize that I have class!" I must have given her a funny look, because she began to point her squatty thumb in my face and shouted, "No shit, Bob. I've got class." Everybody was looking— including my important acquaintances. I couldn't wait to call them the next day and explain what happened. It turned out neither of them thought much about it—apparently one of them knew Ruth quite well. Hughes never rented her house; Ruth sold it to me instead.

The houses and hangars, combined with acreage that Hughes had been buying up for years, gave him a rather substantial investment in the area. At one point, Hughes announced that he was going to get rid of everything in California, completely sever all relations. He said that he was through with the place.

I found myself given more and more responsibility over his day-to-day activities, and was prepared to move with him. The more I wheeled and dealed for Hughes, the more he kept reminding me of the arrangement we'd made back in 1957. He kept telling me that I had to convince the world that I was his only spokesman. It was an awesome and odd responsibility.

Of course, I still had never laid eyes on the Man. And as far as I knew, Bill Gay was the only person seeing Hughes on a regular basis other than his male nurses. At least that was the line he was handing me. Yet, what was even more perplexing was the fact that every time Gay's name came up in our conversations, Hughes would get vehement. He told me not to involve Gay in any of our projects. "Keep the guy out!" he'd scream.

Finally the day came when he began talking about flying to Tucson. By this time, he had an entire entourage taking care of his daily needs, and I asked him how many would be making the trip. Naturally, I assumed Bill Gay would be first on the plane.

"No way am I going to take Bill Gay," Howard told me without hesitation. At this point, I began to realize that perhaps Gay was exaggerating his closeness to the boss. Yet, he did seem to know important things. For example, Gay told me Hughes wasn't taking care of himself; and that he was an absolute fanatic on the subject of germs. In fact, Hughes wouldn't even shake hands with anybody. And if one of his aides coughed, he banished him from the room.

As a matter of fact, Gay showed me a memo that Hughes had written. It was about what to do if a glass shattered: exact directions on how to pick up the pieces. He also had rules about cleaning the staircase. Every step had to be cleaned one inch at a time.

He also had a fetish about his planes and his cars. He kept an entire fleet of cars at the Miami airport for years. They were just sitting there with flat tires, never driven, never serviced. But Hughes didn't want them moved. He was afraid germs would get into the tires if they were inflated—and that he might catch them if he ever went back there.

Hughes's obsession with his health was probably the reason we never made it to Tucson. After several false starts, he abruptly changed his mind and began to talk about Boston. He wanted to go there for a while. I asked him why he wanted to go on the trip, thinking there might be a business reason.

He told me he wanted to see how well he withstood the trip. He confided that he was preparing to move permanently to another country. Maybe he would head to Montreal, a place he'd visited some years back and liked a great deal, he said. Armed with that information, I checked for the availability of a large number of rooms at the Ritz-Carlton Hotel in Montreal, as well as rooms at the Emerald Beach Hotel in the Bahamas. Howard always called those islands his first love, and I always had a feeling he might try to go back there. So strong was my hunch that I even arranged for the rental of a barge in Miami. Should Howard want to travel to the Bahamas, he could take the train to Florida and have his Pullman cars barged across to Nassau.

Although Hughes never told me why he selected Boston as a destination, the rumor mill had it that it was because of Dr. George Thorn. He was the physician-in-chief at Peter Bent Brigham Hospital, as well as the director of medical research for the Howard Hughes Medical Institute. Hughes talked about him a lot and seemed to have complete faith in the man. Perhaps Hughes was scared about being sick and wanted to be near a good doctor involved with his foundation.

Actually, it was nearly impossible to know if Hughes was genuinely ill. He was getting older and he seemed weak. Perhaps the most telling sign, however, was that he didn't want to fly. Hughes insisted on taking the train to Boston.

In the old days, Hughes would have flown himself. He had a fleet of Lockheeds that were just gathering dust. Apparently, he just wasn't physically able to handle playing pilot anymore, and perhaps he didn't feel confident with anybody else at the controls. Whatever the reason, Howard called and asked me to get two Pullman cars ready for the trip. And he wanted it done quietly.

It was July, 1966, and Howard could not have selected a worse time to travel. The airline machinists had gone on strike, and the trains were booked solid. And nobody really wanted to deal with a special order for Pullman cars. I couldn't have pulled it off without getting some cooperation from the presidents of three railroads.

Thank God a friend of mine, ex-FBI agent William John Quinn, was the president of the Chicago, Burlington and Quincy Railroad. I told him the problem and he paved the way. He put me in touch with Ed Bailey, the president of the Union Pacific Railroad, and Ernest Marsh, president of the Santa Fe lines. Hughes ordered me not to tell anybody about the trip. But I didn't want to play games with these men; or worse, have them find out the facts while he was en route. So I took them into my confidence, and told them exactly who they would be carrying.

Hughes picked the date he wanted to leave. The train was set to pull out in the late afternoon. A limo was waiting to drive him to the train station in Pasadena, where the *Superchief* was scheduled to stop; his luggage was packed; and all was arranged. But with Howard, things are never that easy. All of a sudden, he changed his mind. Unfortunately, by the time I got the word, the Pullman cars had already been moved closer to the departing train. Now we had to move them back.

It sounds simpler than it was. To get permission, I had to call the railroad presidents at home and get their personal okays.

This scenario was repeated for the next ten days. Hughes wanted to leave; Hughes didn't want to leave. Things were packed; things were unpacked. Just when everyone was about to give up hope, I finally got a commitment out of the Man. Tonight would be the night, he said.

Then, I'll be damned if he didn't do it again. By the time I received word of the postponement, packers were already loading the Pullman cars with his personal goods, his favorite chair, his papers, his medications, and a supply of Kleenex. As I called to cancel for the umpteenth time, a second phone rang and I heard, "It's back on again. We're going."

Unfortunately, by this time, the train to which our two Pullmans were to be hooked was already loaded with cars. They couldn't or wouldn't take on any additional ones. Right then I learned where the expression "tearing my hair out" came from.

As doors all over the railroad yard began to slam in my face, I realized that my only chance was to call my Chicago contact again and have him apply pressure halfway across the country. Somehow, he pulled off the impossible. A special section was added, scheduled ahead of the regular train—just to accommodate the richest man in the United States.

Right on schedule, our special train arrived in Pasadena. Unfortunately, Howard was still at his home in Bel Air. He just couldn't get himself to leave the bedroom that had been his prison for the past four and a half years.

I finally got him on the telephone. Hughes sounded very weak. "Is there a problem, Bob?" he asked.

"Not as long as you move your ass, there's not," I responded.

Howard stalled as only he could. "Bob, do you really think a train is the proper way?" he asked, sounding like a child.

I was ready to explode. "Howard," I said, and felt myself drawing a long breath. "I don't give a damn whether you go to Boston or you don't. But if you decide you are going, you better get on that train in Pasadena tonight. We've created so much curiosity now that we'll never be able to duplicate this again. So that special section is going to roll to Chicago whether you're on it or not. I'm not canceling it again. Now if you tell me that you're prepared to let that happen, and that you're ready to board a private plane a week from now and go to Boston, fine. Otherwise, there's a limo parked in front of your house, and I recommend that you use it."

Howard still wasn't budging. I pleaded with him, I threatened him, and then I actually started to cry. Nothing worked, until I finally broke down completely and found myself laughing uncontrollably into the phone. For some reason that worked, for Hughes said, "Okay. I'll go."

Things at Union Station were a mess. The special section had taken off for Pasadena to pick up Hughes. But, since he was so late, it was then affecting the regular train's schedule. The conductor of that train made the decision that he wouldn't wait any longer and started to follow the special section.

I wasn't going on the trip, but was coordinating from Los Angeles. My son Peter had the job of getting Hughes on the train. Poor Pete didn't know what he was in for. He was in Pasadena pacing the floor. While waiting for Hughes, he managed to case the station, and found the master switch. If everything went to hell, at least he could throw it and delay the trains, perhaps buying us a little more time.

Just as Hughes was getting into the limo in Bel Air, the stationmaster in Pasadena was blowing a fuse. Passenger or no passenger, the special section was leaving in ten minutes, he informed Peter. Of course, by now the second section, the full *Superchief* itself, was tying up traffic at every intersection. It was just sitting on the tracks near Pasadena with no place to go. Hughes's train was blocking the way. Crossing gates were down for miles in both directions, and cars were backing up on Pasadena streets. People were getting out of their cars and screaming at one another. Pandemonium is the only word that comes to mind.

Finally, Hughes's limousine arrived outside the station in Pasadena, but Howard refused to leave the car. He was sitting there trying to get up the courage to get on the train. Ten minutes passed, then twenty. Only then did Hughes finally get on board. He brought along about six staff members, plus ex-cop Jack Hooper, whom I had given the assignment of security. On the train, Jack briefed his security people. None of them were allowed to carry weapons. It was a regulation. If there was any trouble, the railroad had a detective on the train to handle it.

The regular passengers didn't have a clue that Hughes was on board. But the delays made everybody anxious. And then there was a lot of weird activity going on. People started getting curious. All of a sudden, stories started flying about the "Mysterious Train Headed East."

At one of the stops, a reporter started cornering passengers getting off the train, asking them if they'd seen any guns on board. Obviously nobody could have—the railroad detective was the only person armed, and nobody knew about that. Everybody else, including all those who worked for Hughes, was clean. Even so, one woman said, "Well there was something: a case painted with the word OXYGEN." By the time that reporter was through analyzing her, somehow the oxygen tank had turned into a machine gun.

I was sitting at home watching television when a report came on about the mystery train. It featured a mock-up of a train. The thing had airplane blisters on the side and machine guns on the roof. The reporter had no idea who or what was inside the train. It was just a lot of noise about nothing. The whole thing was a perfect example of what happens to a story. There wasn't much I could do about the report, so this time, Maheu didn't come to the rescue. I had something bigger to worry about—getting Hughes safely ensconced at the Ritz-Carlton in Boston. Howard had asked to be on the top floor of the hotel, but it was under renovation. So, instead, I had reserved the entire fifth floor of the place. Since Hughes didn't want his calls going through a switchboard, I had to get direct lines put in. Everything on that end was working well. No one was asking any questions. Much of the credit went to Walter Fitzpatrick, the man I had assigned to handle all the arrangements in Boston. He was a trustworthy and capable assistant, and did his job so well that he eventually became the general manager of the Desert Inn in Las Vegas. I was certain that he had everything under control. Then, my telephone rang and the roof fell in. Walter was on the line with news I didn't want to hear: it seemed there was a city law in Boston requiring that whoever registers in a hotel room has to be the one occupying it.

Now, Hughes had a lot of rooms and suites, and all of them were in my name. It was obvious I wasn't using every single one of them. And the manager of the Ritz didn't understand what was going on.

I quickly called an old classmate of mine from Holy Cross who was at that time a lawyer in Boston. I had to level with him about Hughes, and asked if he could straighten it out with the hotel manager. And it had to be done fast—the train was going to chug into Boston at any minute. My friend said that he'd work it out. Little did I realize how. When my old classmate called me back, he said our problems were solved. Hughes could stay with him and his wife. They had this lovely home, you see, and would be happy to have him.

I didn't want to offend anybody; yet it was clear that there was no way that Howard Hughes was going to stay in somebody else's home. I explained this as tactfully as I could, then told him that if the hotel needed a list of names, I would provide it. I used names of people I knew and trusted. Then I called each of them and explained—just in case somebody decided to check.

Since there weren't any phones on the train, Hooper called me from each stop with a report. One time, Hooper was frantic. Hughes wanted certain foods, but the train didn't have them. The train's next stop was in Cleveland, but the city was being hit by riots.

I only had a couple of hours to figure things out. I called a former FBI agent I knew who lived outside the city and pleaded with him not to think that I had lost my mind. Then I gave him a list of things to buy—a small grill and some charcoal, ten prime steak fillets at least one-inch thick, six cans of baby peas, six cans of French-cut string beans, a half-dozen semiripe bananas with no black spots, six cans of mixed fruit, a vanilla cake without frosting, and an assortment of freshly baked pastries—heavy on napoleons if possible. I gave him the car number, and asked him to deliver the stuff to Jack Hooper.

I was sitting chewing my nails when my friend from Cleveland called back.

"Mission accomplished, old buddy," he said.

I thanked him and told him to send me the bill. When I received it, I doubled it and sent back a check.

When the train finally barreled into Boston, tension was running high. Fitzpatrick and his people were waiting to whisk Hughes off the train and rush him to the hotel. When they arrived at the Ritz-Carlton, Hughes was smuggled in through the service entrance.

Unfortunately, by that time, some Boston reporters had figured out that Hughes was on the mystery train. I guess they looked at the hotel register and saw my name. It didn't take a brain surgeon to make the connection. So while Hughes was tucked away on the fifth floor, the vultures circled, and the hunt was on.

1. At age two-and-a-half; my parents were preparing me for "snow jobs."

2. When I married Yvette on July 27, 1941, I thought I was the happiest man in the world. I still do.

3. In the basement of the Lewiston, Maine, police department, in 1946, I took my best FBI stance to give a firearms demonstration with my trusty .38 special. Despite their expressions, the police were impressed.

4. Home sweet home in Falls Church, Virginia, when we were trying to pay off our debts, about 1954.

5. After the Greek shipping magnate and client Stavros Niarchos insisted I find a home more fitting with my career, Yvette and I moved into this house in Falls Church, Virginia. We lived happily there from 1956 until Howard Hughes moved us to Los Angeles in September 1961.

6. The large Falls Church home was our first with a pool.

7. Howard Hughes's Hollywood attorney Greg Bautzer was one of the most respected and powerful men in town. In 1966, he joined me in my home in Pacific Palisades, California, to celebrate my twenty-fifth wedding anniversary.

8. X marks the spot where Howard Hughes spent his entire tenure in Las Vegas. From November 1966 to November 1970, he shut himself away in the ninth-floor penthouse of the Desert Inn Hotel. Much of the eighth floor was occupied by his staff, including his doctor.

9–10. Dubbed "Little Caesar's Palace" because of its size and design, this is the house that Hughes had built for me on the golf course of the Desert Inn so that I would never be too far away. While the entrance was imposing (*above*), the backyard was positively overwhelming (*below*).

11–12. Working for Howard Hughes meant spending over sixteen hours a day on the phone behind a desk. I kept his picture on the wall behind me in my office at home (*above*). It was at my office in the Frontier Hotel (*below*) that I literally lived while looking for a vanished Hughes.

13. Joining me in my office for a chat in 1968: California governor Ronald Reagan and Nevada governor Paul Laxalt.

14. In 1968, I was joined at the Desert Inn Country Club by Nevada governor Paul Laxalt (*right*) and Moe Dalitz (*left*), one-time co-owner of the hotel.

15. Four generations of Maheus: my mother, my son Peter, his son Peter, and me in 1966.

16. This is a sample of one of the thousands of memos I received over the years from Howard Hughes. In this one, sent in late 1969, Howard was trying to suggest my loyalty would be rewarded with a voting trust in his corporation. It was as close as Howard ever came to giving anyone a piece of his pie. Less than a year later, I would be history.

Bob, I have your message. I do not feel your apprehension is the least bit unjustified. If I give you my word to find a solution promptly, such as a voting trust for my Hughes Tool Company stock, and if I put the formalities into a state of effectiveness for your scrutiny without any unreasonable delay, will you consider it done as of now, so your mind will not be filled with these thoughts in the near future? I will assume an affirmative answer and proceed accordingly.

17. My official company photo as president of Hughes Nevada Operations. It was taken in 1967, but saw the most action when I was dismissed in 1970.

18. A current photograph of Yvette and me, through it all and still in love.

Chapter Six

INTO THE DESERT

A PACK OF BLOODTHIRSTY HOUNDS: THAT WAS WHAT THE REPORTERS outside the Ritz-Carlton behaved like. Once they got Hughes's scent, there was no stopping them. And they weren't above trying every trick in the book to get past the guard on the fifth floor of that Boston hotel.

I had a lot of contacts in the Boston Police Department from my school days in Massachusetts. We worked out an arrangement for Howard's guards to be off-duty cops who needed to do some moonlighting. Most of them were sergeants or pretty high-ranking officers, so the press couldn't push them around like they could with a rookie. But the press *can* get pretty crafty. One reporter tried to flush Hughes out by pulling the fire alarm on the sixth floor. That kind of stuff went on for weeks.

They even came after me. While Hughes was trying to get settled at the Ritz, I decided to take my family to Maine for a little holiday. We had a cottage there on one of the Belgrade lakes. I figured that I could enjoy some time with my family, but still be close to the action. The press found out about the cottage and assumed I had moved Hughes there for safekeeping. All of a sudden, seaplanes started landing on the lake. It was an invasion. Enemy forces armed with cameras, taking pictures of the cottage.

Back in Boston, things were going no better for Howard. Jean

Peters had flown in from Los Angeles and wanted to see her husband. But Hughes wouldn't let her in his room. Germs, he said. He was afraid that even Jean would contaminate him, so they talked across the room—he in bed and she at the door. Years later, Jean would testify that they discussed plans to buy a summer home in Boston, but Hughes was never serious about it. It was all subterfuge to try to keep her happy.

It didn't work. Jean is a woman of absolute class, for whom I have the utmost respect. In all the years I worked for Hughes, I only had contact with her on a few occasions. The reason was that we rarely had cause to deal with each other. My responsibilities were to deal with Howard's affairs in business and politics, not his personal life. Jobs like buying mink stoles and hiring nurses fell under Bill Gay's aegis. At the time, Gay's responsibilities seemed far less glamorous. Eventually, however, they'd prove the deciding factor in the struggle over Hughes.

I can only recall two occasions where Jean actually asked something of me. The first involved a passport she wanted me to obtain for a friend of hers who was about to marry Jack Lemmon. I believe Lemmon and his future wife were about to leave for Europe, and couldn't wait the two or three weeks it took to go through normal channels. The second request concerned a job in Las Vegas that Jean wanted filled with the son of an acquaintance. But, she stressed, *only* if he was qualified and *only* if the job was available. She made it quite clear that she didn't want us padding the payroll.

Jean was like that: a true lady, and amazingly loyal to Howard. Never—not during the years they spent together, nor during their divorce, nor in all the years that have passed—did she ever speak out publicly against him or his organization, and Howard, despite the compulsive way he chased skirts, absolutely adored Jean. But it was a relationship that couldn't last. Through the fifties and early sixties, Jean became increasingly disenchanted with Howard. The problem wasn't the starlets. It was his sickness and pathological fear of personal contact. As time went on, they spent more and more of their time apart.

Any remnant of physical contact between them ended that day in Boston. When Howard wouldn't allow her in his room, Jean did a 180-degree turn, went right back into the elevator, and headed for home. And that, for all practical purposes, was the end of their marriage. She would never again set eyes on Howard. This was a woman who put up with a lot over the years. But even Jean had her limits. You can fight another woman, but not this kind of paranoia. Jean didn't even try. By 1971, they would be divorced.

No sooner had Jean left Boston and returned to Los Angeles than Hughes himself made noises about leaving. Having spent nearly a quarter of a million dollars to travel to Boston and maintain his seclusion at the Ritz-Carlton, he was still discontented.

He wanted to take off again. First Montreal, and then the Bahamas. He was getting visions of reviving the dynasty he had tried to build there in '57. He vacillated for weeks before deciding to fly up to Montreal for a day or so. But since we didn't know when he wanted to leave, we had to charter a plane and keep it on hold. We knew that when Howard finally made up his mind to go, he would want to go at a moment's notice.

It was ironic how much Hughes wanted to travel. It really made little sense since he never saw anything when he did. After we finally moved him from Boston to Las Vegas, the windows of the train were sealed with drapes so no light could get in. We could have taken him from the Ritz-Carlton to the Boston railroad yards for a few days, brought him back to the Ritz, and said, "Mr. Hughes, welcome to Las Vegas." He wouldn't have known the difference until he turned on the TV and discovered the truth.

Yet, none of this changed our intense preparations. While the chartered plane was sitting at the airport, fueled and ready to head for Montreal, it became increasingly tough to keep a hold on it.

The charter company nagged me about whether Hughes was going to use it or not. In the meantime, I was also juggling reservations for the Bahamas. If Hughes got that whim, he would need an entire floor of a hotel.

The fact is, he outsmarted us all. In October, 1966, as my juggling act was in full gear, Hughes called me. I was certain this meant that he would be off to Canada or the Caribbean. Either way, I had things covered.

"Lake Tahoe, Bob," he said. "We're going to Lake Tahoe. Arrange it." Few things ever catch me by surprise, but that order was one of them.

Hughes had been a frequent guest at Tahoe's Cal-Neva Lodge in years past and had always enjoyed it. And Nevada still held an attraction for him. The tax laws were very good, and it still had a flavor of "the frontier." It was the proverbial small pond, where a big fish like Hughes could be an absolute behemoth.

Howard decided that he was going to buy some property and settle down there. He told me to find a place for him to stay and to wait for instructions. Some contacts helped get me the accommodations. They even knocked out a wall to make the place bigger. But true to form, three weeks later, Hughes had a better idea.

"No more Tahoe. I've decided on Las Vegas."

The Dunes Hotel is where he wanted to stay. And he wanted the *entire* top floor. Unfortunately, Hughes couldn't have it. It seemed that the Dunes already had a restaurant up there, and I figured Hughes didn't want to spend the night in a booth. So I booked all the suites and rooms on the floor below.

That satisfied him. We tied up the hotel for a week. And when Hughes once again put off the trip, I was able to get an extension. But the Dunes was having a celebrity affair and needed some of the suites for its high rollers. It made me give up at least half of the space we were holding. And Hughes wasn't happy about it.

He said, "Find me another location where I can have the

whole floor to myself. I will not accept anyone else being on the floor."

The Desert Inn had space for Hughes. I took the whole top floor and promised that we would be there for not more than ten days. The management was reluctant at first. Those suites were for the big-buck players. And they were beautiful: high ceilings, bars, enormous living rooms. Fortunately, this time we didn't have long to wait. On November 22, 1966, Howard decided it was time to make the move.

He had planned the basic elements himself. According to the memo he sent me, the train

...must be routed through Chicago. Must be 20th Century and Union Pacific streamliner City of Los Angeles. Maximum security should be possible. Ready now to definitely leave very earliest departure possible by train consistent with maximum security. Will leave present local men here, but in a room not visible to public or hotel employees. Expect bring them west and make a part of permanent group, but not until I give signal. This location will be permanent for foreseeable future, but don't disclose that. This should make a practical and happy arrangement.

We arranged this train trip the same way as the one to Boston, but now we had to deal with the press. They were staked out at every exit of the Ritz, so we had to set up a decoy operation. It wasn't complicated, but it had to look like the real thing. First we hired a fake Hughes and put him in a limo. The reporters spotted him taking off and followed the decoy. Meantime, Hughes slipped out of the Ritz and was taken to the train station. And for all their effort, the press didn't have a clue.

The train began its journey to Las Vegas with Hughes safely aboard. Everything was going fine until I received word that the train was having brake problems. Jack Hooper called from Ogden, Utah, and said that the faulty breaks were causing a delay. The train was supposed to arrive in Las Vegas around 5:00 A.M. the day before Thanksgiving. Now, it was going to get there later in the morning, or worse still, in the afternoon.

There was no way we could let this happen. It was absolutely vital that Howard arrive in Las Vegas when it was still dark. I pressured Hooper to determine how long it was going to take for the engineers to fix the brakes and get moving again. While Hooper couldn't give me an exact time frame, it certainly looked like hours. So I said, "How much will it cost us to have them make up another train? We'll pay for another engine ... a caboose ... whatever it takes." Jack called back with a quote of $18,000. I said, "Hook it up right now."

Within minutes, the cars on Hughes's train were being moved and shuffled around. The Man himself had no idea what was happening, of course. All he knew was that after sitting on a track for a little over an hour, his train was headed toward Las Vegas again.

Meanwhile, I had checked into the Desert Inn Hotel in Las Vegas under the name of Robert Murphy. But somebody recognized me and the rumors started flying: Hughes was coming to Las Vegas. We were afraid that the press would swarm the train station. I called a railroad agent and swore him to secrecy. Arrangements were made to stop the train outside of town, at a location to be determined.

I sent my son Peter to find the ideal spot, four or five miles outside of town, where Hughes and his entourage could be safely removed from the train and taken into town. After canvassing along the tracks, Peter found a location that was accessible by road, yet still hidden from public view. The only problem was that highway construction was causing traffic to be detoured almost directly past the spot. Peter managed to change the signs long enough to divert traffic, while I calmed the railroad engineer, who was upset at being told by the station to stop his train. As I looked over my shoulder, I saw a stretcher being removed from the train, and realized that I had missed another opportunity to see the Man. I never thought it would be my last.

It was a little before 4:00 A.M., on November 27, 1966, when Hughes was taken off the train just north of the city. He was brought by a van to the Desert Inn. The service door is usually the best bet for getting someone inside secretly. But the service door also had access to the front entrance, so we needed a distraction. We had a half-dozen limousines pull up to the hotel entrance as decoys. As we drew attention away from Hughes, he was hustled up to his penthouse suite without being recognized.

My relationship with Hughes started to change as soon as he was ensconced in his blacked-out room on the Desert Inn's ninth floor. Communication between us significantly expanded, in both frequency and intensity. I had always talked to him on the phone, but now he was sending me handwritten memos. Security men were bringing me notes. Sometimes they waited for me to write the answer on the back, with memos going back and forth between us twenty or thirty times a day. All this was a sign that Hughes himself was entering a new phase, one that would mean big changes not just for me, but for the gambling mecca in which we had been transplanted as well.

I innocently thought that Hughes's stay at the Desert Inn would be a temporary situation; the kinds of plans Howard had cooking in his head almost never crossed my mind. But Las Vegas was ripe for expansion, and Hughes wanted to be a part of the last frontier. A very *big* part.

Our first ten days at the Desert Inn were so packed with activity that none of us realized how much time had passed until the hotel management came knocking on the door. The hotel wanted the rooms back—or rather, the *floors* back. At that point, we had almost two floors tied up: Hughes on the top level, and the staff on the floor below. These were prime suites, and the hotel wanted him out. It was getting very near Christmas; and while at the time that was not a real active period in the city, the hotel was gearing up for New Year's—the biggest event of the year.

Ruby Kolod, one of the owners, gave me an ultimatum. Actually, it was more like an order. Basically, he said, "Get the hell out of here, or we'll throw your butt out." Kolod had every right to be testy: he had been convicted of federal conspiracy charges after he tried to extort repayment of a debt from a Denver businessman and was caught in the act. A real tough character.

The hotel's majority owner was Moe Dalitz. Dalitz was reputed to have been involved in rum-running operations as well as illegal gambling for years in Cleveland and areas of Kentucky, long before Las Vegas came into existence. That was back in the old days when hoods like Bugsy Siegel came to play in what wasn't much more than a desert outpost.

Anyway, Kolod made it clear the honeymoon was over. I told Howard about it, but he wasn't a big help. Unwilling to budge, he merely told me, "It's your problem. You work it out." Obviously, he had no intention of leaving. I started to scramble through all my contacts and came up with only one name: Teamster boss Jimmy Hoffa. If anyone could get us a stay of eviction it was Hoffa, so I took a chance and picked up the phone.

I knew that the hotel had a loan with the Teamsters, so Hoffa pulled a lot of weight around there. I had met Hoffa a few years back during my Washington days. He knew about the work I'd done for the Steel Workers and at one point had wanted me to help his union. I'd turned him down. I just didn't want to be associated with the Teamsters. But I had promised that I wouldn't tell anybody about his request. That was important to him. Hoffa remembered that I had kept the faith with him. We also had some mutual friends—lawyer Edward Bennett Williams; Eddie Schafitz, a top lawyer and labor negotiator; and Edward P. Morgan, an ex-

FBI agent and prominent Washington attorney. I got in touch with
Hoffa through Ed Williams, and Hoffa called the Desert Inn management and made a request. Actually, that's putting it nicely; it
was more like a demand. Long story short: Hughes was allowed to
stay through New Year's—but we didn't win any popularity contest.

After we lived through that last weekend, Hoffa or no Hoffa,
our time was up. Kolod wasn't putting up with any more excuses
and wanted us out immediately. Hughes wouldn't even listen to my
pleas for guidance in the matter; he just wanted to lie in his darkened room, watch old movies, and be left alone.

Being pushed from both sides, I finally told Howard he should
buy the damned place and put an end to this pressure on us all. It
was more than the best idea anyone had; it was the only way we
weren't going to get kicked out. So we started negotiations to purchase the Desert Inn.

The hotel wasn't officially up for sale, of course. But word had
it that the hotel's chief management people were trying to get their
estates in order because most were getting on in years. The decision was made to sell the place. But none of them were in a hurry.
And they wanted to sell it on their own terms.

I knew there were two people who could help pull off this deal.
One was Ed Morgan. In the late thirties, Morgan had been an outstanding FBI agent. And in 1941, he had written the official FBI
report about the Japanese raid on Pearl Harbor. It was truly elo-
quent. After he left the Bureau, Morgan formed his own law firm,
and now had tremendous connections in Washington, particularly
with ex-FBI agents. He also had connections in Las Vegas, having
been called in from time to time by *Las Vegas Sun* publisher Hank
Greenspun.

The other facilitator was Johnny Rosselli. Over the years, I had
maintained a distant friendship, and now I put it to good use. No
matter what I thought about him, Rosselli was like a key to the city,
the ultimate mob fixer in the desert. Hughes never knew Johnny—

just knew of him. Both of us agreed he was a source that had to be used. We hooked him up with Ed Morgan and the ball started to roll.

Johnny smoothed the way while Morgan moved in to make the arrangements, representing Moe Dalitz and the Desert Inn. I did all the talking for Hughes, and it didn't take long before the talk turned ugly. First of all, Hughes was a tough trader. The minute we would get them to agree to something, he would always want to change it.

In the meantime, Kolod began to check with his contacts. They told him that we were still paying rent on the rooms in Boston, and they were right. Hughes had never given me the authority to give them up. While I was in a meeting with the negotiating committee, Kolod walked in and started calling me every name in the book. He was yelling that the whole deal about buying the hotel was a scam. It was only a ploy to buy time—so they wouldn't kick us out. Kolod started to blab that he knew all about the rooms in Boston. I guess in his mind that meant Hughes could pack up tomorrow and leave. I certainly could understand his logic. Very few people would keep that many rooms in another hotel if they didn't have any intention of going back. The man was livid. I tried to calm him down. But nothing worked. Adding insult to injury was Hughes's method of negotiating.

He said, "Take it down to this point, but make sure not to commit. You've gotta come back to me." But every time I delivered the offer he wanted, Hughes would say, "Okay, now knock them down another quarter of a million dollars. And again, don't commit." After doing that four or five times, he said, "We've reached exactly the price I want."

I had been through the ringer, so I became a little hot. "Why the hell didn't you tell me that in the first place?"

Hughes said, "It would have never worked. You had to do it piecemeal. We did it the only way that it would work."

That was a valuable lesson in negotiating: keep asking for a little bit; then a little bit more. Just keep the dialogue going. Don't give anything that even sounds like an ultimatum.

Finally we arrived at a sale price for the Desert Inn that Hughes thought was fair. The total came to $13.25 million. Hughes agreed to pay $6.3 million in cash and to assume $7 million of the hotel's liabilities. The terms called for Hughes to immediately place half a million down in escrow. When it came time for the cash to appear, Hughes had me go back to them and say forget it. He wanted to pay the entire nut—$6.3 million up front. The sellers were in ecstasy.

As I was about to walk out of the room, signed deal in hand, Kolod came up to me. He put out his hand, as if he wanted to shake and be friends. But I grabbed his wrist instead. Then I looked him right in the eye and said, "Don't you have something to say before we shake hands?"

He froze. He didn't answer. So I looked at the other people in the room and said, "Don't the rest of you men think he has something to say? How he berated me forty-eight hours ago?"

Finally Kolod opened his mouth. "Bob, I'm sorry."

There was no way he was going to leave that room without that apology. I wanted to get things straight. And I always figured it was best to end old battles before making peace.

When the Desert Inn deal was closed, Ed Morgan received a huge legal fee: $150,000. He shared a third of it with Johnny. Ed felt that because Rosselli had helped us get to the bargaining table in the first place and smoothed things out along the way, he was entitled to see some kind of reward. I didn't know about it at the time. It was Ed's call, and he kept it between himself and Rosselli.

Evidently, the money wasn't enough for Johnny. He felt he was entitled to stick his nose into the way I ran things. Right after the takeover, Johnny asked to see me. It was a meeting I'll never forget. We ended up at a lounge in the Desert Inn. I was seeing a

Johnny I'd never seen before. He looked me right in the eye and said, "Now, I want to tell you who the casino manager is going to be here, and who your entertainment director is going to be."

Johnny and I had decided in Miami that we wouldn't ever do business together again. I reminded him of that. He still insisted, "I'm just telling you," and he named the two men he wanted to be casino manager and entertainment director.

I couldn't believe this guy. I said, "Johnny, go to hell. If you want to remain a friend of mine, we'll never discuss this subject again."

Johnny said I was making a big mistake. I told him I didn't care—case closed. And I'll tell you, it was the smartest decision I ever made on the spot. If I had let Johnny order me around then, it would have never stopped.

Rosselli had some idea that Las Vegas was his world—and that I was supposed to sit at his knee. No longer was I merely a social friend whose children called him Uncle Johnny. Now that I was a player in Las Vegas, I was under his thumb, or so he thought. When I told him to go to hell, I changed his mind.

I knew Johnny was pissed, but I don't think he ever tried to get back at me in any way. Anyway, I always felt that somebody was covering my rear. In retrospect, I think it could have been Sam Giancana. I hadn't talked to Sam since our Fidel Castro days. But when I first started running the Desert Inn, I would get these strange phone calls. The voice would tell me to watch what was happening in this particular craps game or at a card table on a certain shift. I asked who was calling, but never got an answer. So I would have someone watch the game to find out if anything was wrong. Sometimes we would catch a bad dealer. Or somebody was getting signals. Or somebody paying $100 at the craps table and getting back $500 in chips. I never knew who was tipping me off, but something told me that Sam had people around who were trying to protect me.

Thirteen and a quarter million dollars bought us the Desert Inn operating company only—not the actual property. That meant we had the right to run the hotel and casino—assuming we were awarded the license.

The property and the building were actually owned by Desert Inn Associates, a division of the Helmsley-Spear Corporation out of New York. Harry Helmsley ran the real estate conglomerate—the same Harry Helmsley who married Leona and got into big tax trouble in the past few years. At any rate, Hughes kept saying, "One of these days, we'll buy the property." And I had a very good price worked out for him. But as usual, you couldn't get the Man to make a decision. And, as usual, it was one of many deals that should have happened but never did.

The deal for the hotel was unofficially closed on March 27, 1967. Since gaming taxes are paid on a quarterly basis, it's always best for a new buyer to close a casino deal at the beginning of the quarter. In this case that was April 1. So we waited the extra few days before becoming hotel and casino operators.

There's something very important to do when you make a big deal: make certain you actually receive what you *think* you bought. And we figured the best way to do just that was through Moe Dalitz. Moe was a hard-nosed businessman who let nothing escape his attention, particularly where money was concerned. So I went to him and said that I was ready to pay him the biggest compliment of his life.

"Howard has asked me to appoint you as fiduciary agent for the remaining period until the end of March," I told him. "He knows you'll give him a fair count."

What that essentially meant was that Moe had to make sure all the accounts were in order—to determine what we had, and what we earned in the meantime. It would have been all too easy to suddenly end up with a lot of phony markers in the till and no way to collect them. In Las Vegas, it's amazing how fast cash can disappear, only to be replaced by worthless pieces of paper. People have since told me that nobody had ever worked so hard as Moe did to keep things straight, and I believe he was square with us.

At this point, we were about twenty-four hours away from closing the deal. Yvette and I were having dinner in the Monte Carlo room of the hotel, when we were suddenly interrupted by Eli Boyer, the accountant for the current owners. He called me aside and told me all hell had broken loose. Hughes was suddenly arguing about some item totaling about $13,000.

All the owners were at the hotel for the closing, and they were eating in another dining room. Hughes was causing such a stink that they were going to throw him out of the hotel. Suddenly they didn't care about the deal; they cared about proving who was still boss to the Man on the ninth floor.

I went to their table and Kolod looked up at me. He said that I had one hour to clarify the issue or lose the deal entirely. "We've made up our minds. Let's see you magic this one up," he sneered.

It was obvious that he didn't think anyone could save the deal. Right then and there, I took his challenge. I grabbed the accountant and headed to Hughes's penthouse suite. The guard was standing there and wanted to know what I was doing. There was a suite across the hall from Hughes's quarters. I used it once in a while to do some work. We went inside and I started writing Hughes a letter of resignation.

"I've given my word," I wrote Howard. "And now you're playing games for a matter of peanuts. I just don't want to be involved with you anymore."

I showed it to the accountant. He thought I was kidding, but I was dead serious. I went across the hall and knocked on the door. The aide on duty took one look at the letter and said, "I can't give him this." I told him to step aside and I'd give it to Hughes myself. He finally took the letter in. I waited outside for a while, then headed downstairs to Kolod's table.

"How's your miracle working?" Kolod asked. I told him my hour wasn't up yet.

A couple of minutes later, the accountant walked into the room. He was smiling and told us he had just had a call from Dick Gray, the Houston attorney I had brought in to help with the legal aspects of the transaction. "We're to close immediately without this item being involved," the accountant said.

Then the phone rang for me. It was Hughes, and I kept playing my hand. I told him I was packing up and leaving that night.

"Bob, I'm not going to argue," Hughes told me. "I'm too tired to argue. Please promise me that you'll at least be in your suite tomorrow morning at eight. I want to talk to you. Please promise me that."

The next morning, the call came at eight on the dot. Hughes persuaded me to stay, and said, "Don't you ever, ever scare me like that again."

Then he told me I was right. "We can't get involved in this world and start playing games at the last minute. You were absolutely right. Please forgive me. And please don't pack." He went on making a lot of promises about my future, saying that he and I would be working together for the rest of our natural lives.

There's no doubt that Hughes and I understood each other. And I truly believe that, most of the time, I did "tame the beast" better than anyone else could have. But as Hughes told me many times, "Just remember, Bob: there's not a man that I cannot buy or destroy. Including you."

Though Hughes's eccentricities amazed me, I knew another side of him. But to people like Kolod and Dalitz, Hughes was a total enigma. They knew of Hughes from the old days, when he was this handsome guy who would go out on the town and charm the women. They now saw that he never left his room, even to come down to dinner, but they did not suspect how his condition was deteriorating.

As soon as we'd arrived in Las Vegas, Hughes had had a physician placed on staff. He had persuaded a Beverly Hills doctor named Norman Crane to give up his practice and work just for him. While we were negotiating, everybody would ask when Hughes was going to show up. I'd just say, "Well, you know we have a doctor here. The Man is not well. He'll get better and then you'll see him." It was an easy out. And that seemed to satisfy everybody. Then, once we made the deal, it didn't make any difference.

So it was that on April 1, 1967, Las Vegas entered a new chapter in its history, and Hughes in his. The Desert Inn, long described as a citadel of organized crime, went legit. The hotel that had hosted presidents, chief justices, the king and queen of Nepal; the showroom where Noel Coward had made his only Las Vegas appearance; the pool in which Johnny Weissmuller had done aquacade dancing and diving; the elegant, darkened penthouse on the ninth floor—all belonged to Howard Hughes.

The Desert Inn agreement wasn't just good business. We didn't know it at the time, but it wound up being a real blessing for Hughes in terms of taxes. When we were structuring the sale, Hughes informed me that he had learned that the gross revenue of the casino qualified as "active" income.

When Hughes sold his TWA stock, we had to get that check deposited as soon as possible. With the check amounting to $546,549,771, we were talking about tens of thousands of dollars in interest per day, even at the rates they were paying back then.

Hughes's attorneys structured him into something called a Sub-Chapter S Corporation. It was designed for a small individual—not somebody with the kind of money Hughes had—but there wasn't anything that said Hughes couldn't use it, and it meant a big tax break at the time.

When Hughes began to earn enormous amounts of capital in interest, he found out that a Sub-Chapter S Corporation was a double-edged sword. Hughes told me that interest money was classified as "passive" income. It was taxed just like earned wages, unless it could be offset with "active" income. The ratio is four or five to one; in other words, the active income had to be four or five times greater to offset the interest money.

The taxes on Hughes's interest alone were a killer, until he learned that the gross casino revenue could be used to offset the interest. Suddenly he was saved, and in one giant whoosh his tax problems went out the window. He called me right away to tell me the great news. Then he asked, "How many more of these places are available? Let's buy 'em all!"

I was speechless. Here was a man I never thought would put his name on a gaming license. It required too much outside investigation into your personal life to get one. If somebody had suggested it a couple of years back, I would have bet ten to one against any of this ever happening. I would have been very wrong. Howard wanted every casino in town. He wanted to become King of the Strip. He was acting like the Howard of old. Yet, before we could make any more moves, Hughes would have to receive one important piece of paper: a gaming license. Without that, there would *be* no casinos, at least not in Howard Hughes's name. The tough part was trying to persuade the authorities to give Hughes the license without ever laying eyes on him. Under normal circumstances, they insisted on meeting the applicant face to face. But Hughes wasn't coming out of his suite. All of which, once again, left me trying to pull this off with an impromptu song and dance.

When I started looking for an attorney to help with the licensing process, I asked the governor of Nevada, Paul D. Laxalt, for a recommendation. He suggested Tom Bell, an honest and well-respected young lawyer. Then I talked to both of the state's senators, the sheriff, and the district attorney. They all said Tom Bell. You can't argue with that kind of support.

While we had Bell doing the paperwork, the man who really

made rain in the desert was Laxalt. The former governor and senator is a good friend of mine, has been all these years, and there has been a lot of controversy about what he did for Hughes. There's been talk about payoffs and personal gain. Not a word of it is true. Laxalt never did anything that wasn't strictly kosher, and anybody who says differently is, quite simply, a liar.

The controversy surrounding Laxalt's honesty began when some memos written by Hughes to me in the late sixties became public. Hughes was instructing me to get in touch with the governor and tell him to drop whatever he was doing and to instead help us try to buy Harrah's Club in Nevada. After the memo was made public, the conclusion drawn by many was that Laxalt was on Hughes's payroll. That was never the case. What no one realized was that I never acted on many memos Hughes sent me.

I believed that an important part of my job was helping save Hughes from himself. If I had gone to Laxalt to tell him to stop everything he was doing and concentrate on us, he would have flipped me on my back. He was, and is, a totally honest man.

Laxalt started his political career as a district attorney in Ormsby County, and was elected governor of the state in November, 1966, just a few days before Howard Hughes arrived on his doorstep. Laxalt believed—and I think rightly—that Hughes was just what Las Vegas needed. Hughes's arrival brought respectability to a city overrun by organized crime.

The syndicates were starting to get a lot of heat from the Feds. Many of them were looking to get out of Las Vegas. Laxalt saw Hughes as a better option than the mob: he was an excellent businessman, and he was totally legitimate—the kind of sugar daddy Las Vegas needed.

Laxalt approved of Hughes and told that to the Nevada Gaming Commission to smooth the way. He did something that will never happen again: he helped Hughes and myself get seven gaming licenses without Hughes ever appearing before the commission. But Paul didn't break any laws to do it.

He was convinced that when he spoke to me, he spoke to Hughes, and he convinced the commission that I could be Hughes's surrogate before them. Laxalt didn't do it to get something from Hughes; he did it to get something good for Las Vegas, and in return, Howard Hughes gave the town new life.

As a way of securing Laxalt's cooperation, and to suggest how serious Howard was about his plans for Las Vegas, Hughes sent a handwritten letter to the governor three days before the Nevada Gaming Control Board was to vote on the Desert Inn's new gaming application. In the letter, Howard offered to finance a medical school at the University of Nevada in Las Vegas, donating $200,000 to $300,000 annually for twenty years. Three days later, Hughes had his first gaming license.

That hurdle overcome, we started snapping up real estate right and left. First we bought the Sands. It was a relatively quick acquisition for $14.6 million and about $9 million in debt that we assumed. The deal included both the hotel and acres of property around it. Once again, Ed Morgan represented the owners, and once again he received a nice fee—this time $225,000. And as before, he paid off Rosselli, to the tune of $45,000.

The Sands had always been associated with stars since its opening in 1952. It was where the Rat Pack worked and played—Frank Sinatra, Dean Martin, Joey Bishop, Sammy Davis, Jr., and Peter Lawford. On August 1, 1967, the Sands officially became the property of Howard Hughes.

For his part, hidden away atop the Desert Inn, Hughes's attention was scattered. While I continued to pursue the availability of additional casinos and hotels, Howard turned his attention to films. Up until this point, Hughes would spend hours and hours watching films on his bedside movie projector. When he moved to Las

Vegas, he found that KLAS-TV, the local station owned by Hank Greenspun, ran old films into the night. But not late enough for Howard. You must remember that this was a man who slept very little, and never in the evening. He kept pestering Greenspun to keep the movies on later and later, and always tried to get him to program the films he wanted to see, until finally the publisher offered to sell the station, just to get Howard off his back. The station cost Hughes $3.6 million, a small amount for a CBS affiliate. Before it became official, of course, the Federal Communications Commission had to be sold on granting Hughes a license without his making the mandatory personal appearance in Washington.

I once again went to Ed Morgan. And once again he didn't disappoint me. Morgan convinced the FCC to put the application in the name of Raymond Holliday, the top executive at the Hughes Tool Company in Houston, and Howard had himself a TV station.

During this same period, Howard was actively trying to convince Jean Peters to join him in Las Vegas. Despite the fact that he hadn't seen her since she'd stood in the hallway of the Ritz-Carlton in Boston, he wanted her nearby. They continued to talk nearly every day by phone, and Howard held out a carrot—several beautiful homes in the area. He went so far as to have me arrange for a friend to purchase the magnificent estate of Major A. Riddle, who was a part owner of the Dunes Hotel. The gigantic home was located near the Las Vegas Strip and the Desert Inn.

In addition, Hughes decided to buy a 518-acre ranch outside the city. It was owned by the ex-wife of Alfried Krupp, the German munitions kingpin, and it seemed like the kind of place where Jean Peters could maintain the same privacy she enjoyed in Beverly Hills. At one point, she even agreed to move, but only if Howard would move there first. He never made that commitment, leaving both properties empty for years. Eventually, they became the first places I looked for Howard when he vanished years later.

He hadn't satisfied his thirst for casinos as yet, either. I continued the buying spree with the small Castaways Hotel and Casino, and then the much larger Frontier Hotel and Casino across the street from the Desert Inn. Hughes was now running three of the major spots in town, and one smaller one. But it wasn't enough; he wanted more. I received word from his penthouse to keep buying, though we were beginning to run out of potential properties.

Soon even hotels weren't enough. He bought a small charter airline and its fixed-based operation at McCarran Airport; the North Las Vegas Airport and a motel that adjoined it; a subdivision next to the Desert Inn; and every vacant piece of land I could find up and down the Strip.

In less than twelve months, I had invested millions of Hughes's money in property and casinos, yet he still wasn't satisfied. Howard started to work with overlay maps of Las Vegas, until he knew every inch of the city. He would put them on top of one another, charting development over several years, assessing the potential for growth. Hughes predicted the development of the city's west side long before it took place.

Insatiable, he next announced that he wanted to build a super-jet airport of gargantuan proportions away from downtown Las Vegas. It would be the airport of the future, connected to Los Angeles via high-speed trains. Since Las Vegas already had an international airport, Hughes told the county that he would acquire that property and turn it into a facility to handle private planes and nonscheduled aircraft. He had studies made showing that climatic conditions were perfect for airplane landings. The airport had only closed a couple of times, because of a sandstorm, but never for rain or fog. That meant full-time operation. Howard even toyed with the idea of moving the Hughes Aircraft plant from Culver City to land he already owned in Nevada. The potential for development was tremendous.

Immediately, I started working out a deal with authorities that said Hughes would do all the construction and then give the super-jet airport back to the county at his cost. Before relinquishing the McCarran property, the county was to have an appraisal made of its worth, with the value deducted from Hughes's total cost for the new airport. Altogether, the super-jet airport would have cost between $400 and $500 million, but the deal never came to fruition.

In the meantime, Hughes was also buying up all the land surrounding McCarran. Not directly, of course; that still wasn't his style. We had other people making the deals and then turning the property over to Hughes.

We also started looking at the Stardust Hotel and Casino (the majority of whose stock was owned by Moe Dalitz) and the Silver Slipper, a small-stakes casino best known for all-you-could-eat breakfasts. For a while it seemed like the Hughes empire was the only game in town.

Then the Feds trumped up a notice from the Justice Department's antitrust division in San Francisco. The Feds advised Hughes not to buy the Stardust. If he went ahead with the deal, they would try and block it, they said, calling it a violation of antitrust laws. By purchasing the Stardust, Hughes would have controlled more rooms in town than one single owner was allowed to have. Rather than fight the Feds, Hughes dropped plans for the Stardust. We bought the Silver Slipper instead. The place didn't have any rooms, just a casino.

Hughes was on a roll that didn't seem to be losing steam. Soon after buying the Silver Slipper, he had me start negotiating to buy the Dunes. And Caesars Palace. The fact that the government might slap us with the antitrust rule again no longer seemed to bother him. He even started talking about an auto-racing track and a book operation. He wanted to put Indianapolis right out of business.

Hughes loved the pace and the power. And I began to enjoy it as well. It *did* have its advantages. When we bought the Desert Inn property, we also acquired a house that belonged to Moe Dalitz. It was right on the grounds, next to the clubhouse. So in 1967, right after my children got out of school for the summer, the Maheu family moved in. At the time, my son Robert was fourteen, my daughter Christine was thirteen, and my son Billy was seven. My oldest son, Peter, was already married with children of his own. He moved to Las Vegas shortly thereafter.

Hughes loved the idea that I lived on the Desert Inn property—insisted on it, in fact. However, Bill Gay was getting scared. Gay saw that house as just one more sign that I was next in line to the throne. He began to worry that my power was growing as his own was slipping fast. On two occasions, Gay asked if I'd help him get Hughes declared incompetent. One time he asked me in front of Ed Morgan, and at one of my birthday parties, he tried again while I was talking to Dr. Robert Buckley. Not fully realizing the extent of Howard's condition, I was shocked at the suggestion. Morgan, Buckley, and I all considered Gay's scheme diabolical, and we told him so. Moreover, I told Howard about Gay's plan. His only response was, "Bob, as long as you and I are talking, those bastards will never succeed."

At the time, Dr. Buckley had been on staff at St. John's Hospital in Santa Monica for years. Howard knew of him through Jean Peters. Buckley had helped Jean's maid, who had been having some problem with her son. He also helped save Jack Hooper's life in 1967. Hooper had just been released from a Las Vegas hospital after having some tests. He was talking to Buckley on the telephone, expressing his pleasure at his release, but continuing to complain about some minor symptoms. Something he said made Buckley suspicious, for he excitedly told Hooper to check back into the hospital immediately, and said he would be on the next flight to

Las Vegas. Alerted by Buckley of his suspicions, Dr. Harold Feikes performed surgery for an aneurysm that very night on Hooper. Thanks to Buckley, his life was saved.

Hughes was very impressed. He insisted that I move Buckley and his family to Nevada; get him a house; put him on a private retainer. Buckley was supposed to remain available for Hughes, although it would be months before Hughes would need him.

As I said, there was already one doctor on the Hughes payroll. Dr. Norman Crane had been hired when we first hit Las Vegas. Howard had persuaded him to give up a pretty lucrative practice in Beverly Hills, placed him on a retainer of $80,000, and given him a big suite at the Desert Inn.

Hughes had also promised Crane that he could go home every weekend. But when that first weekend came, Hughes wouldn't give him permission. This went on for about three months. Eventually, the doctor also was moved from his big suite to a much smaller room. Here was a man who'd left his family, a nice home, and a good practice, only to find himself living in virtual captivity. He started drinking heavily.

One night, Crane was summoned to see Hughes. Hughes was bleeding and needed a blood analysis. The doctor was about to have dinner, but the aides told him he couldn't go down to the dining room. Hughes was afraid that he might pick up some germs and pass them along.

Unfortunately, the poor doctor had had too much to drink on an empty stomach that particular evening. He was shaking so bad that he couldn't even find a vein in Hughes's arm. This scared the hell out of Howard. So he called me and said to bring Buckley over immediately.

Buckley and I had been buying a lot of equipment and setting it up in the suite across the hall from Hughes—it was like a mini-hospital—so when the call came, we were ready. Before Buckley had a chance to leave, however, Howard was back on the telephone questioning me about Buckley's background. He wanted me to send over his curriculum vitae, a complete rundown on his credentials. Buckley gave me a copy. It showed he had a strong background in psychiatry. Hughes took one look at it and told me he couldn't use Buckley anymore. "If word ever got out that I was seeing a psychiatrist," Howard said, "all hell would break loose. It would have an effect on the government contracts and everything else."

In retrospect, one can see how Hughes's reluctance came from the fact that he needed a shrink more than anything else. His mind was becoming more dangerous than any of those germs he feared. Bill Gay knew it. Rather than get Hughes some help, he was using his mental instability as a secret weapon. At the time, I didn't know the threat was growing bigger every day. This was just a warning sign.

Moving into Dalitz's old house was convenient, but I wasn't happy with the setup. The place was right in the middle of everything. And it wasn't the kind of atmosphere to raise your children. They were being spoiled rotten. Everyone was kowtowing to us, bringing gifts, offering favors.

Yvette and I tried to lay down some discipline—not only on the children, but on ourselves. One thing that we decided was never to go to any midnight shows. We were family people with responsibilities. Our time together was more important than catching somebody's act.

There was something else about living so close to the business that began to drive me nuts: my phone wouldn't stop ringing. It didn't seem to matter what time it was. If there was a problem in the casino, the employees would just say, "Well, the boss is on the premises. Let's call him."

That's not my idea of running an operation. You have to

appoint managers to make the decisions. If they make a mistake, you talk to them. If they don't listen, you fire them. But you can't run the whole show alone.

I started fighting with Hughes to let me move, but he wanted me to keep my home on the Desert Inn property. I began to beg him to help me provide my family with a normal life, until finally he decided to give an inch. He would build me a new house—still on the property, but not so close to the casino. That was the best deal Hughes was going to offer, so I took it.

We built the house on the golf course for over $600,000. The home was stately, pillared, and enormous—a French Colonial residence that was quickly dubbed Little Caesars Palace. We had room to entertain several hundred people at a time. The kitchen had five stoves, there were two magnificent staircases, six bedrooms, and as many baths. It was ready in September, 1969. My family and I spent two Christmases there. The children never did like the place. They thought it was too cold, too institutional. But it had something I loved: there was one beauty of a wine cellar. When Baron de Rothschild found out that his Chateau Lafitte '59 was my favorite wine, he sent me two cases. It is a gift I've savored over the years. I still have a few bottles left, as a matter of fact.

My main office was at the Frontier Hotel. It was a real showplace, on the second floor overlooking the tennis courts, with a beautiful desk and conference table, both made of rosewood. The maintenance crew at the Sands built them especially for me. I wasn't your standard executive type, so I didn't like doing business from behind a desk. The only time I sat there was when I had to fire somebody. The office also had a hidden wet bar. I didn't feel that liquor should be out in the open; it gave a bad impression. Perhaps there was even more of a reason I felt that way—during this period I began to drink more heavily than I should have.

The pressure always seemed to be on me, and my only way of escaping it was by going to a chalet I'd built on Mount Charleston.

It was like being in the Swiss Alps. The home of rough, natural wood was rustic, isolated in the middle of a big pine forest, up about 7,400 feet. From Las Vegas it was thirteen minutes by chopper. We used a landing pad at a restaurant I owned with two partners that was located across the valley.

The road to the cabin was treacherous. There was a fire station at the bottom, so I worked out a deal: I put up this security system, and then wired it into the fire station. That way, the men down there could keep an eye on things.

After a while, not even the chalet worked to calm my shattered nerves. I started to get the feeling that keeping up with the casino business would drive me into an early grave. After the initial publicity about Hughes taking over the Desert Inn, mail started to pour in, bundles of it every day, and the phone never stopped ringing. Everyone was after something. People I hadn't seen for years began asking me for comp tickets to shows. There were people who wanted to sell me meat, linens, plumbing ... everything! On top of that I was getting a barrage of offers for property. Ten different real estate agents were trying to sell me the same piece of land.

I knew I had to devise some sort of system to gain control, a way to log and answer all this communication so that, at the very least, we didn't get slapped with lawsuits. Negotiations were moving fast. Occasionally things had to fall through the cracks. I kept worrying that one day somebody would read about a deal we had just closed, then claim he had something to do with it, demanding a fee. It became imperative to keep track of every offer or request that came in, and how we responded.

We also had to deal with malpractice suits. People would get sick at the hotel, and the employees would recommend a doctor. If some hotel operator made a referral, it was as if the recommendation had come straight from Hughes. He became responsible if anything went wrong. I worked with Dr. Buckley to organize a group of local physicians. These doctors formed a committee, and they would make the recommendation when a guest needed help.

Then there was the matter of markers—the casinos' version of IOUs. We had to tighten up the way they were handled. In the old days, if a player didn't make good on a marker, the Mob would send some thug to break his legs. But Hughes couldn't use the old methods. There was no way he could send out some goon to rough up a bad customer. Nor was I going to put up with pimps or hookers either. I put the word out to the bell captain that providing women for guests was going to stop. I knew that Las Vegas was a wide-open town and that rackets were going on at some of the other hotels. But I didn't want Hughes to be part of it. I took a lot of heat for it around town.

Despite the strain, I got a thrill out of calling the shots. Being on top in Las Vegas is an awesome, almost indescribable feeling. Not only were we on top, we were getting bigger every day. Hughes was steamrolling his way through the desert. And, most surprising of all, he was *enjoying* himself. He liked the power and the action. He even got a kick out of the press attention he started getting again, attention he had been avoiding for years.

It was true: Hughes had become the King of Vegas. And as he remained invisible, cloistered high atop the Desert Inn, I served as Crown Regent. But you have to be careful when you're riding that high. You've got to make sure that you don't get swept away. And pulled under.

Chapter Seven

TROUBLE IN PARADISE

IT'S OFTEN BEEN SAID THAT A LITTLE POWER IS A DANGEROUS THING. A lot of power is even worse.

As Howard was busy severing ties with his Hollywood base on Romaine Street, I settled into my new life in Las Vegas, establishing a division called Hughes Nevada Operations and appointing myself chief executive officer. I did it to anchor our arrangement. Remember, although I was essentially calling all the shots for Hughes, I still had no employment contract with him, not even an official document that gave me the right to wheel and deal on his behalf. While all of that was exactly how I had planned it, it confused other people. With Hughes's Nevada, I at least had a title and an organization that people could see. My son Peter became my administrative assistant, and I hired an old Holy Cross classmate, Major General Edward Nigro, as my deputy CEO. Two ex-IRS employees, Walter Fitzpatrick and Henry Schwind, were brought on board to look over the casino and hotel operations. The onetime head of the FBI bureau in Nevada, Dean Elson, handled a variety of sensitive assignments, while Jack Hooper officially headed up the entire security force.

Howard, in his penthouse, surrounded himself with his aides—Roy Crawford, Howard Eckersley, George Francom, John Holmes, and Levar Myler. All were Mormons, except for the

Catholic Holmes, and all had been handpicked by Bill Gay. Even though Romaine Street was now far away, Gay's boys on the scene kept him well informed on Howard's condition. As it turned out, Gay was far better informed than I was.

The aides' backgrounds had hardly prepared them for their tasks. Myler used to run a milling machine; Holmes had been a wax salesman; Eckersley, the most pompous of them all, had worked for a finance company; Francom had done construction work; and Crawford once repped an oil refinery.

Their power came from their close access to Hughes—each of them saw him every day and dealt with his increasingly strange behavior as if it were normal. Unlike my dealings with other Hughes employees, my dealings with Gay's men were limited. They would relay messages to and from Howard and me. For the most part, however, Howard and I talked directly or exchanged memos. It wouldn't be until years later that I realized how little attention I was actually paying to the activities of his personal assistants. It would prove a fatal mistake.

It was almost a year into his run as King of Vegas that Hughes's paranoia began to blossom fully. The occasion was the annual Easter Egg Hunt at the Desert Inn. It had been a long-standing event for kids in the neighborhood. In 1967, just days after the Desert Inn officially became a Hughes property, the event went off as usual without a hitch. The next year was to be different, however. Howard became convinced that an Easter Egg Hunt with hundreds of "ever-lovin' little darlings" could prove disastrous if it got out of hand. Worse still, he feared it might provide the perfect setting for his enemies to sabotage his good intentions. I was told to cancel the event. It was as if the mere presence of hundreds of screaming kids could somehow affect his tranquillity in his ninth-floor penthouse. He was convinced that disaster was afoot, and nothing I could say would change his mind.

It reminded me of one of Howard's demands when we first

took over running the Desert Inn. It had long been the site of the Tournament of Champions golf tournament, and Howard wanted the event out. At the time I received the call, the tournament start was only ten days away. The tickets were already printed, and the players had made their arrangements to come to Las Vegas.

I argued long and hard in an attempt to change Howard's mind. He turned a deaf ear and refused to even consider allowing the event to continue at the hotel. He said he felt trapped by the thought that the thousands of people in attendance would know where he was living—perhaps even gain entry to his rooms.

Knowing the battle was lost, I telephoned Moe Dalitz to break the news. I invited him to an urgent breakfast at his old house. When I told him Howard's decision, he looked at me blankly. He simply couldn't believe that Hughes would give up the gold mine that the Tournament of Champions represented.

I told Moe we could make an announcement saying that when the Desert Inn was purchased, Moe and the other owners had not sold the rights to the Tournament of Champions with it. Instead they were planning on holding the event at another one of Moe's hotels, the Stardust. Moe hesitantly agreed, despite the fact that the Stardust's golf course isn't even connected to the hotel—it's a mile away.

Moe pointed out that on such short notice, the added costs incurred in moving the event would generate a huge loss. I told him that Hughes would cover his losses, and signed over the rights to the tournament that afternoon. Howard had made an enormous mistake. The tournament was a class event that created a great deal of excitement. People would check into the hotel a week or ten days ahead of the event, just to watch the players practice. The night before the event, there was a Calcutta where people would bid on different teams. During the tournament, you couldn't even get to the golf course without walking through the casino, a fact that further increased the hotel's profits. It also brought a wealth of celebrities and the prestige they attract. The tournament eventually ended up at La Costa Spa in California, in which Moe Dalitz was a minority shareholder.

I had acquiesced and followed his orders then; and I did it again with the Easter Egg Hunt, silly as his worries seemed. Frankly, my plate was too full to give these things much thought. In addition to the ongoing fight with TWA, I was about to take on another giant corporation—the ABC television network. For months, Howard had been suggesting that he was interested in buying a controlling interest in the network, primarily to gain access to ABC News. Howard believed that, by controlling the content of ABC, he could influence political decisions in Washington. Freedom of the press was fine with Hughes, as long as it worked to his advantage.

I had argued with him against attempting the takeover. In addition to being costly, I felt it could only lead to another protracted court battle, even if Hughes were successful. I could not imagine the Federal Communications Commission allowing such a transfer of ownership without Hughes having to make a personal appearance before it. And obviously he would never do that. Undaunted by my reasoning, for months Howard continued to toy with the idea of making a bid for the network, his enthusiasm vacillating back and forth. Mere months before he made his move to acquire ABC, he sent me a memo stating that he no longer wanted the network, and for the most bizarre reason.

> Bob, I just got through watching ABC's "Dating Game" and "Newlywed Game," and my only reaction is let's forget all about ABC. Bob, I think all this attention directed toward violence in TV dramatic shows is certainly misplaced. These two game shows represent the largest single collection of poor taste I have ever seen.
> The first show—"Dating Game"—consisted of a small negro child selecting, sight unseen, one of three girls (adult girls) to make a sexually embellished trip to Rome with his father.

Two of the girls were negro and one was a white girl. The child chose the white girl, who then was introduced to the negro father of the child and informed that she (the white girl) was to make an all expense paid vacation trip to Rome on TWA.

Bob, the entire handling of the show was, in every way, carried out in a manner best calculated to titilate [sic] and arouse the sexual response of the audience. The whole show was of such a marginal character, sex-wise, that if it had been presented as a motion picture to the governing body of the movie industry, its acceptance would have been very uncertain at best.

But, let me explain that I make the above comment based upon the subject matter and the treatment of the show, without any consideration whatsoever of the racial issue.

Then, on top of the very marginal show of miserable taste, which I have attempted to describe above, they have to compound the abuse of any conceivable moral standard by arranging a sexual rendezvous between a beautiful white girl and a negro man in Rome, which may even be in violation of the law.

And all of this is done solely for one purpose: to shock and arouse the sexual response of the audience so as to obtain a higher rating from the TV polls for the benefit of the sponsers.

Please consider this entire affair most carefully, Bob, to see if it gives you any ideas. Many thanks, Howard.

While I was happy that Howard had at least momentarily given up his desire to acquire ABC, I had to point out to him that the "beautiful white girl" he saw on the program was actually a light-skinned black, and sure enough, within months he was hot in pursuit of ABC once more.

Over my protests, Howard finally made it public and announced his intention to buy two million shares of ABC stock from the current stockholders, and offered them two weeks to tender their stock. Hughes had waited for the third-rated, cash-poor network's stock to plummet to a low point before he made his move on Sunday night, June 30, 1968.

Right before his announcement, he telephoned to alert me to

his plan. By that time, I realized that the early-morning papers would already be hitting the newsstands on the East Coast, so there was little I could do other than voice my displeasure. I went on to tell him that the next time we talked about ABC he would be asking me to implement something I labeled "Operation Extricate" to get him out from under what I saw as a major blunder.

As word spread about Hughes's offer, the reaction across the country was immediate. Newspapers throughout the United States suggested that Hughes would be coming out of hiding to wrestle control of the network from ABC chairman Leonard Goldenson. Howard, of course, had no intention of leaving his ninth-floor penthouse, and promptly put me to work to "condition" the individual members of the FCC for his no-show. Once again, I placed a call to attorney Ed Morgan to accomplish the impossible, and Ed assured me that he felt that the FCC might be agreeable.

Within days, Morgan was back on the phone alerting me to the fact that the FCC had unanimously voiced its intention to make Hughes testify in person before the collected commissioners. At the same time, Goldenson announced that Hughes was attempting a hostile takeover of the network and began to fight back. Sensing the disaster I had long predicted, Howard was nervous when he called me on July 7 and asked me what I had called my plan.

"Operation Extricate," I told him.

"Put it into action, immediately," he said.

I informed him that I would have to call on Chester Davis for help. At the time, Davis was on the outs with Hughes for his fumbling of the TWA fiasco, yet he was the only attorney I knew who was devious and obnoxious enough to tie ABC up in the courts long enough to allow the deadline on the stock offer to pass, thereby removing Howard from his obligation by default. On July 9, ABC played into our hands and slapped Howard Hughes with legal action. The network asked the federal courts to issue an injunction prohibiting Hughes from continuing to pursue his stock purchase. Unfortunately for our plan, the courts made quick work of the action. That very afternoon, they denied ABC's effort at an injunction, and eventually went on to refuse an ABC demand that Hughes testify.

While the federal courts were busy clearing the way for a takeover, the Justice Department was threatening to become involved. The antitrust implications of a Hughes-ABC buyout were obvious. Hughes was already the owner of CBS affiliate KLAS-TV; Hughes Aircraft was manufacturing communications satellites; he had dabbled in cable TV franchises; and he even produced components used in the transmission of TV signals. When I alerted Howard to the Justice Department involvement, he became even more nervous. Now fearing that the courts might actually clear the way for his purchase of the ABC stock, he wanted to have a backup plan, and asked me to get an immediate reaction from President Lyndon Johnson, whom Howard considered a friend. He had been a supporter of Johnson since his earliest senatorial campaigns and had contributed heavily to Johnson in his losing bid for the presidential nomination in 1960, which ultimately went to John F. Kennedy. Hughes wanted Johnson to give his approval to the takeover, halt any Justice Department intervention, and at the same time assure him that an appearance before the FCC would not be required. Howard expected a lot; too much, to my mind. I finally persuaded him to drop the LBJ idea and to instead handle the situation through Ed Morgan and his contacts.

Davis continued to attempt to stall the tender offer in court while giving the appearance to outsiders that Hughes was still anxious to buy the network. Fortunately, Davis's tactics created enough doubt in the hearts of the stock brokerage houses that less than 100,000 shares had been tendered on the day before the two-week deadline was up.

Much to Hughes's glee, the ABC attorneys worked overtime filing one charge after another, intent on blocking the sale and further intimidating stockholders who feared becoming involved in the legal brouhaha. ABC had continued to tie the offer up in federal court right up until hours before the final deadline. A last-minute ruling in Hughes's favor, however, brought us an avalanche of over a million and a half shares on the final day.

Hughes was frantic. While his buyout was obviously an enormous success, the prospect of spending over $180 million to pay for it made him anxious. If that weren't enough, the FCC had publicly announced it would put his ownership in a trust until after he appeared in person before its members. With the clock ticking, we needed only a little under 400,000 shares to be tendered to reach Howard's announced goal of two million. Luckily, when the clock struck midnight on July 14, 1968, we were still several hundred thousand shares short. Hughes could have extended the offer, of course, and easily been handed the necessary shares to acquire the network. Yet, with ABC in his grasp, Hughes had me make a public announcement stating that we would not extend the offer, and we all breathed a sigh of relief—one that was echoed in New York by ABC and Leonard Goldenson.

Howard's contentment would not last long. He lathered up over the formation of Air West that same month. The airline was a combination of three small commuter lines—Bonanza Air Lines, based in Phoenix; Pacific Air Lines, headquartered in San Francisco; and West Coast Airlines, whose hub was Seattle. Former West Coast Airlines CEO Nick Bez was heading up the new company, which was overwhelmed with problems from its first day of service. Not only was the airline undercapitalized, it had installed a new computer system that was broken more often than it worked. Nicknamed "Air Worst" for its performance record, the airline was a primary carrier of passengers between Los Angeles, Las Vegas, and Reno. If it failed, it would deny potential gamblers easy access to the sister cities and mean millions of dollars in lost revenue for Hughes's casinos.

More important to Hughes than forestalling lost profits, however, was the fact that a takeover of Air West represented an opportunity for him to reenter the airline business. Suddenly he could think of nothing else. He was enthusiastic to the point of insisting I arrange to buy the airline immediately. I chose not to fly Air West when I traveled to Los Angeles on July 30, 1968, to meet with Bez and present Howard's takeover proposal at the Century Plaza Hotel. Bez was a big diamond in the rough, a native of Yugoslavia, and a multimillionaire himself. Aware that his problems at Air West were growing daily, he was receptive to the idea of Hughes's involvement, suggesting a simple stock-buyout plan that I relayed to Howard.

As it turned out, it was anything but simple. I hadn't counted on the jealousies and differing management philosophies of the Air West board members. They were asking far more for their stock than it was worth, and I attempted to convince Howard that if he waited six months to a year, the board of directors would be begging us to buy them out. Howard couldn't or wouldn't wait and insisted I reenter negotiations with Bez. After weeks of dickering, we finally arrived on a price of $22 a share, still inflated, but at least within reason. Bez promised me he would make an effort to deliver the other board members. I didn't want to take any chances, and went to speak with each one myself. Before I had the opportunity, the board found me. The day after Hughes's bid for the airline was announced, its president, G. Robert Henry; its executive committee chairman, David R. Grace; and its vice chairman, Edmund Converse, all notified me of their opposition to the sale.

Clearly facing an uphill battle, I found an unexpected ally in the airline's rotten service. So many complaints were flowing into the offices of the Federal Aviation Administration that business on the airline dropped dramatically. Faced with a money crunch, the full board of Air West capitulated and signed an agreement that had been prepared by Chester Davis. It did more than spell out the terms of the purchase; it inserted a clause which guaranteed that the net worth of the airline would be at least 75 percent of what it was on July 31, 1968. With the airline in deep trouble, the chances of its value maintaining that strong were slim, and Hughes knew it. The clause provided him the perfect opportunity to renegotiate the terms at a later date.

Complicating matters was a sudden turn in the health of Nick Bez. He was diagnosed with terminal cancer of the liver, and his condition was worsening daily. In an effort to remove the burden of running the airline from his shoulders, he offered to turn the operating reins over to Converse if the stockholders would approve the sale to Hughes. Realizing that the opposition was on the ropes, Chester Davis, at Hughes's instructions, refused to consider such an arrangement. Despite the inhumanity of the move, it proved a smart business decision. Bez would be dead within ninety days and an internal fistfight over control resulted that only helped our position.

In late December, the stockholders voted to sell their shares to Hughes. The following day, Chester Davis and I were sitting in San Francisco's Thunderbird Hotel bar while the Air West board was ratifying the sale upstairs. But, as usual, all was not as it seemed. A last-minute pitch from Northwest Airlines to buy Air West convinced the board not to proceed with the sale to Hughes. It would prove a stupid mistake. With the help of Chester Davis and fellow attorney George Coulson, the stockholders of Air West immediately prepared a lawsuit against the board of directors that was filed two days later in a Delaware court.

In addition, Howard had asked me to arrange for several of his friends, including Hank Greenspun, to sell their stock in Air West, promising to make up for any loss. Together they owned some 86,000 shares of stock, and dropping it on the market all at once caused the price of a share to fall three points.

When the Northwest executives heard about the drop in Air West's stock, and the board members were informed of the filing of the stockholders' lawsuit, it wasn't long before the white flag was raised. Northwest quietly retreated back to the security of its own corporate nest; and on December 31, the board members agreed that selling their airline to Howard Hughes would be in everyone's best interest after all. And to make it official, all that was needed was Bez's signature on the contract of sale.

While the news was great, the timing was awful, for it was already mid-afternoon on the 31st, and Hughes's deal with the airline expired at midnight that night. With less than nine hours to close the sale, I sent Hughes Tool's director of aviation, Francis Fox, ahead to Seattle to make the last-minute arrangements for our arrival. I pulled Chester Davis away from the craps tables and we raced to catch a company jet.

Davis wasn't thrilled to be spending New Year's Eve in a last-ditch effort to save the Air West deal, and told me so, endlessly. Only news of a snowstorm heading toward Washington State ended his tirade. Our pilot kept us updated every few minutes, and the more we heard, the less we liked. What had begun as snow flurries escalated into a full-scale blizzard within an hour, effectively closing down all of Seattle—including the airport.

Franny Fox, who had begun his aviation career as head of the airport in Worcester, Massachusetts, took the situation in stride. After arranging clearance for an emergency landing, he assembled a crew of maintenance workers at the airport and proceeded to plow a runway long enough to accommodate our De Havilland 125. With visibility nearly zero and air turbulence frighteningly rough, we made several passes at the airport in a futile attempt to land.

As seconds passed like lifetimes, I tightened my seat belt and attempted to remain calm. I remember saying a silent prayer as the pilot maneuvered us closer and closer to the runway. When the wheels hit the macadam, the plane swerved as it fought the cross-wind, finally slowing against the freezing sleet and snow.

Exiting the jet, I saw Franny Fox, breathless from working side by side with the crew. Shielded against the freezing snow in a heavy windbreaker, muffler, and knee-high galoshes, Fox's outfit was in comic contrast to my cashmere topcoat, polished shoes, and homburg. As I reached the bottom of the flight steps, I kidded Franny by asking, "So where's the limo?"

"You son of a bitch," he laughed, the words turning to icy vapor as they hit the air. "You'll never change."

It was after ten by the time we arrived at Bez's apartment, and we rang in the New Year overlooking Shilshole Bay and toasting the official launching of Hughes Air West. Moments later, I called Howard and relayed the news of our success. His jubilation at owning another airline was obvious—so much so that I suggested he thank Nick Bez personally for making the deal a reality. Howard refused instinctively, retreating like a disturbed clam back into his shell. Hughes was callous and uninterested when I reminded him that Bez was dying and that he had literally used his last few ounces of strength to see that the Air West deal went through. Howard was not about to break his isolation for a stranger, even over the phone, and as I hung up the receiver, I couldn't help feel sorry for the selfish hermit Hughes had become.

Ten or fifteen minutes later, the telephone rang. Howard Hughes was on the line, and he wanted to speak with Nick Bez. We watched as Bez crossed the room and picked up the phone, shaking with joy. They talked aviation for twenty minutes, and I can truthfully say, I was never more proud of Howard Hughes. Bez could think or talk of nothing else the rest of the night. But high points have a way of fading into memory. In another two months, Nick Bez was dead; Howard was back to his frustrating ways; and I was fighting for my future.

* * *

It all started in 1968, when investor Kirk Kerkorian announced plans to build the largest hotel in Las Vegas. Howard used every trick he could think up to convince Kerkorian not to do it. It wasn't so much that Howard minded having another hotel in town; it was the fact that it would be the biggest. And when something was the biggest or the richest or the fastest, it had to have the name "Hughes" connected with it. At first, Howard tried to buy the land from Kerkorian. Our offer fell on deaf ears. Kerkorian was intent on creating his resort, which he would call the International. Sensing an attack on his kingdom, Hughes fought back and announced plans that he would construct an addition to the Sands Hotel that would make it the largest hotel in the *world*. He pledged $100 million to the project. I don't think Howard ever really planned on enlarging the Sands, but rather wanted to make it more difficult for Kerkorian to get the financing he needed. That didn't work either.

As Kerkorian began construction on the International, Howard changed course again. He announced cancellation of the Sands expansion due to plans by the Atomic Energy Commission to increase its testing of underground nuclear weapons in the area. He advised Kerkorian that these tests would surely damage a high-rise building such as the one Kerkorian planned to build. Once again, Kerkorian ignored Hughes, and within the year the International was nearing completion.

Prohibited by the Justice Department from investing in any more hotel-casinos, Hughes's ego was battered with each new publicity release on the glamorous new resort Kerkorian had under construction. He desperately needed to make a major move in Las Vegas, and to make it quickly. The answer came in the form of the bankrupt Landmark Hotel. The space-needle structure with a huge bubble on top had been a Las Vegas eyesore. Because of financial problems since its construction, the Landmark had never opened. It stood empty for eight years until the government agreed to allow Hughes to bail out the place under its "failing-business concept." I was vehemently against the purchase of the hotel because its design limited its profit potential. But Howard was insistent. In the gambling business, profit wasn't his only concern; it was a big game, and he enjoyed it. By agreeing to pay 100 percent on the dollar, he got himself a new hotel and casino. Hughes now owned more rooms than anybody else in town—Kirk Kerkorian included. And we didn't hear a peep from the Justice Department. Besides, thanks to Howard, a lot of people had jobs.

The opening of the Landmark was planned as the most glamorous event to hit Las Vegas in years. For Howard, it meant more than just another hotel; it certified his ability to triumph over the Justice Department's antitrust blockade. For me, it was a celebration of the triumph of the Hughes-Maheu team. In retrospect, it also marked the beginning of its end.

Thirty-one stories high, with a glass elevator that climbed along its side, the Landmark afforded an unprecedented view of the city that was Hughes's kingdom. It also offered a bird's-eye view of Kirk Kerkorian's International Hotel—much bigger and scheduled to open the first week of July, 1969.

The Landmark was slated to open on July 1 to take advantage of the July Fourth weekend. At least, that's what I planned. Hughes, however, didn't agree. Although Howard wanted desperately to have a grand party, he didn't want it to be overshadowed by the opening of the International, scheduled for the following day. For weeks we argued over the opening date, and for weeks we could not agree.

The planning for the party continued, however. The absurdity of trying to organize a major event without knowing the date didn't seem to make any impact on Hughes's mind. In addition to disagreeing on when we should have the party, we couldn't agree on who should be invited. Obviously, Hughes himself wouldn't be in attendance; and he seemed determined to see that no one else was either. We dickered over every name on the proposed invitation list. Back and forth it went, with Hughes first crossing off names, then adding them back. And all the while, my proposed opening date of July 1 crept nearer and nearer.

Hughes was also concerned that the International's showroom headliner, Barbra Streisand, would steal the Landmark's thunder as well. It was impossible for me to even open negotiations with a star without knowing for certain the date he or she would be needed.

I continued to pressure Howard to set a new date or to agree to July 1. By mid-June, I had gotten nothing but runarounds. I was ready to head out of town from embarrassment, and told him so. In return, I received a memo that placed our entire arrangement in jeopardy.

Bob, you have done a good job for me and I appreciate it. I also appreciate your several statements to me that you have a low flash point and that I should learn to accept this in its proper relevance.

However, Bob, there are some things in life beside [sic] money and success. I am afraid I have reached the point where I have a greater reserve allowable tolerance in my money-success column than I have in my health-and-remaining-years column.

If, under these circumstances, you think my failure to give you a specific date has placed you in a position of embarrassment under which you dont [sic] want to be in Las Vegas, I think maybe the time has come when, for my health's sake, a somewhat less efficient and less successful man, but one who would not find it so difficult to put up with my admittedly less-than-perfect operation, should perhaps be the resident managing executive here in Las Vegas.

Re: the Landmark opening, I have told you repeatedly that I dont [sic] want the Landmark to open until after the International.

Bob, I say this only in the interest of harmony. If I were indifferent to your barbs and inferences, it would be no problem, but I am not indifferent, and some of your implications get under my skin and my blood pressure goes higher than the Landmark Tower, which is not good.

It was an ultimatum that suggested to me for the first time how concerned Hughes was about his health. It also made it clear that I had better cut back on the pressure I had been placing on him, or risk winning the battle and losing the war. Yet, as the days passed, Howard showed no sign of cooperating, despite his insistence that he was doing his best. Guest lists were sent to the penthouse for approval, seemingly endless lists of qualifications for each guest were prepared, names were dropped as quickly as they were added. By June 27, just five days before the event might or might not take place, we had yet to send out a single invitation.

Finally, I had had enough. After Howard sent me a memo asking for my latest revised guest list, I simply gave up. At this point, I honestly didn't care what happened, and shot off the kind of memo that I hate to write.

> Howard: We don't have a revised guest list because, as of right now, we don't know whether we're going to have one group or two groups—or any groups. If we don't have any invitees at all, then it becomes moot to furnish a guest list.
>
> I have given you the schedule of events about ten times now. Unfortunately, I have been so busy with this and many other of your problems, that I have no idea about the menu, except that, as I indicated to you in a previous memorandum, it will cost us about $10 per head to feed the beasts.
>
> At this point, I couldn't care less whether we have an affair on the 30th, on the 1st, or whether we ever open up the damned joint. My recommendation to you, Howard, seriously, is that we put this whole caper aside, not take advantage of the fact that we can make the International look foolish. Instead, let them make us look foolish and wait until you are satisfied that you have capable people around you to have your opening, at which time I wish you the greatest success.

It was taking a chance, but it worked. Or did it? Howard's response was to approve three names to invite to the opening. Three. And I couldn't even invite those three since we still had no date. It was as if he was challenging me to fail, and I told him so in no uncertain terms.

Howard: I really don't know what you are trying to do to me, but if your desire is to place me in a state of complete depression, you are succeeding.

I don't mind making myself available to you every moment of the day, 24 hours a day. It is a hell of a sacrifice to do so, but your staff can verify that in the last 2 ½ years they have never spent but a few moments to locate me. I feel, however, that all of my efforts to cooperate with you in this matter are becoming an exercise of complete futility.

Now, Howard, I am getting pretty damned disturbed about what seems to be developing into a compulsive need to give Bob hell. I find it very depressing to pick up the telephone and, practically in each instance of the recent past, I am catching hell for what I did, or what I did not do. I am being second-guessed at each corner.

Now, Howard, this may come to you as a shock, but we are soon entering the realm of not being believable. All I know is that we have an opening taking place in a few days. Everyone seems prepared for it, except you. There have been many hours of sweat and blood poured into this project, and all we need is evidence of confidence from you. After all, Howard, in the last analysis, only you have something to gain or lose. In my present state of mind, I couldn't care less if it takes place or not.

Howard, all I can tell you in conclusion, is that I have no desire to be identified with a fiasco. But if you are hell-bent on being the author of one, I am afraid that there is nothing else I can do to prevent you from accomplishing just that.

If this whole thing means nothing to you, why in the hell should I be concerned about it?

The opening, if we have one, is now only days away, and as much as I want to help you, we have almost, already, run out of time. It is becoming urgent that we announce a definite date.

If on the other hand, you would prefer that I not be involved at all in the Landmark caper, just simply tell me, and you will never live long enough to see how quickly this Frenchman can make the disappearing act thru the nearest escape hatch.

The fat was in the fire and Howard was apparently eager to see it flame, for his return memo spelled things out, not only in relation to the Landmark party, but also to our entire business relationship.

Howard opened his memo by referring to my "pent-up condition of resentment that is just boiling over." I had gotten his attention, and now he was about to get mine.

It is just absurd for two people in the position we are in, where each depends as completely on the other as we do, to have the compressed, bursting package of bitterness and resentment, bottled up inside one of us as you disclosed this morning.

And I assure you, Bob, it is not a one-way street because for every feeling of injustice, or whatever it is that is bugging you, I feel just as strongly in the opposite direction.

Just as convinced as you appear to be that I am wrong and that you are getting the bad end of the deal, just as convinced as you appear to be that you are mistreated, and that you have to take some kind of revenge, just as firmly convinced of this as you seem to be, you may rest assured I feel equally strongly that you are 100 percent wrong.

So I am sure this walled-up bitterness must not be permitted to continue between us.

Howard then went on to tell me not to do any more planning on the Landmark party, not to approve a specific date, not to invest another second in planning for a major event that was due to take place within forty-eight hours, until we straightened out our personal problems.

"Bob, the above is really important if we are to have any chance at all of healing this breach between us," he concluded.

In truth, we never did. On June 29, he finally supplied a guest list with the names of forty-four people whom he had personally approved.

However, he had not officially signed the closing papers on the hotel itself. On top of throwing a party with only forty-four invited guests, at that moment it looked like it would be in a hotel that we didn't even own. Finally, on the evening of June 29, he closed the sale and the Landmark was added to the Hughes empire.

By the day before the party, our communication had degenerated to the point of strained politeness. Each of us knew that a single wrong word would end a partnership that had brought us both money and great satisfaction. Howard made a point of sending a memo telling me: "I will tell you what I propose for the remainder of our relationship after the Landmark is opened."

With those ominous words on my mind, I entered the glass elevator to rise to the top of the Landmark Hotel and Casino on July 1, 1969. In addition to the forty-four people Howard had authorized, on my own I had complemented the guest list with four hundred more—enough to pack the Landmark showroom.

Hughes had finally allowed me to order food, a mere two hours before people started to arrive. As I stood among the party guests and gazed out across the lights of Las Vegas, I reached into my pocket and pulled out a memo Hughes had sent over moments before the event began.

"Bob: You and your people have my wishes for good luck tonight, in every way. Is there anything further I can do to be helpful?"

Chapter Eight

ALL THAT GLITTERS

WITH THE OPENING OF THE LANDMARK HOTEL, HOWARD HUGHES reached his pinnacle of control in Las Vegas. He not only owned more hotel rooms and casinos than any other single individual in the history of the gambling mecca, he was also the state's largest private employer, revered as the Piped Piper who had brought Las Vegas back to economic life. Yet, the illusion was far different from reality.

Despite the size of Hughes's Nevada empire, we were consistently losing money, and lots of it. With the addition of the Landmark, our losses were $8.4 million in 1969 alone. While on the surface the red ink appeared to be caused by mismanagement, the real reasons went far deeper. Howard would purchase property to boost his ego, rather than as sound business investments. He acted on impulse, rather than recommendation.

The Landmark was a perfect example. I had advised him against the purchase since I'd first learned of his interest in the property. Until Hughes came to its rescue, the hotel had been a Las Vegas eyesore for years. It had stood unopened since its construction chiefly because its space-needle design predetermined its low profit potential. To effectively run the hotel and casino, the necessary employee-to-guest ratio was far higher than normal. Hoping to dissuade Howard from the purchase, I asked Moe

Dalitz to prepare a study that would estimate our potential loss. Moe calculated the hotel would lose $5.5 million in its first year of operation. He was close; in actuality, we lost $5.7 million.

Yet, Howard didn't seem to mind. While the casinos' losses continued to help his tax situation, he had a plan to recoup his capital in another arena—mining. Like Howard Sr. had done in his youth, Howard Jr. intended to prospect for gold and silver. Not with a pick and shovel, of course; Hughes had decided in early 1968 to buy up broad stretches of land in Nevada, complete with their mining rights.

At the time, the United States was going through a severe money crunch. For the first time since the Great Depression, speculators and bankers alike were flooding the gold and silver markets with orders to buy. In March, 1968, gold reserves in the U.S. were so low that Congress removed the gold standard. Federal Reserve notes were no longer required to be backed by the precious metal. Gold fever was in full force, and the frenzy did not escape the notice of Howard Hughes. He wanted to corner what he could of the market, and immediately placed John H. Meier in charge of all Hughes mining acquisitions. I was shocked when I heard the news.

I had first met Meier in 1960 while I was still living in Los Angeles and had my offices at the Kirkeby Building. It was in the same office complex where Bill Gay had decided to open a new Hughes division called Hughes Dynamics. Gay had a plan for Howard to become a major supplier of computer software, and hired a staff of "experts" with a background in computer science. One of those people was John Herbert Meier.

Gay took over a portion of the top floor of the Kirkeby Building, and designed extraordinarily elaborate offices. To sit with him on the board of directors he invited Raymond Holliday, the top officer of Hughes Tool Company. Unfortunately, the one person he failed to notify was Howard Hughes.

Hughes eventually learned about the existence of Hughes Dynamics from Jean Peters. Jean was having lunch one day in the restaurant that occupied the remainder of the Kirkeby Building's top floor when the maitre d' struck up a conversation with her. He was excited to be sharing a floor with her husband's newest company, he said. When Jean went home that night, she told Howard what the maitre d' had said. Hughes went absolutely berserk. By that point, Gay had spent nearly $10 million of Howard's money, totally without his permission. It was an enormous breach of business ethics, one that Hughes handled at once. He ordered the business liquidated, and within days, Hughes Dynamics was history.

Soon afterward, a humiliated Bill Gay called me and begged me to find John Meier a job within my organization. He told me that Meier was "absolutely brilliant, and had two doctorate degrees." He went on to say that Meier's wife was dying of cancer and that the poor man needed money for her medical treatment. Based on Gay's recommendation, I automatically put him on the payroll as a scientific advisor to Robert A. Maheu Associates.

A few months after we completed the purchase of the Desert Inn and moved our base of operations to Las Vegas, Howard became concerned that the Atomic Energy Commission was proceeding with plans to continue its underground testing of nuclear bombs in the Nevada desert. What began as a casual concern turned to terror in 1968 when Hughes learned of plans by the AEC to explode the largest atomic device in history—a bomb equal to a million tons of TNT—in a deserted region 150 miles northwest of Las Vegas. The AEC labeled the test "Operation Boxcar."

Upon hearing the news, Hughes became frantic. He was terrified by the danger of nuclear fallout and became absolutely obsessed with getting all testing stopped. He asked me if I had anyone on my staff with scientific know-how. I immediately thought of John Meier. Hughes told me to get John involved with

Ban the Bomb groups and any other organizations interested in stopping underground testing. Meier's only restriction was that he not involve Howard Hughes's name directly. Because Hughes was the nation's largest private defense contractor, he could ill afford to appear to be antigovernment.

While Meier joined numerous antiwar groups, Howard sent me to the Capital to lobby for a postponement. He asked me to use my influence to get the AEC to delay Boxcar for three months in order to allow further study into the effects of nuclear fallout. Hughes was prepared to fully fund the study, and anxiously awaited the AEC's reply.

He didn't have to wait very long. Within days, the AEC had denied Hughes's request, dismissing it as civilian meddling in a classified operation. When I told Howard the news, he flew into a fury, and threatened to use his entire fortune to fight "those bastards in Washington." The day before the test, he even sent a hastily written but typically long-winded letter to President Johnson:

> Based upon my personal promise that independent scientists and technicians have definite evidence, and can obtain more, demonstrating the risk and uncertainty to the health of the citizens of Southern Nevada, if the megaton-plus nuclear explosion is detonated tomorrow morning, will you grant even a brief postponement of this explosion to permit my representatives to come to Washington and lay before whomever you designate the urgent, impelling reasons why we feel a 90-day postponement is needed?

Hughes went on to add that he was not a "peacenik." In fact, he said, the purpose of his writing was actually to help the defense movement. "I can positively prove that if my appeal is heeded, the nuclear test program will proceed more rapidly than at present."

It was a desperate letter that went on for two additional pages, replete with false statements attributed to unnamed (and nonexistent) researchers whom Hughes claimed to have hired to study the situation. It was delivered to President Johnson through the office of Secretary of Defense Clark Clifford that afternoon. The following day, April 26, 1968, Boxcar was detonated in the Nevada desert on schedule.

Hughes was devastated but not defeated. Months later, I met with Johnson at the LBJ ranch in Texas. Hughes had sent me to personally meet with the outgoing president. Johnson was to be told that Howard was prepared to give him a million dollars as soon as he left office, if only LBJ would stop the atomic testing while he was still in power. The thought of being able to bribe the president of the United States appealed to Hughes's innate need to exercise his control over everyone. It disgusted me, so much so that I never did bring up the matter of money during our conversation.

Instead, I asked the president how Howard might be able to help him in the future. He told me that perhaps Hughes could make a small contribution to his pet project, the Johnson Library, which was being built in Austin, Texas. Near the end of our conversation, Johnson mentioned that he had received a letter from Howard several months before "relative to atomic energy." As he shook his head, he told me that the letter would be one item that would never be placed on display in the library. Johnson felt that it was so full of inaccuracies that it would have been an embarrassment to them both.

Through it all, John Meier continued to weave his way into political circles, making various trips to Washington, D.C., for the Ban the Bomb cause. He had the look of a football player, standing over six-foot-three and weighing over two hundred pounds. He also had an ego that matched his frame, an ego fanned by his association with Howard Hughes.

At first I began to get reports the Meier was tossing Hughes's name around, in direct violation of his instructions. Even more amazingly, he was telling people that he was in daily contact with the Man. When I later called Meier on the carpet and demanded an explanation, he stammered something about a misunderstanding that wouldn't happen again. But I wasn't satisfied.

During my next conversation with Howard, I told him I wanted to fire Meier, and I told him why. Howard was adamant that Meier remain on the payroll. He told me that he was "his man on underground testing" and that I was never to fire him for any reason. Soon afterward, Meier was placed in charge of all Hughes's mining acquisitions as well. Once again, I tried to dissuade Howard, but there was simply no changing his mind.

Hughes's first mining purchases attracted national interest and started speculation on his real intent. While mining engineers made statements to the effect that the area's gold and silver deposits were minimal, others suggested that Hughes was developing a high-tech method for extracting ore and was privy to information not available to the public.

The *Las Vegas Sun*'s headline of April 4, 1968 screamed "Hughes Buys N. Nevada Mines" in bold type. Hughes had acquired the rights to several mining properties owned by investor Jack Cleveland and Nevada Gaming Commissioner George Von Tobel for the sum of $225,000. The 260 acres, located in Lyon County, Nevada, included four mining claims. It was to be just the beginning.

Meier began to flood my office with recommendations to add to Hughes's mining properties. According to Meier, the Nevada desert held vast untapped veins of precious metals, waiting for discovery. He told me that his research had revealed that $150 million worth of silver, lead, zinc, gold, and copper could be reaped from mining properties currently on the market. Meier estimated that Hughes could purchase the property for $2.5 million and reap a sizable net profit. When I informed Howard of Meier's projections, his enthusiasm was unbridled. The rush for gold was on.

In August, Hughes authorized the purchase of eleven mining

claims from Mr. and Mrs. Denny Hill for just under a quarter of a million dollars. The mines were located in Goodsprings, Nevada. Later that same month, Meier went back to Jack Cleveland and paid $146,000 for five claims in Churchill County. Now on a roll, Meier added another eighty-five mining claims in October from a variety of sources and spent an additional $1.9 million. By the end of the year, he had spent another $1.6 million for claims in Esmeralda, Nye, and Humboldt counties.

Hughes's claims were scattered across the state of Nevada like a blast of buckshot. They covered 114,000 square miles, and shared only a single common denominator—John H. Meier.

Despite the incredible outpouring of cash, Howard remained enthusiastic. His confidence in Meier's ability as a surveyor was unshakable. By this point, I had long since given up trying to talk Hughes out of trusting Meier, and in fact, was not even made privy to his purchases until after the fact. After the initial land buys, I had placed a high-powered Las Vegas attorney on retainer to handle the clearing of all future mining transactions. The actual checks were then drawn directly by the Romaine Street offices, and given to Meier.

My mind was elsewhere—the continuing TWA lawsuit, the operation of the hotel properties in Las Vegas, and Hughes's increasing interest in the 1968 presidential campaign.

Having failed to stop the testing of nuclear devices through the current administration, Hughes dedicated himself to buying the attention of the next president of the United States. Caught in the political quicksand of Vietnam, President Johnson had announced his decision not to seek reelection on March 31, 1968. Within a month, Democrats Robert Kennedy, Eugene McCarthy, and Vice President Hubert H. Humphrey had all declared their candidacies, while Richard Nixon was running on the Republican ticket.

Although Nixon continued to be Howard's favorite, Hughes was torn by the reality that the Republican was strongly in favor of continued underground testing. Humphrey, on the other hand, had views far closer to Hughes's own on the issue. In an effort to cover all his bases, Hughes made the decision to contribute $100,000 to each of the two candidates' campaigns, with an additional $25,000 token contribution to Robert Kennedy. Because these contributions were far larger than any Hughes had previously made to other political candidates, he decided to camouflage his donations, dividing the contributions to Nixon and Humphrey into two parts: $50,000 in cash and $50,000 via check, made payable through Robert A. Maheu Associates. Furthermore, Hughes wanted me to personally give the contributions to each man to insure that both Humphrey and Nixon knew that he was behind the sizable sums.

Months earlier, John Meier had become friends with Humphrey's son Robert, and had arranged for him to be placed on the payroll of Robert A. Maheu Associates. Through Meier and Robert, I arranged for a secret meeting with the vice president on May 9 at the Denver Hilton Hotel. During a lengthy discussion, I expressed Howard's views on nuclear testing and his hopes of bringing it to an end.

Humphrey was intrigued, and thought that a reasonable way to proceed would be to form a committee of six distinguished scientists whom he personally knew to be experts in the field. These men were respected by both the administration and the Joint Committee on Atomic Energy, he told me, and could study the consequences of continued nuclear testing with authority.

It was only at the end of our conversation that I mentioned Howard's intention to contribute to Humphrey's presidential campaign. I told him that I was authorized to pledge $100,000, half in cash and half via check. Humphrey was surprised and elated, and expressed his delight repeatedly.

The following day, I sent Hughes a memo confirming Humphrey's assurance of cooperation:

The following reflects the suggestions and procedures set forth by the Vice President. It is imperative, he states, that we not become involved in an all-out war in the press with the AEC and the Department of Defense. He feels we should have two objectives—(a) delay the future plans of those big blasts until (b) the propitious moment at which the Administration will urge that underground testing be added to the Ban Treaty. He feels very strongly that we have a good chance of accomplishing these goals. He pledges his support and that of the Administration.

Additionally, I wrote to Hughes:

Humphrey is convinced there is nothing to be gained by having conferences directly with the AEC. These people are irrevocably committed to the continuance of the tests, and he thinks that if we get trapped into allowing them to brief us, they will immediately issue a release stating that their technicians have met with the "Hughes people" to explain the safety features of all facets of the program. The Vice President will work with us very closely and confidentially. He is very anxious to get your reaction to these above mentioned plans.

Howard's reaction was one of impatience. He wanted action, not studies by handpicked scientists. While he went along with the plan, including a commitment to pay $300,000 to fund the study, he continued to pressure me to deliver the contributions and put both Humphrey and Nixon in his debt.

When Robert Kennedy was assassinated on June 4, 1968, Hughes's only thought was of himself. A part of him was delighted that a gunman had removed the single candidate whom Hughes considered too pompous and difficult to be influenced. Another saw the potential for personal gain in the situation. Hughes wrote me the night of the assassination:

I hate to be quick on the draw, but I see here an opportunity that may not happen again in a lifetime. I dont [sic] aspire to be President, but I do want political strength. ... And it seems to me that the very people we need have just fallen smack into our hands.

Howard wanted me to hire Robert Kennedy's entire campaign organization. He liked the way they moved within big-money circles and accomplished difficult tasks with seeming ease. Moreover, it appeared to Howard that hiring these people would be a victory over the Kennedys:

> The Kennedy family and their money and influence have been a thorn that has been relentlessly shoved into my guts since the very beginning of my business activities. So you can see how cruel it was, after my all-out support of Nixon, to have Jack Kennedy achieve that very, *very* marginal so-called victory over my man.
>
> So, as I point out, thru this long-standing feeling of jealousy and personal enmity, I have become fairly well informed about the organization of people that sprung up, first around Jack, and then around Bob. Essentially the same group. They have moved over. But think of the experience they have had in the two campaigns combined.

Hughes was relentless. Memo after memo badgered home the reality that he would not rest until he had hired Kennedy's staff. In particular, he wanted to put Kennedy's campaign manager, Larry O'Brien, on the payroll. O'Brien had served the Kennedys for sixteen years. He was behind Jack's first Senate campaign, went with him to the White House, stayed on as a member of Lyndon Johnson's cabinet, and then left to lead Robert Kennedy's ill-fated drive to the presidency. He was now a man without a job, and was quite available to discuss the possibility of involvement with Hughes when I contacted him in late June about the prospect. I had never met Larry O'Brien when we arranged our first meeting in Las Vegas on July 4, 1968. He ended up becoming one of my best friends.

Outgoing and exceedingly gracious, Larry listened as I

informed him of Hughes's misunderstood and underappreciated efforts on behalf of the American people. It hit a chord with O'Brien as he sat in the living room of my Las Vegas home. He said that both Jack Kennedy and Lyndon Johnson had felt the very same way about themselves.

He listened as I told him about Hughes's problems with TWA, the antitrust threats he was enduring in Las Vegas, his efforts to rescue Air West from bankruptcy, and his push to take control of the ABC television network (announced just days before). O'Brien was clearly impressed by the scope of Hughes's involvements, and returned to Washington committed to aiding our cause.

When I informed Howard about our successful meetings, he was so excited that he wanted me to put O'Brien into action immediately. He suggested that I instruct Larry to storm into the Oval Office and confront President Johnson about the continuing threat of underground nuclear tests. It was an ill-conceived plan at best, and one that I never conveyed to O'Brien.

At the same time, Howard continued to express concern over the slow pace of Humphrey's presidential campaign. Hughes urged me to complete plans to deliver the first part of his donation in an effort to inject some excitement into Humphrey's effort. Although I never admitted it to Hughes, I was deliberately procrastinating. Despite the fact that in those days cash contributions were entirely legal, the thought of handing $50,000 to the vice president of the United States weighed heavily on me. It had to be handled delicately, with a minimum of intermediaries. On July 29, 1968, Humphrey was to speak at a $5,000-a-plate fund-raising dinner at the Century Plaza Hotel in Los Angeles. Although I never mentioned the cash directly during several telephone conversations with the vice president, I had made arrangements to deliver "the item" to him that night. I told him I would place an envelope in a briefcase and find the occasion sometime following his speech to have him receive it.

On Howard's instructions, I had borrowed the money for the contribution from Chester Sims, the manager of the Frontier Hotel Casino. It was Hughes's way of keeping the contribution hidden from his Hollywood accountants, and he had me repay the debt a year later. I was uneasy about making the contribution in cash, and repeatedly told Howard, to no avail. I also didn't cotton to carrying $50,000 in my pocket, so I made the decision to bring $25,000 in cash with me on the plane from Las Vegas, and arranged to have Gordon Judd, a Hughes employee from Nevada, bring me an additional $25,000 in new $100 bills.

After settling into my seventeenth-floor suite at the Century Plaza, I went downstairs to greet the vice president at a VIP cocktail party. During the dinner, I sat with Lloyd Hand, a former U.S. chief of protocol, who was then traveling with Humphrey. Hand told me he was accompanying the vice president and his wife to the airport immediately following the dinner. Humphrey had to catch a plane to San Francisco, and Hand invited me to come along in the vice president's limousine.

After the dinner, I returned to my suite and carefully packed my briefcase with the cash. While Judd waited for me in the suite, I carried the $50,000 in cash through the lobby and out to the curb, where Humphrey was waiting for me in his limousine. I got into the car, relayed Hughes's concern over atomic testing, told Mrs. Humphrey how radiant she looked despite the rigors of the campaign trail, said good-bye, and got out of the limo half a block away—without the attaché case or the cash.

Despite sworn statements from witnesses to the contrary, Hubert Humphrey would later state that he never received the $50,000, eventually recanting his statement to indicate that perhaps someone within his campaign had accepted the money. He also said that while he remembered talking to me in front of the hotel, he could not remember my leaving the briefcase with the money in the car. I don't want to call him a liar; let's just say that he had a conveniently poor memory. Particularly is this true since a few days later he had sent me a communication thanking Hughes for the contribution.

The remaining $50,000 was paid to Humphrey by checks drawn on the account of Robert A. Maheu Associates on October 17, 1968, and reimbursed by Hughes. The checks were made out to various Humphrey reelection committees in amounts not over $3,000—the legal limit for such contributions—and delivered to former governor Grant Sawyer, Humphrey's campaign manager in Nevada. Sawyer, in turn, passed them along to the vice president.

Just two days after I had my short limo ride with Hubert Humphrey, I found myself in Washington, D.C., meeting again with Larry O'Brien. In my pocket was the $25,000 cash that Hughes had promised to Robert Kennedy; I felt obliged to fulfill the pledge. O'Brien later passed the envelope along to Bobby's brother-in-law Stephen Smith.

O'Brien was extremely grateful for my loyalty, and continued to express an interest in working for Hughes. He told me, however, that he had been approached to head up Hubert Humphrey's presidential campaign, and had accepted the offer. I told him that Howard was also eager to see Humphrey in the White House, and urged O'Brien to become a consultant to Hughes. To avoid any seeming conflict of interest, we eventually worked out an arrangement in which we paid $15,000 a month to the public relations firm of Joseph Napolitan Associates in Washington, D.C., with O'Brien overseeing the company's work. That arrangement continued until October, 1969, when O'Brien opened his own consulting firm, Lawrence F. O'Brien Associates, Inc. and went officially on the Hughes payroll.

With the Humphrey camp solidly in the Hughes corner, I next turned my attention to our old friend Richard Nixon. Since getting Nixon to accept contributions had never been a problem, I didn't anticipate any as he made his second bid for the White House in 1968. How wrong I was.

Late in August, I received a call from Ed Morgan in Washington. Ed had heard from Richard A. Danner, then working with the Nixon campaign, who wanted to know how much Hughes might be willing to contribute. Danner had been the head of the FBI office in Miami at the time Morgan was an agent there. Subsequently, Danner became the city manager of Miami, and had heavy Republican connections himself. It was Danner who introduced Nixon to Bebe Rebozo in the early fifties; and it was Rebozo who was now requesting a substantial donation—and in cash (then perfectly legal).

Hughes laughed when I told him about the call, since our plans were already in full swing. I informed Dick Danner that we would give him $50,000 in cash for the Nixon campaign, with an additional $50,000 to be donated by check. Danner and I arranged for the money to be handed to Morgan, and he in turn hand-carried it to Rebozo. Rebozo knew Ed was a lifelong Democrat and refused to take any money from him, probably fearing he would use the transaction to embarrass the Republicans later, so Ed brought the money back to me.

Ironically, on October 14, 1968, when I was processing the second $50,000—this amount to be paid via smaller checks to the "Win with Nixon Committee" fund—the original $50,000 was still in my safe. Ed Morgan wanted no further involvement with the money, and I finally came to realize that if Nixon was ever going to get it, Danner or I would have to deliver it.

It would be early December, 1968, before I could make the arrangements. By that time, Nixon had won the presidential election and was confidently waiting to be sworn in in January. He was set to address the Republican Governors Convention in Palm Springs, California, on December 6, and I made the decision at the last minute to try and arrange a rendezvous at that time.

As it turned out, all the hotel rooms in Palm Springs were booked solid, and I was only able to arrange accommodations by pulling some strings with the chief of the Secret Service, James J. Rowley. Rowley and his men were guarding Nixon, who was staying at the home of publishing magnate Walter Annenberg.

Governor Paul Laxalt was also attending the convention, and made the arrangements for me to meet with Nixon before his speech. I remember being nervous as we approached Annenberg's palatial Palm Springs estate. Here I was again with $50,000 in my briefcase, only this time I was about to hand it to the next president of the United States.

When we arrived at Annenberg's home, I decided to remain in the car with the money while Laxalt went in to see if Nixon could see us. It was only a matter of moments before he reemerged. The governor told me that Nixon had been running behind schedule and he had no time to see anyone before his speech that evening at the Continental Hotel.

That night, Yvette and I joined Governor Laxalt and his wife to hear Nixon speak. Before we left our hotel, I had placed the $50,000 under the carpet in the trunk of my car. At the Continental Hotel, I asked some friends within the Secret Service to do me a favor and watch the car. It seemed like a fair trade-off, since the money they didn't realize they were guarding was intended for their new boss.

That night passed, and the next day as well, with no opportunity for me to deliver the cash. As we were boarding our plane to return to Las Vegas on Sunday afternoon, the well-traveled $50,000 was still in my possession. When we returned home, I placed the money in a special hidden compartment in our staircase. There it would remain for several months. At the time, my son Peter was building a new home, and when it was completed he installed a safe in his bedroom. The first cash to be placed in the safe was the $50,000 with Nixon's name on it. I told Peter it was for disbursement at a future date.

By February of the following year, Nixon was firmly seated in the White House, and I had hired Dick Danner as managing director of the Frontier Hotel. Hughes liked the fact that Danner was a former FBI agent; he liked it even better that he had a direct pipeline to Nixon. It wasn't until late fall or early winter that I sent my son Peter over to Danner with the $50,000 cash contribution to pass along to Nixon. Danner in turn gave it to Bebe Rebozo, and Hughes's presidential pledges were finally achieved.

During the first year of Nixon's administration, John Meier continued to increase both his presence in the nation's Capital and Hughes's portfolio of mining properties. Although I was unaware of it at the time, Meier had formed an alliance with Jack Cleveland, the wily promoter who had sold Hughes his very first mining claim the year before. It was Cleveland who had encouraged his buddy Clarence Hall to sell some of his mining claims to Hughes, snaring a large percentage of the purchase price for himself. Hall, in turn, had a lifelong friend named Harry Vonderheide. Vonderheide, too, had mining properties, and ended up selling Hughes his claims at inflated prices—all on the recommendation of Meier. Vonderheide gave a kickback to Hall; Hall gave a kickback to Cleveland. It was a new version of the old-fashioned pyramid scheme, and given the thickness of Hughes's wallet, the potential seemed limitless.

So encouraged was Cleveland by the possibilities of continuing to con Hughes into paying bloated prices for mining claims that he formed a company he called Basic Industries and opened offices in Tonopah, Nevada. The town held a special place in Howard's heart. It was there that he had gone on January 12, 1957, to marry Jean Peters in a secret ceremony. And before 1969 was ended, Howard Hughes would own much of the town, in the form of a variety of worthless mining claims and hundreds of acres of property.

Adding to the uniqueness of Basic Industries was the appointment of John Meier as a special consultant. While I was paying Meier a healthy salary to find legitimate mining properties for Hughes, Basic Industries was paying Meier to make certain it was B.I. claims that Hughes bought. I later learned that Meier had also made contact with the deputy mine inspector for the state of Nevada, a man named Leonard F. Traynor. Having sold his first mining claim to Hughes in 1968, Traynor began to systematically buy claims one day, then sell those same claims to Hughes through Meier literally the next day, at enormous profit.

While at the time I never realized the extent of the snowballing purchases of mining properties, I had inadvertently given it a shove of my own. In reaction to a memo I received from Meier, I informed Hughes that the gold and silver ore that would be extracted from his mines could be held without paying taxes on their net worth, thus showing a loss on the properties for IRS purposes. The merest mention of tax savings was enough to reassure Hughes. He encouraged further purchases; it was exactly the vote of confidence that John Meier needed.

Meier apparently figured out that the kickback scam that was working so effectively with Basic Industries could work equally as well with other firms. He made contact with a company called Arivaca Mining Corporation and arranged to buy some mining claims in Hughes's name from the firm. Meier's wife, Jennie Elizabeth Cravotta, was a stockholder in the company. Meier also was linked to another firm, the Georgetown Research and Development Corporation. Headquartered in Washington, D.C., the company was owned by Thomas E. Murray, Jr. Murray was placed on Hughes's payroll by Meier as a consultant, and within months the Georgetown Research and Development Corporation was also doing a brisk business in mining claims sold through Meier to Hughes.

In subsequent court proceedings against Meier, the full extent of his dealings would eventually become known. Yet, at the time, of all of Meier's associates, the only one I was aware of personally was Richard Nixon's younger brother Donald. Having gone through the Donald Nixon loan scandal during the 1960 presidential campaign, I thought I had seen the last of the man. I was wrong.

John Meier had struck up a relationship with Donald soon after his brother moved into the White House. At first Hughes had encouraged the connection as still another link with the presidency. It took less than six months for things to get out of hand. With Meier circulating throughout Washington and informing anyone who would listen that he was Howard's favorite, and with Donald hanging onto Meier's coattails, the relationship began to be an embarrassment for the president. Despite their denials, word began to spread that the pair were involved in some sort of unorthodox real estate deals—Don using his brother's clout and Meier using Hughes's credentials.

At the request of the White House, Bebe Rebozo called his friend Richard Danner. Rebozo was direct and to the point. He wanted John Meier to stop associating with Donald Nixon, and any common activities to be collared. Danner came to me and I, in turn, warned Meier to toe the line. I had had my fill of Meier's clandestine dealings, and immediately tried to shorten his leash. He was told to report daily to Dean Elson, the Hughes executive who at one time had been head of the FBI in Nevada. Additionally, I instructed Elson to begin to look into the escalating number of mining claims being purchased by Meier under Hughes's name.

For its part, the White House began to have Don Nixon followed, and even went as far as having a tap put on his telephone. On July 6, the tap revealed that Nixon had phoned Meier and that the pair had arranged to meet two days later at the Orange County Airport in California. Meier also mentioned a man named Tony— later identified as Salt Lake city businessman Anthony G. Hatsis—

through whom Meier had bought some mining claims for Hughes.

The White House team trailing Don Nixon took photos of the pair's meeting and informed me that it was taking place. I wasted no time getting my own men to Orange County, and when Meier stepped off the plane after returning to Las Vegas, Elson escorted him into my office. Meier had never received permission to leave Nevada, and now had little hope of keeping his job, as far as I was concerned.

I placed an urgent call to Howard in his penthouse, requesting that he allow me to fire Meier on the spot. Through an aide I learned that Howard had again refused my request, ordering me "not to fire Meier under any circumstances." Once again I acquiesced against my better judgment.

While the White House attempted to keep Donald Nixon in his place, we did our best to muzzle John Meier. Meier was busy initiating the purchase of more mining claims, most through his association with Tony Hatsis. Among his many business efforts, Hatsis was the president of the Toledo Mining Company. Meier had arranged for Hatsis to sell Howard Hughes a group of claims to mines in northern Nevada. A subsequent suit brought against Hatsis by Hughes Tool questioning the legality of the property sale revealed that Meier had instructed Hatsis to deal with a Hughes intermediary, Everd B. Van Walsum of a firm known as Maatschappij-Intermovie N.V. The Dutchman, headquartered in the Netherlands. In reality, Hughes never heard of Van Walsum, who turned out to be another Meier connection. Out of the money paid to Hatsis, a portion would be sent Van Walsum, who in turn would funnel it back to Meier.

It was a plan that Hatsis not only accepted, but which he embellished upon. During the latter part of 1969, Hatsis was negotiating the purchase of mining claims that he would turn around and sell to Howard Hughes through Everd B. Van Walsum at enormous markups. All of this was done without my knowledge or consent.

But, my feelings for Meier hit an all-time low when I received a letter in late August from attorney Ed Morgan. Morgan had had lunch with the former governor of Colorado, Steve McNichols. McNichols, it seemed, had just made a deal to sell a mining property he owned in Tonopah to Howard Hughes:

> He had the top man, so he said, in the Hughes organization lined up to make the purchase—the only man who sits at Hughes' right arm. I inquired as to who this man of influence might be and learned, to my great surprise, that it was your Mr. Meyer [sic]. I suggested to Steve that I understood that a fellow named Maheu was Mr. Hughes' top man. He seemed undismayed in the certain knowledge that Mr. Meyer was *the* man who truly had Mr. Hughes' ear. According to advice from Mr. Meyer, the only thing holding up the purchase of the mine was Mr. Hughes' absorption with the Air West deal. I did not disillusion him. Where ignorance is bliss, 'tis folly to be wise. So sayeth the bard.

Meier's blatant arrogance finally went too far in November, 1969, when Dean Elson informed me that he had learned that Meier was once again planning to meet with Donald Nixon. I had promised the White House that I would keep the two men apart, and I intended to keep my promise. On November 2, I called Meier into my office at the Frontier Hotel, and gave him a choice—resign from the Hughes organization or be fired. He resigned. According to the *Las Vegas Sun*, it was to form a research foundation "to apply system analysis and practical research to a solution of ecological problems in and around Nevada."

My terse official comment on the resignation: "John Meier has made a significant contribution to the Nevada Division of the Hughes Tool Company." I figured the less said the better.

When I subsequently told Hughes that Meier had resigned, Howard tried to persuade me to get him back. By this point there was absolutely no way I would even consider Hughes's request, and told him so.

"Howard, if you want him to reconsider, you talk to him," I

said. "I've had my bellyful of this guy and I'm happy he's gone."

I gave Meier four weeks' severance pay, but I didn't allow him to remove any of his files. For several months before his resignation, Meier had been successfully dodging Dean Elson's demands for the legal paperwork detailing our mining acquisitions. As soon as he was history, Elson began reviewing what files he did have. It was an enormously involved process; and when he was done, he didn't like what he had found. On April 14, over five months after Meier resigned, Elson submitted a report to me that sent shock waves through my system:

> When [John Meier] left the organization in November, 1969, I again demanded from him that he produce his records regarding the acquisition of claims, and at that time I was astounded to find that he had no records whatsoever regarding any of the properties we had purchased, even as to legal documents. He informed me that he did not know who had possession of the Deeds, Titles, and other records that pertained to our purchase of mining properties. To say the least, I stepped into a chaotic condition, with absolutely nothing to refer to or work with.
>
> Due to John Meier's reluctance to produce his records regarding the acquisitions of mining claims, I began to have some strong suspicions that something was wrong, and from that point I began endeavoring to reconstruct files as best I could. It has not been until the last several days, and through tedious effort, that I have finally assembled a group of records—though no means a complete group as yet.
>
> ... In reviewing what transpired while John Meier was in charge of the mining operations, it appears to me that there have been many irregularities in the purchasing of various mining claims. Although the situation looks very serious, at this point I am not in a position to give you a final reading as to the extent of this situation.

It proved to be the first snowflake of an avalanche that would hit me full force in time. I remember that I took Dean's memo, which promised to keep me updated as he uncovered further evidence, and attached a little Post-It on which I wrote, "Howard, here is what appears to be a case of illegal activity per the enclosed memo. My recommendation is that we turn this entire matter over to the authorities forthwith and let the chips fall where they may." I never heard back from Howard about the memo, and only years later did I learn that it was intercepted by an aide friendly with Meier and never delivered.*

With the exit of Meier, Hughes's involvement in mining ceased. Meier had spent over $20 million of Hughes's money on property later valued at less than $2 million. I am not convinced that Howard ever did learn that his trusted advisor, John Meier, defrauded him out of millions of dollars.

In February, 1970, I was in Los Angeles to be near my wife, who was to undergo some minor surgery. I was in my suite at the Beverly Wilshire Hotel when I received an urgent call from Larry O'Brien asking me if he could fly out to see me. I knew Larry was never a man to waste my time, so, despite my concern about Yvette, I told him to come as soon as possible. The next day, O'Brien joined me at the hotel.

Soon after O'Brien became a consultant to Howard Hughes in mid-1968 and subsequently agreed to become the national campaign manager for Hubert Humphrey, he was selected to chair the Democratic National Committee. It was a position without pay, but an enormous power base. Several months after the campaign

---

*Meier went on to join Toledo Mining in Salt Lake, where his old pal Tony Hatsis gave him a job as a consultant. Within three years, the IRS had indicted Meier for income-tax evasion. To escape the charge, he fled to British Columbia, where he remains to this day. Subsequently, in 1978, the Hughes organization successfully prosecuted Meier for fraud in connection with the various worthless mining acquisitions he made using Hughes's money. The $7.9 million judgment still remains uncollected. Meier never had two doctorate degrees as he claimed. In fact, he never even attended college, although he was reported to have had some scientific training in the military. Meier's wife, Jennie, never died of cancer, nor did she apparently ever have the disease. She is currently living with her husband in Canada. John Meier occasionally still telephones me at my home in Las Vegas. He never mentions the mining scandal.

concluded and Nixon had beaten Humphrey for the presidency, O'Brien resigned his position as head of the DNC to become president of the New York brokerage house of McDonnell & Co. Within months, Larry realized that he had made a mistake and quit to open his own public relations firm, Lawrence F. O'Brien Associates, Inc., with Howard Hughes as his first client.

O'Brien arrived in Beverly Hills with important news. He wanted to alert me to the fact that the Democratic National Committee was pressuring him to come back aboard as its chairman. "You know, my company has an enormous deficit, the DNC job is unsalaried, and I've made clear to them that I cannot take it unless I can continue to work for Hughes." Larry basically wanted Hughes's permission.

When I broached the subject with Howard, he was excited. To once again have the chairman of the Democratic National Committee on his payroll represented control, Howard's favorite pastime. Larry accepted the position while continuing to perform a number of important tasks for the Hughes organization, including advising Howard on the direction of tax legislation, FCC rulings, and the antitrust movement, as well being our top contact in the Capital.

At the time, Hughes's mind was totally occupied with preventing further underground testing. With his man Nixon now firmly in the White House, Howard believed that he might be able to control the situation and forestall further tests, at least temporarily. The subject was never far from the front of his mind.

When Danner first came on board, Hughes eagerly wanted him to approach Bebe Rebozo and to urge him to persuade the president to halt underground testing.

"Good God, that's a tough one," Danner said, shaking his head in disbelief when I relayed Hughes's request. "But, let me make the approach."

A few days later, he came back into my office, excited and anxious to share some news.

"Bob, you won't believe what I'm about to tell you. The president himself is prepared to discuss the whole thing with Hughes personally, and explain chapter and verse why we have to go on testing for national defense!"

Dick was so excited, I hated to inform him that not even the president of the United States could meet face to face with Howard Hughes. Still, it was an honor, and I relayed Dick's message to the penthouse.

As I suspected, Hughes turned down Nixon's offer—flat.

"Okay," I countered. "Perhaps there's still a way to take advantage of the president's offer. If he's willing to see you personally, sure as hell he'll talk to you on the phone. What an opportunity! Let me set it in motion," I begged.

Howard wouldn't consider it. He began to mumble about the president cornering him on the telephone with "important requests." He said he didn't want to be in a position of having to say no or make promises.

"Howard, please, just talk to the man!" I heard myself saying. "He's not going to start making demands of you on the telephone. You owe this to him, particularly since you disagree. You might even be able to convince him that you're right. You keep saying you have all these technical facts available; well, make them available to him."

Silence. Then Hughes spoke again, this time with the faintest tinge of apology in his voice. "Bob, frankly ..." More silence. "Bob, I'm afraid I'll be embarrassed if he gets into certain technical data that he feels I may know, and in fact I don't."

Howard Hughes—exposed. A man afraid to show his inadequacies, in mind as well as body. It was a revealing moment. It would not, however, change Howard's determination to stop underground testing—testing that continued despite his protests. Every two or three weeks, with predictable regularity, the underground explosions continued. Some were announced; most were not. For Hughes, each blast was like an incredibly volatile version of the Chinese water torture, with no end in sight.

Hughes's preoccupation with the continuing blasts hit an all-time high in March, 1970. I was in New York at a meeting of the board of directors of Hughes Aircraft Company, having lunch at the Regency Hotel when I received a call. It was from one of Howard's aides, and he wanted me to go immediately to a pay phone and call him back. There was a telephone booth in the corridor outside the dining room, so in less than a minute, I had one of the aides back on the phone. He read a note from Howard, almost whispering the words: "Go to Key Biscayne and offer Nixon through Rebozo one million dollars to stop this goddam testing."

I caught my breath. The aide sensed my hesitation.

"The Man is serious, Bob. And he wants you to take Danner along to warm up the contact with Rebozo."

As I walked slowly back to my table in the dining room, I knew that I could never make such an offer. At one point, I even caught myself smiling. I was probably the only person in the entire world who was ever asked to bribe two different presidents of the United States for a million apiece. The idea didn't sit any better the second time than it had the first.

Later that evening, I phoned Danner and arranged to meet him at JFK Airport the following day. I didn't tell him why. Twenty-four hours later, I still hadn't thought up a logical story to explain our sudden trip to Florida, so I decided to take Dick into my confidence and level with him. His first reaction was shock, followed by a certain hopelessness.

"I promise you, Dick, we're only going to Florida to keep Howard happy. I will not ask you to make any pitches to Bebe.

We've just got to think this thing through together and come up with a reason why we can't make the contact."

I will never forget the look on Danner's face. Slowly his stare of disbelief changed to a smile. "What the hell. I needed a vacation anyway."

Once we arrived in Key Biscayne, we put our plan into action immediately. At first, I told Howard that Bebe was unavailable. Then I told him that every time we got together, Bebe was never alone and I couldn't broach so delicate a subject with anyone within earshot. After four days of stalling, Danner became bored and returned to Las Vegas. Yet, when I spoke to Howard and suggested that I return as well, he would not hear of it. "No, no, Bob. Keep on it," he said, refusing to give up on his impossible plan. Days more in the Florida sun went by—so much time, in fact, that even Rebozo was beginning to wonder what I was up to.

Finally, my stalling paid off. The TWA litigation was hanging around Howard's neck like an anvil, and without support, it became too much to bear.

"You might as well come back, Bob," he finally called to say. "We'll keep this on the back burner, and when the atmosphere is better, perhaps when Nixon himself comes to Key Biscayne, we'll try again. Come on back, Bob, and let's get going on this damn TWA thing."

When I returned, somehow the subject of Bebe Rebozo, Dick Danner, and cash followed me like a shadow, and not a month later I found myself back on the telephone, this time alerting Howard to a call I had received from Bob Hope.

Hope was making a personal plea for a $50,000 contribution to the new Eisenhower Medical Center then being built in Palm Springs. Bob and his wife, Dolores, had donated the land, and Hope told me to tell Howard that the White House was interested in seeing that the drive was an enormous success.

"Hell, Bob, if the administration is that much interested, why don't we placate them in some other way?" Hughes responded. "Let's get as much mileage out of this as we can. See if we can get by with a ten-thousand-dollar contribution to the Eisenhower Center, and get word to the administration that we'll give them fifty thousand to use in their congressional campaigns."

When I informed Bob Hope that Hughes would donate $10,000 to the Center, he wasn't pleased, but nevertheless accepted the donation graciously. Richard Nixon was far more excited. I ran Hughes's suggestion past Richard Danner, who in turn conveyed the offer to Bebe Rebozo, who then ran the plan past Nixon himself. Within days, Danner had an affirmative response from the White House, with Nixon requesting that the money be delivered once again in cash and once again to Rebozo.

It all sounded simple enough. Danner was to make the arrangements to deliver the money to Rebozo during one of his visits to Washington. At this point, Danner was making several trips per month, actively conferring with Attorney General John Mitchell. Howard had taken an interest in purchasing the Dunes Hotel and Casino in Las Vegas, but before he proceeded, he wanted to be assured by Mitchell that he would no longer be accused of violating any antitrust laws—the memory of the Stardust debacle still fresh in his mind. It has been rumored that Danner was instructed to offer Mitchell $50,000 if the Justice Department would bend on the Dunes matter. This was never the case. Hughes wanted the money to go directly to congressional campaigns that would be helpful to Nixon. By mid-1970, other businessmen had added additional rooms to their hotels and acquired others, leaving Hughes no longer the largest fish in the Vegas pond, even with the addition of the Dunes property. It was that fact alone that gave Mitchell the ammunition he needed to fight any antitrust action should Hughes make another Las Vegas purchase.

Howard was eager to make the Dunes purchase, and had been

for almost a year. In fact, he had told me to make a $3.5 million personal loan of his funds to Dunes majordomo Sidney Wyman to secure the purchase.

In early August, 1970, Richard Danner and I headed first to Miami and then to Key Biscayne in the private De Havilland 125, with Danner carrying the $50,000 donation in a manila envelope. Danner had picked up the money earlier in the day from the cage in the Silver Slipper casino.

After we settled into our hotel, Dick placed a call to Bebe Rebozo, and was told that we should stop by around five that afternoon. Rebozo's home was directly next to the one Nixon had bought after the 1968 election. Since this was now the Florida White House, it was rigorously guarded.

At a little after five, a chauffeured limousine pulled up to our hotel and took us the short distance to Rebozo's house. When we arrived, Bebe was standing outside. He greeted us with his usual enthusiasm, and welcomed us inside. As we walked into the living room, Danner handed the envelope containing the $50,000 to Rebozo, who disappeared briefly into a back bedroom and emerged without the money.

Rebozo was in a cheerful mood, and offered us a drink. I opted for a gin martini on the rocks. How well I remember Bebe going to the refrigerator and pushing a lever. Suddenly, ice cubes started to drop into the glass he was holding against the refrigerator door. It was the first time I had seen the novelty that has since become so commonplace.

There was never a mention of the $50,000. Instead, we talked about the Reverend Billy Graham. Graham was a close friend of Bebe's and was interested in getting conservative programming on television. Rebozo quizzed me about Hughes's reported plans to create a fourth network and his failed effort to gain control of ABC. After our drinks, Rebozo drove Danner and me to a restaurant, where we had a particularly lavish meal. Before midnight, we were back in our hotel rooms, mission accomplished. I had the feeling that we had done our job well. What I didn't realize was the way that Danner's deliveries of two $50,000 envelopes would continue to haunt me.

Returning to Las Vegas, I threw myself into the continuing negotiations to buy the Dunes Hotel and Casino. With Danner's assurance that the United States attorney general was firmly in Hughes's corner, there seemed to be little to stop the deal from being finalized. I was mistaken.

With the beginning of 1970, Howard Hughes's life underwent a decided change. First, Jean Peters, his wife of thirteen years, had decided to sue for divorce and announced publicly her intention to leave the world's most private man. Despite the fact that he had not set eyes on Jean during the entire time he was in Las Vegas, Howard was heartbroken. If any one situation contributed directly to his worsening health and unstable mind, it was the dissolution of his marriage.

As the months passed and Howard grew increasingly distant and irrational, my contact with him lessened. Complicating matters was the growing arrogance of Chester Davis and Bill Gay in Hollywood. They began to send me irritating memos questioning my actions. At the same time, they were planting seeds of doubt in Hughes's mind concerning my ability, through selective comments delivered by Howard's personal aides. I was so consumed by my work load that I took their interference in stride, the majority of the time ignoring their criticisms and handling any problems directly with Howard just as I had always done in the past. Finally, at the end of May, 1970, what had begun as a festering administrative pimple came to an ugly head.

Davis and Gay called an emergency meeting of Hughes executives at the Presidential Suite of the Century Plaza Hotel in Los Angeles. Raymond Holliday and Calvin Collier, the two top officials at Hughes Tool Company, were in attendance, along with Francis Fox and me.

I am convinced that Davis's sole purpose in calling that meeting was to attempt to embarrass me in front of the others. The only thing he succeeded in doing was making a fool out of himself. As the confrontation began, Davis demanded to know the meaning of a recent release put out by Los Angeles Airways in which the company announced its purchase by Hughes Tool Company.

I told Davis that Howard had made a commitment to Los Angeles Airways to purchase the company and that negotiations had been ongoing for months. They had begun about the same time as the original inquiries were being made into Air West, and I told him so. The commuter company operated a fleet of helicopters that serviced much of the Los Angeles area. Several years before, the company had had a crash that had killed the grandson of the owner, Clancy Berlin. Upon hearing the news, Howard had immediately called me and told me to see about buying the company. He wanted to hit them when they were down.

Subsequently, Hughes had authorized me to guarantee two loans to Los Angeles Airways to keep it flying until we could conclude our purchase. LAA received its first loan in the amount of $1.8 million in late 1969, with Hughes's Sands Hotel guaranteeing repayment. In January, 1970, LAA borrowed an additional three-quarters of a million dollars, again using the Sands as a guarantor. Howard not only knew about the loans, he encouraged them, to make the airline more vulnerable to our takeover effort.

Davis was also questioning a $3.5 million loan that Howard had offered to give to Sidney Wyman. Davis began to scream that I had no authority to offer Wyman the money. He was wrong, but I wasn't about to argue the point. Since I was still the only one of the executives in the room in direct contact with Hughes, he had no proof to back up his contention, and I needed no proof to back up mine.

I left the meeting to go to the bathroom, and when I returned, everyone was gone, with the exception of Raymond Holliday. During the entire meeting, he had been drinking. Now he was so drunk, he had fallen asleep, a burning cigarette in his hand. I removed the cigarette and left him to sleep it off, right at the table.

Gay and Davis were not about to ease up on the pressure. Although I still failed to realize it at the time, they were preparing for their ultimate takeover of the company, and I was the only thing standing in their way. Using the most powerful weapon in their arsenal, they began to tighten their grip on the flow of information to Hughes. Patiently and methodically, they were cutting the Man off from his own company. Unfortunately, Howard was too sick, and too tired, to even notice.

Planting phony complaints about my behavior in Hughes's ear, they began to sow the seeds of doubt that would grow untamed over the next several months. Slowly Howard retreated into himself, almost unnoticeably at first. The endless streams of memos written on yellow legal pads and sealed in plain manila envelopes slowed to a trickle. My phone calls went largely unreturned.

While I was busy delivering the $50,000 to Rebozo in Key Biscayne, Gay prepared to build a foundation for his continuing accusations of my incompetence. He sent his assistant, Kay Glenn, to Washington, D.C., to meet with a private security firm called International Intelligence, Inc. Nicknamed Intertel, the organization was run by Robert D. Peloquin, a onetime attorney with the Justice Department. Glenn told Peloquin that he wanted the firm to come on board to sling mud in my direction. They were convinced there was dirt under my rug, and they wanted Peloquin to find it.

I first heard about the Intertel investigation from Governor Paul Laxalt. Returning from a convention in Hawaii, Laxalt called me to say that he had heard that Peloquin had been hired by Gay and Davis to dig around in my business. I remembered Hughes's warning about letting "those bastards in Hollywood wedge their way between us," and I asked Laxalt if he would write a memo to Howard alerting him to what he had heard.

When several days passed, and Laxalt hadn't received a response from Howard, I telephoned Hughes's suite, determined to get satisfaction. Howard Eckersley was the aide on duty and he refused once again to put me through to the Man. This time, I wasn't about to let the subject drop, and insisted that Eckersley come to my house for a powwow. He was as pompous as ever when he glared at me across my desk, but I was not about to be intimidated by an overpaid hand-holder. I told him that I was fully aware that memos intended for Hughes were not being delivered and that I wasn't going to tolerate it for another instant.

"If you continue to block communications between Howard and me, I'm going to go up to the ninth floor and throw each of you guys out the window, one by one, until the only person left is Howard Hughes," I openly threatened.

"Don't be too conceited, Mr. Maheu," Eckersley shot back. "We're the only ones constantly with the Man. So don't screw around with us, or we'll cut you off completely."

I felt my blood pressure rising as he continued to stare unflinchingly in my eyes. Since he worked for Hughes and not for me, I could hardly fire the guy, so I did the next best thing: I bodily threw him out of my house, telling him to take his best shot. He did.

Repeatedly, I attempted to reach Howard by phone. Each of his aides told me the same story—the Man was extremely ill, and unable to speak to anyone. I phoned Dr. Harold Feikes, and Hughes's private physician confirmed the report, telling me that Howard had needed extensive blood transfusions and was indeed very weak. By this point, it had been several weeks since I had spoken to Hughes. Our last conversation had concerned my son Robert, whom I was enrolling in school in West Germany. I had planned to travel to Europe with Yvette to place him in the school, and Hughes had begged me not to go. He didn't want me gone for any extended period of time.

For the entire month of October, I operated in a virtual vacuum. No calls from Hughes; no memos, either. Nevertheless, I continued to flood his penthouse suites with memos of my own, in the continuing hope of getting a reply. In Hollywood, Davis and Gay proceeded to meet in private sessions with Peloquin, a fact I would not learn until much later.

During the first week of November, I made up my mind to remove Davis from the TWA case. We were appealing the landmark decision against Hughes, and all my advisors in Washington indicated that Howard didn't stand an ice cube's chance in hell of coming out of the thing in one piece unless Davis was dropped from the case. He had made so many enemies along the way with his vulgar behavior and hostile attitude, that I finally decided to terminate his handling of the lawsuit.

In late 1968, at Hughes's specific request, the board of directors of Hughes Tool Company gave me carte blanche in handling the TWA case in general and Howard's defense in particular. I had the authority to dictate every detail, including the selection of our attorney of record. On November 6, 1970, I shot off a telegram to Davis that read in part:

"You and your firm are hereby advised that you are not to be officially identified with the appeal of the TWA judgment and that neither your name nor that of the firm is to appear on the appeal itself."

Many have speculated that I sent this telegram as an end run to try and eliminate Davis from the power circle and therefore increase my own importance within the Hughes empire at an extremely volatile moment in its history. Such is not the case. I honestly believed that Davis was hurting Hughes's chances of gaining an effective appeal, and others agreed with me—Edward Bennett Williams among them.

It was several days before Davis replied to my telegram, and then he did so in a rather casual manner, requesting a statement of my reasons for wanting him off the case "so that the matter may be properly evaluated." I had never expected Davis to fold easily; nor was I surprised by the arrogance with which he questioned my authority.

"You are being dismissed," I wired back, "because of my firm conviction that a successful appeal will be more likely if you are not officially associated with it. To date you have lost this case at every level with catastrophically adverse financial injuries to the defendants. This consideration alone dictates that responsibilities for the appeal should be placed in other hands." Additionally, I reminded Davis of my full authority over the litigation.

Even as I was preparing my reply, Davis was doing some rug pulling of his own. He had gotten the board of directors of Hughes Tool to vote to revoke my authority and place it squarely in Davis's lap. When I was informed of the vote via a letter from Calvin Collier, I was on a plane to Houston within two hours. I stormed into the office of Raymond Holliday demanding some answers, particularly whether he had personally heard from Hughes on this matter.

Holliday admitted that he had gotten instructions to remove my authority over the TWA case from one of Howard's aides. The news didn't surprise me. Holliday was a onetime $17,000-a-year clerk within the Hughes Tool operation who had been given his job by Gay as his puppet. And now, he was performing well.

When I returned to Las Vegas, I still had confidence in my ability to turn the situation around. For a brief moment, I even considered using my passkey and taking the elevator up to the ninth floor of the Desert Inn and forcing myself into Hughes's suite to alert him to the situation. I have always regretted that I didn't do it. If I had, perhaps what happened next never would have taken place.

On November 14, an unusually cold Saturday morning in Las

Vegas, Chester Davis and Bill Gay sent a fax to Howard's suite in the Desert Inn. Fat, bespectacled Levar Myler was on duty, along with belligerent Howard Eckersley. The fax was a proxy and power of attorney naming Davis, Gay, and Holliday as Hughes's "true and lawful attorneys" and awarding them the ability to "vote and otherwise exercise all rights" in regards to Hughes's Nevada holdings. Myler would later testify that he saw Hughes sign the proxy, which Eckersley also "witnessed."

If Hughes actually signed the document, he effectively placed control of his entire empire in the hands of three people he'd specifically told me on numerous occasions he could barely tolerate. I would not learn about the existence of the document until weeks later. At the time, I still earnestly believed that I could control the situation. So certain was I that at the time I was more concerned about finding a thirty-five-pound turkey for my Thanksgiving celebration.

November 26, 1970, was crisp and beautiful in the snow-covered hills of Mount Charleston. The aroma of turkey had filled the chalet all morning. I had placed the huge bird in the oven the previous night, set the thermostat to 225 degrees, and let it bake for over ten hours.

I was just carrying the turkey to the table, preparing to slice the heavy breast meat, when Yvette told me Jack Hooper was on the telephone. She handed me the receiver, and I remember putting into my mouth a dollop of filling that had fallen out of the turkey cavity. As I savored its magnificent flavor, Jack said the words that would alter my life forever.

"The Man is gone."

Chapter Nine

INTO THE DARKNESS

DISBELIEF. I HEARD JACK HOOPER SAY THE WORDS, YET MY MIND refused to accept the situation. As my guests and family watched the color drain from my face, I felt a slight tremble in my hand as it held the receiver to my ear.

Howard Hughes—gone? Impossible, I continued to tell myself. Gone where, and how? Hughes was sick, he was old, but most important, he wouldn't have set foot out of his self-imposed isolation on his own. There was absolutely no way.

My first reaction was to tell Jack to be certain that the penthouse suites at the Desert Inn were actually vacant. He called me back within minutes and assured me that they were.

"No action; they're gone," he confirmed.

As I hung up the phone, there was a flurry of questions from those seated at the table. Then there was an unnatural silence. My mind raced through different scenarios of what might have taken place. The theory that made the most sense to me was that Gay and Davis had taken the Man against his will. I didn't want to believe it, however, and fought hard to put it out of my mind.

Yvette, God bless her, continued to serve our Thanksgiving meal. While the others proceeded to eat their dinner, I went to the telephone and began canvassing hospitals in Las Vegas and the surrounding towns. I gave Hooper the assignment to check the various houses that Hughes had bought and never occupied, his proposed love nests for Jean Peters, including the Riddle estate in the fashionable section of Las Vegas, and the 518-acre Krupp ranch outside of town.

As the sun was setting over Mount Charleston, my family and guests piled into a Hughes corporate helicopter to return home. It was the only time that the beauty of those isolated pine forests had failed to move me. My mind was elsewhere and nowhere at once.

After saying good-bye to Larry O'Brien and his family and swearing them to secrecy, I went to my offices at the Frontier Hotel and proceeded to call Pat Hyland, the head of Hughes Aircraft. Pat knew nothing about Hughes's change of location and was as shocked and worried as I was. Next, I tried reaching Hughes's Hollywood attorney, Greg Bautzer. I pulled Greg away from his Thanksgiving meal to learn that he too knew nothing. Ditto, Raymond Holliday in Houston. Both were amazed and promised to contact me the moment they heard any information.

With the dawn of a new day, there still was no clue as to Hughes's location. I was nervous. I feared for Hughes's future. If Davis and Gay were behind the disappearance, I feared for my own. Having seen what they were capable of doing, the way they'd maneuvered Holliday and the board of Hughes Tool Company, their threat was real and I wasn't taking it lightly.

By the end of that evening, a full forty-eight hours had passed since Hughes had left his Desert Inn penthouse. Since I had yet to receive any ransom demands, it appeared more and more likely that this was indeed an inside job. In the days that had passed, Jack Hooper had repeatedly scoured the local hospitals, as well as Hughes's Las Vegas properties, all to no avail.

Moving Howard out of Nevada unseen would not have been an easy task. We began to look for witnesses. The sole guard on duty at the time had heard nothing. In order to have eluded him, Hughes would have had to have been carried bodily down the exterior fire staircase of the Desert Inn nine flights to the parking lot below. The desert air on Thanksgiving Eve was below freezing, posing an enormous risk to an aging and sick man with a propensity for catching pneumonia.

While I had Jack Hooper, Dean Elson, and my son Peter running down every lead, I placed a call to hotel entrepreneur Del Webb. Webb was about to make a trip to Washington, D.C., to meet with FBI director J. Edgar Hoover. I begged Webb to attempt to get Hoover to look into the possibility that Hughes had been kidnapped. Webb unsuccessfully broached the subject. Hoover remained reluctant to proceed with any investigation into Hughes's disappearance, citing a lack a evidence that he was forcibly removed. Not willing to give up, I called attorney Ed Morgan and asked him to fly to Las Vegas to assist me in my search. By this point, I was living out of my office, barely sleeping or eating.

Finally, on November 30, we received a break in the case. A source at McCarran International Airport told me about an unscheduled flight on Thanksgiving Eve from Nellis Air Force Base. Upon further checking, Dean Elson managed to find an Air Force captain who confirmed that a Lockheed Jetstar had landed at Nellis Air Force Base at 8:00 P.M. on the evening of November 25. Captain David Van Dyke was the airdrome officer on duty at Nellis when at 9:00 P.M. a small van, a station wagon, and a two-door car drove onto the taxiway and six people hurried toward the waiting plane. They were carrying a man covered in a blanket and lying on a stretcher.

We later learned that the flight schedule of the plane indicated that it had headed to the Bahamas. Peter and Dean Elson took off immediately for Miami to set up a base of operation from which we could determine if Hughes was now back in Nassau. If we succeeded in finding Howard and were able to determine that he was being held against his will, I wanted to have a contingency plan set up to get Howard back. I even flew in Doug Priest, the captain of my yacht, in case we needed to sail Hughes to safety.

Despite the lack of reliable communications and political stability, the Bahamas were always a favorite with Hughes. And if Davis and Gay were behind Hughes's sudden departure, it was a convenient place to relocate the Man. Hughes had maintained suites at the Britannia Beach Hotel on Paradise Island for over a year. It was just one of many sets of suites we had continued to keep at our disposal in various cities in case Howard's wanderlust should get the best of him once again.

Peter hired a team of private eyes from Investigators Inc. of Miami—the same company we'd used to help Sam Giancana. He sent the men over to Nassau, and told them to head to the Britannia Beach Hotel. The investigators quickly gained the confidence of an employee, who confirmed that Hughes was staying in a suite on the hotel's top floor. The men placed a bug in the ceiling of the suite below Howard's in an effort to determine whether he was being held against his will.

Las Vegas is a very small town, and when its biggest fish jumped off the hook, we didn't have a chance in hell of keeping it quiet. On Dec. 2, 1970, I received a call from *Las Vegas Sun* publisher Hank Greenspun. Hank had received a tip that Hughes had left town, and as an old friend I wasn't going to lie to him. I told him what I knew, and in a special edition of the paper that evening the banner headline read: "Howard Hughes Vanishes! Mystery Baffles Close Associates." Greenspun himself had bylined the story.

Suddenly, it seemed that every reporter on the planet was parked outside my office at the Frontier. The news story made headlines across the world, including Los Angeles, where Davis and Gay were preparing to let the next ax fall—and right on my neck.

At noon on Friday, December 4, Ed Morgan came into my office and told me he had been summoned to a meeting at the

Century Plaza Hotel by Chester Davis. I presumed that they were finally going to admit to me where Howard was and attempt to work out some compromise. That would have been too easy. By 3:30 P.M. that afternoon, Morgan had flown to Los Angeles, had a short meeting with Davis and Gay, and was back in my office. I'll never forget the look on Ed's face as he told me the news. He was drawn and there was sadness in his eyes as he delivered his "I hate to tell you this, Bob" speech. Ed relayed the message that I was fired and stepped back. He knew by the look in my eyes that I was not about to give up. I took a deep breath and prepared for the fight of my life.

Round one began with a call from Al Benedict at 5:00 P.M. that same night. Al was responsible for running all of Hughes's hotels, and he was frantic when I took his call. According to Benedict, Chester Davis and Bill Gay had just arrived at the Sands Hotel and demanded that the entire top two floors be cleared for their use. Almost simultaneously, I started to receive calls from each of the hotel's casinos. Accountants from the firm of Haskins and Sells, accompanied by agents from the Intertel organization, were moving into casino cages to take charge of the money and the files. The battle lines were drawn and I came out swinging.

I immediately issued orders to security at all our hotels that no members of Gay's attack team were to be allowed to remain in the cages. Davis and Gay had failed to realize that according to Nevada law only authorized representatives of the holder of the gaming license are allowed in casino cages. You don't get authorized just by showing up. It's an intricate process designed to maintain the integrity of the cages.

On December 5, I obtained a temporary restraining order from the Nevada District Court barring the Davis-Gay forces from distrupting the affairs of the Hughes casinos. Davis wasted no time in getting a court order issued against me as well. I too was barred from Hughes properties, though not from my own office at the

Frontier. He succeeded in having the court order issued by finally making public the proxy Hughes was purported to have signed three weeks before.

During this entire time, one of my strongest allies had been Nevada Governor Paul Laxalt. More than merely a friend and fabulous tennis partner, he was squarely in my corner. But, on the following Monday, all that changed.

At 1:00 A.M. the morning of December 7, Laxalt was requested to come to the eighteenth floor of the Sands Hotel, along with George Franklin, Jr., the district attorney for Clark County, and Frank Johnson, Gaming Commission chairman. Bill Gay told them that Howard Hughes wanted to speak with them personally on the telephone. Before he left for the Sands, Laxalt called me expressing his skepticism. When I heard from him next, that skepticism had disappeared. About 2:30 A.M., Paul came to my home, and his expression was one of sadness. He was clearly about to say something that was difficult for him, and I guessed that he was about to put my hide out to dry. He did. He told me he had spent over a half hour talking with Howard, and that Hughes had told him that I was fired. At this point, I felt a great deal of energy leave my body. I remember asking if Hughes was all right, and Laxalt assured me that he was.

"Howard told me that he flew to Nassau aboard a Lockheed-owned jet and that the flight was quite comfortable. He said he was feeling well, and confirmed that he did indeed sign the proxy which authorizes your termination," Laxalt said. Paul even said that Hughes was joking with him about all the fuss, explaining that he was simply trying "to fire a couple of guys and go on vacation." Hughes assured him that he would return soon to Las Vegas.

I later learned that when Franklin got on the phone, Hughes joked with him as well. He said that his exit from the Desert Inn was so simple that he questioned how well he had been guarded for the past four years.

"That was some security Hooper was providing," Hughes quipped to Franklin. "I could have been chloroformed and carried out of there. I've been paying a lot of money for this kind of security."

The two weeks that followed found me in court almost daily. During this time, I took the precaution of removing all my files from the Frontier offices. There were ten or twelve enormous files, and I shipped them all to California for safekeeping. As the Hughes-Nevada faction squared off against the Hughes-Hollywood group, I found myself faced with an uphill struggle to keep control of an organization that I had essentially created out of funds provided by an employer who was nowhere to be seen. At the foundation of all the Davis-Gay claims was the November 14 proxy, which they brandished in court like the sword of Excalibur.

For a short time, it appeared as if I had the opposition on the run. I had brought in a highly regarded handwriting expert named Charles Appel who testified that Hughes's signature on the document was a forgery. Appel had worked with the FBI for many years. In fact, the Hughes organization had used his services several times in the past. His testimony was refuted, however, in subsequent statements made by a documents examiner named Ralph Bradford, hired by the David-Gay contingent.

Midway through the hearing, my position was further damaged when a memo from Hughes to Chester Davis and Bill Gay was photocopied and leaked to the press. Even I had to admit privately that it appeared to be genuine. Howard wrote in part:

Dear Chester and Bill: I do not understand why the problem of Maheu is not yet fully settled and why this bad publicity seems to continue. It could hurt our company's valuable properties in Nevada and also the entire state [sic]. ... You told me that, if I called Governor Laxalt and District Attorney George Franklin, it would put an end to this problem. I made these calls, and I do not understand why this very damaging publicity should continue merely because the properly constituted board of directors of Hughes Tool Company decided, for reasons they consider just, to terminate all relationship with Maheu and Hooper. I ask you to take whatever action is necessary to accomplish the objective briefly outlined above. I do not support Maheu or Hooper in their defiance of the Hughes Tool Company board of directors, and I deeply desire all concerned to be fully aware of this immediately. I ask you to do everything in your power to put an end to these problems, and further I ask you to obtain immediate [*sic*] a full report accounting of any and all funds and/or property to which Mr. Maheu may have had access.

It was, for all intents and purposes, the final blow.

On December 19, District Judge Howard Babcock denied my request for a preliminary injunction against Davis, Gay, and Holliday while accepting the Hughes proxy as valid. With his decision, I spoke to the press—this time as the ex-Chief Executive Officer of Hughes Nevada Operations.

"The judge has ruled," I told them. "Needless to say, I'm disappointed. My only hope is that the eight thousand Hughes employees in the state of Nevada will really cooperate in protecting the properties of Mr. Hughes. I can assure you that I intend to cooperate fully." And I did. What I did not do, however, is capitulate to Davis and Gay.

After spending a very solemn Christmas in the house that Howard Hughes had built for me to occupy as his alter ego, I reached a decision. On December 31, 1970, I filed a $50 million lawsuit against Howard Hughes for breach of contract, and stated that I fully intended to force Hughes to give an oral deposition. The suit did more than take my mind off my problems—it gave me renewed energy to face them.

At the time, my dismissal wasn't my only worry. Within forty-eight hours of my being officially dismissed by Davis, the IRS was at my doorstep, serving me with notice that it intended to audit my tax records for the previous three years. I was later told that Richard Nixon had instructed the tax people to sink their teeth deep into my hide; and they obliged. When they were done with their audit, they estimated my tax liability as $3.5 million, a figure that far exceeded my gross income for the period. They decided to use a loophole in the tax laws to include as unreported income all of the money that I'd used to entertain on Hughes's behalf. I spent the next fifteen years fighting that decision. In the end, I reached a settlement. It was the last of many compromises I agreed to as a result of my years under Hughes's control. The first occurred the same day as the suit.

I was getting ready to ring in the New Year when some agents from Intertel knocked on my front door and served me with eviction papers. They gave me thirty days to vacate the home the Gay group had dubbed Little Caesars Palace. I looked over the legal document and then nodded and said, "Okay."

The investigators looked back at me quite puzzled. "We're not getting the reaction we were told to expect," they said, almost gratefully. "We were told you were going to start screaming and raising hell."

"No," I responded calmly. "As a matter of fact, I think I do have some papers in my possession that would allow me to stay in this house the rest of my life if I select to, but quite frankly I've got bigger fish to fry." They turned to leave, but I wasn't quite finished. "You go back and tell those pinheads you work for that they can have this house in a week, not a month."

The men looked back, obviously more confused now than ever.

"And we'll leave this in exactly the same condition that we've left every house we've ever sold, rented, or borrowed—in immaculate condition. There won't be a speck of dust; the carpets will be cleaned. We'll handle this house the same way as the others, with one exception."

"And what's that?" one of the men asked, a chip on his shoulder.

"We usually leave flowers." With that I shut the door. Within the week, we had moved out completely and into the house that we still occupy on a fairway of the Sahara Golf Course.

With no more money coming in from Hughes, I suddenly found myself deeply in debt. I had borrowed heavily against my salary to have a yacht built in Newport Beach. Hughes had told me to replace a smaller yacht that I had owned with one that was more appropriate for my position. And he had made arrangements for a local bank to loan me the funds to have the boat constructed. Now I was on my own, and Gay ordered the loans called in immediately.

Gone was the penthouse at the Balboa Bay Club. Gone was the De Havilland jet at my disposal. I was no longer wining and dining with heads of state and movie stars. There were no more tennis matches with the governor, no more multimillion-dollar deals for airlines, hotels, or mining claims. In what seemed like an instant, I had lost it all, and my spirit, too.

To the outside world, I was a man still fighting back. My attorney, Mort Galane, was battling my case for breach of contract in court. He was doing a superb job as my viceroy dueling an elusive foe. He won a judgment that required Howard Hughes to be a personal defendant in my case. At the very least, the ruling suggested that Hughes would have to give a deposition in the suit and address the issue of my firing directly. Before the year was over, we had taken our plea all the way to the Supreme Court of the state of Nevada. Yet, despite the fact that many of the preliminary judgments were going in my favor, I found myself losing ground on another front.

Gradually during 1971, I began to slip into a deep and uncontrollable depression. While Yvette brilliantly managed to keep the wolf from the door, paying off our bills a little at a time, I became more and more introspective and found myself unable to deal with even the smallest problem. For hours, I did nothing but sit and stare into space in a trancelike state. I was a prisoner of my past, reliving my glories while retreating from reality. For months, my depression continued to deepen, and it seemed as if there was no escape. If I traveled outside my rented home, I couldn't drive a mile without coming across a hotel or casino that I had previously controlled but now could not even enter. From the privacy of my terrace, I could not even glance up for fear of spotting a Hughes Air West plane leaving a trail of vapor across the sky. Although I never entertained thoughts of suicide, every night I would get down on my knees and pray to God to allow me to die in my sleep.

I had grown very adept at avoiding what friends I had left, preferring my solitude to any interaction. Even the planned wedding of my daughter, Christine, couldn't shake me from my despair. The day before the wedding, as relatives and out-of-town friends began to arrive at our home, I braced for what I felt would be a barrage of questions about my mental health. Unlike any feeling I've had before or since, I dropped into an emotional abyss that frightened the hell out of me. Like a helpless child, I fled to take shelter at my son Peter's house. I begged him repeatedly that night to take my place, to walk my only daughter down the aisle. Fortunately, Peter refused, insisting I keep the commitment I had made. On Saturday, June 5, I got dressed and was taken to the church in time for the wedding. I walked down the aisle as if in a trance, unable to look at anyone directly. While I kept my word, I was hardly the warm and loving father Christine had always known.

Returning immediately home with Yvette, I shut myself up for over a month, without purpose or direction. Even when I received a call to visit my bedridden and dying mother in Maine, I had difficulty facing my responsibilities. Not wanting my mother to see my condition, Yvette reserved us a cabin near the ocean not far from my mother's house. It was a beautifully secluded spot, dotted with giant boulders that braced themselves against the crashing surf. The morning after our arrival, I awoke before dawn and went out on the rocks alone. As I sat there watching the sunrise, I began to think about how the mighty had fallen.

Here I was, the great problem solver, unable to pull my own

life together. The man who had dealt with the likes of Howard Hughes, Aristotle Onassis, Richard Nixon, and Sam Giancana without flinching an eye was now too scared and confused to look at himself. I suddenly realized that the reason I wasn't able to solve my own problems was that I hadn't been talking to myself. While everyone had been talking to me or about me, I had separated myself from the conversation.

I remember walking slowly back to our cabin. As I entered the room, Yvette watched me in silence. I moved over to the night-stand and began to set the alarm clock. It was odd behavior for a man who had prayed not to wake up. When Yvette asked me why I was setting the alarm, I told her that the sunrise I had just seen was so incredible, I didn't want to miss the next one. Right then, we both realized, my depression was over.

While I had changed, my situation, unfortunately, had not. The uphill battle I faced as a result of continuing debt plus pressure for back taxes from the IRS left me sprinting at top speed only to keep from falling behind. The few clients who Robert A. Maheu Associates did manage to obtain were minor when compared to those of the past.

When I lost my lawsuit against Howard Hughes in December, 1971, I thought the Man was out of my life forever, but he returned in a major way the following month, courtesy of a con artist by the name of Clifford Irving. Irving was an American novelist living on the Spanish island of Ibiza who had eight books to his credit. Number nine was to be the autobiography of Howard Hughes. He claimed to have been working on the book with Hughes for the past year. When publisher McGraw-Hill announced that it had acquired the rights to the Hughes book, it released a statement attributed to Howard that said, "I believe that more lies have been printed and told about me than any living man—therefore it was my purpose to write a book which would set the record straight." The Hughes Tool Company was quick to label the autobiography a fraud. And to prove its point, it provided direct word from the supposed source.

On January 7, 1972, the voice of Howard Hughes echoed through a conference room in the Sheraton-Universal Hotel in Universal City, California. Seven journalists representing a variety of newspapers were seated around a semicircular table to hear my ex-employer debunk the authenticity of his purported autobiography. The book, which was also going to be serialized by *Life* magazine, was said by McGraw-Hill to consist "almost entirely of verbatim transcripts recorded by Mr. Hughes over a period of many months in various hotel rooms and parked cars throughout the Western hemisphere." Irving was supposed to have written the book based on Hughes's transcripts.

It was, of course, utter nonsense. I knew very well that Howard had never set foot outside of the Desert Inn until the moment he left Las Vegas in November, 1970. If McGraw-Hill had been interested in verifying the facts, all it had to do was contact me. It never did. Instead it paid Clifford Irving $300,000, and got itself involved in an incredible amount of litigation.

During the interview, Howard was asked a series of questions by each of the reporters, who were attempting to verify that it was indeed Hughes speaking from three thousand miles across the ocean. One reporter asked Hughes why he had fired me.

"Because he's a no-good, dishonest son of a bitch, and he stole me blind," Hughes responded. "I don't suppose I ought to be saying that at a news conference, but I just don't know any other way to answer it. You wouldn't think it could be possible, with modern methods of bookkeeping and accounting and so forth, for a thing like this with Maheu could [*sic*] have occurred, but, believe me, it did, because the money's gone, and he's got it."

While I had known about the book, I didn't know about the plans for a press conference with the Man. I learned about the telephone conversation and Hughes's comments about me from a reporter for the *Los Angeles Times*. He played me a tape of that portion of the interview and wanted to know if I recognized Hughes's voice. Unfortunately, I did. His statement caused me more than just outrage. It was further testament to what I had come to realize: the Davis-Gay group had filled Howard's head with lies, and he obviously believed them.

A month later, I decided to prove who the liars really were. I sued the Hughes Tool Company and its public relations firm, Carl Byoir & Associates, for slander and libel and asked damages totaling $17.5 million. There were some who said that I was still trying to live vicariously in the shadow of Howard Hughes. Little did they realize that I was finally trying to escape it. My deposition in the case wouldn't be taken until the first week of July, 1973—such is the slow churning of the U.S. legal system. Yet my comments were timely enough to make headlines around the world. During the course of my deposition, I revealed the fact that Hughes had given $100,000 in cash to President Richard Nixon as well as $50,000 in cash to presidential hopeful Hubert Humphrey and an additional $25,000 to Robert Kennedy, and I made it quite clear why.

"Howard Hughes wanted to own the president, choose his successor, members of the Supreme Court, senators, congressmen, and politicians at all levels," my deposition read. The information about the cash contributions was hardly news by this point. Columnist Jack Anderson had printed a fragmented account of the cash gift two years earlier and was largely ignored. At the time, I had said nothing. Now, my direct confirmation of the donations, as well as Hughes's continuing attempts to control every level of the federal government, was too much to be overlooked. My comments would touch a myriad of exposed nerves and get me involved in the most tragic moment in the political history of the United States—Watergate.

In June, 1972, the nation was shocked to learn about the break-in of the headquarters of the Democratic National Committee in the Watergate complex in Washington, D.C. What it didn't yet realize was the tie between Hughes's cash contributions to Nixon and the head of the Democratic National Committee, Larry O'Brien. While head of the DNC, O'Brien was being paid as a consultant by Hughes to report on tax legistation and antitrust rulings. To the Davis-Gay league, however, he was "Maheu's man in Washington." Soon after I was summarily fired by Hughes, O'Brien was released from his contract with the organization as well, and replaced by Robert Bennett, president of Robert R. Mullen and Company Public Relations.

This was not good news to Richard Nixon. Nixon was fully aware that I had handled the details of the $100,000 in cash contributions to his campaign. What he didn't know was how much, if any, of the information I had passed along to O'Brien.

On January 18, 1971, H. R. Haldeman, Nixon's chief of staff, wrote a memo to White House counsel John Dean. He wanted to know the extent of the relationship between Howard Hughes and Larry O'Brien. Eight days later, Haldeman got a response, under the subject: "Hughes' Retainer of Larry O'Brien." Midway through the memo, Dean stated:

I have also been informed by a source ... that O'Brien and Maheu are longtime friends from the Boston area, a friendship which dates back to early or pre-Kennedy days. During the Kennedy Administration, there apparently was a continuous liason [sic] between O'Brien and Maheu. When O'Brien left the White House prior to become [sic] Postmaster General, it is alledged [sic] that Maheu offered O'Brien a piece of the Hughes action in Las Vegas (believed to be about a $100,000 arrangement). O'Brien apparently did not accept the offer.

Had anyone bothered to check with me, I could have offered a more accurate picture. At the time of the memo, Larry and I were certainly not longtime friends. I had known the man less than three years, having met him after the assassination of Robert

Kennedy. There was no "continuous liason," as Dean suggested, no exchanges of trade secrets or confidential information. And no one, including Larry O'Brien, was ever offered "a piece of the Hughes action in Las Vegas."

Despite its inaccuracies, the memo struck home. Everyone apparently took it to heart, including the president of the United States. Nixon's men believed that O'Brien was in possession of documents which could prove that the president had accepted the unreported $100,000 in cash contributions. It was not the kind of information that they wanted freely circulated, especially among the Democrats.

For more than a year, Nixon quietly had O'Brien investigated. He attempted to launch an IRS investigation into O'Brien's returns, in much the same way as he had mine. O'Brien was so squeaky clean that the White House came up with an empty hand. But the innocence of others has a way of haunting the guilty. So it was with Richard Nixon and his fear of the evidence that he continued to imagine Larry O'Brien held in secret.

Subsequent hearings into the Watergate break-in established numerous possible reasons for the extraordinary attempted robbery and wiretap. One of the most common theories implicated Howard Hughes himself. Indeed, circumstances did seem to point in his direction. E. Howard Hunt, convicted of the Watergate break-in, was an employee of Robert R. Mullen and Company, the public relations firm handling Hughes's Washington affairs. When this was coupled with Hughes's close ties with Richard Nixon, the rumor mill worked overtime. In reality, Hughes was far removed from any involvement. By the time of the break-in, Hughes had moved from his Paradise Island isolation to a blacked-out suite at the Bayshore Inn in Vancouver, British Columbia, and knew only what he learned about Watergate via television.

In February, 1973, the Select Committee on Presidential Campaign Activities was formed by the Senate to investigate the Watergate conspiracy, with hearings begun the following May. Nixon, seeking to free himself of the Hughes stigma, ordered Bebe Rebozo to return the hidden $100,000 to its sender in June. Rebozo insisted the money had never been touched. It had, however, mysteriously multiplied. When Rebozo returned the money to Chester Davis, there was an extra $100 bill.

Less than a week later, I gave my deposition for my slander suit against Hughes. And with it came the truth that Richard Nixon had hoped to hide forever. The $100,000 in cash that Hughes had given the president was suddenly big news. And the Senate Watergate Committee was anxious to learn more. I was interviewed in private by the seven members of the committee on four different occasions. They asked about a possible Hughes connection, and I merely repeated my story. That's the nice thing about the truth. It never changes.

The committee subsequently interviewed Bill Gay, Nadine Henley, and several dozen others. All of their conversations were taken off-the-record, and none of the contents of those interviews have ever been made public. Whatever was said didn't completely satisfy the committee. It wanted more. In January, 1974, Terry Lenzner, the committee's assistant chief counsel, wrote to Chester Davis requesting an in-person interview with Howard Hughes himself. Since the break-in, Hughes had moved to the Intercontinental Managua Hotel in Nicaragua, and then on to the Inn on the Park in London. And not even a Senate hearing was going to break his self-imposed exile.

When Nixon eventually resigned from the office of president of the United States on August 8, 1974, the Watergate conspiracy had placed all the burglers behind bars. In addition, nine of the president's closest advisors, including Attorney General John Mitchell, were found guilty as well. Watergate had brought the executive branch of the government to its knees. The only unanswered question remained the motive.

It's obvious that the Hughes cash contribution played a large part, and the O'Brien connection cannot be disputed. How ironic it is that all of Nixon's suspicions about a breach of confidence concerning the funds could have been laid to rest with a simple phone call to me. Instead, the history of the United States and its presidency was altered forever—most say for the better.

As a die-hard Republican, I wish I could say that I felt sorry for Nixon, but I can't. Quite frankly, I didn't have enough time to even care. For while Nixon's character was being questioned by the Senate Watergate Committee, my name was being dragged through the mud in Los Angeles.

My libel suit against Hughes Tool Company, and the Summa Corporation as it was later called, went to trial on February 26, 1974, in the U.S. District Court in Los Angeles. It was branded from the start as a historic confrontation in the law of defamation. It was a contest that continued for five months—an unbelievable five months in which my life was laid out before the public and picked clean.

I had moved to the prestigious Jonathan Club in Los Angeles to live during the trial. The private club provided me with the seclusion that I needed to maintain my sanity under such intense day-to-day scrutiny. And during the first weeks of the trial, I was scrutinized indeed. The Summa Corporation's attorneys numbered an even dozen and were prepared to defend Howard's statement calling me "a no-good, dishonest son of a bitch," no matter what the cost.

My attorney, Mort Galane, had taken my case on a contingency basis. A recent book on trial attorneys names Galane as one of the six best in the world. It goes on to say that Galane's reputation as a courtroom killer began with Maheu vs. Summa. The book is correct on both counts. Galane was a master in litigation even then, and aggressively maneuvered me through a mine field of insinuation and slurs from dozens of witnesses brought to the stand by

Summa's lead attorney, Norbert Schlei. During the thirty-six court days spread over nine weeks that it took Schlei to present Summa's defense, the most controversial testimony concerned the $50,000 that I had given Hubert Humphrey during the summer of 1968. At the time, the former vice president turned U.S. senator continued to maintain that he never received the cash that night in the limousine in front of the Century Plaza Hotel. The Summa Corporation suggested that I had kept the money myself.

Galane subpoenaed ex-Humphrey aide Lloyd Hand and Hughes employee Gordon Judd to testify on my behalf. Both men corroborated my story. When I took the stand, I told the court that not only had Humphrey received the cash, but he'd called me at my home in Las Vegas after losing the election to ask me to thank Howard for the money. My daughter, Christine, who was fifteen years old at the time, answered the phone and overheard the entire conversation on the extension. Although I think he was an honest man, as a result of the testimony given during my libel case, Humphrey's integrity during the last few years of his life was perceived as something less than lily-white.

Try as they might, the Hughes attorneys repeatedly failed to impugn my character or present a single example of theft. Ironically, it was Hughes's own character that ultimately was questioned. In addition to his continual efforts to buy political favors, Hughes was depicted as a man prone to impulsive executive decisions. One of the most classic was illustrated by publisher Hank Greenspun, who testified about the sale of television station KLAS. Greenspun declared that Hughes paid $3.65 million for the station so that he could watch old Westerns and aviation movies in the hours before dawn. Even the members of the jury found the testimony amusing. They were far more serious when listening to Hank talk about a loan he had given me for $150,000—a loan I hadn't repaid. When the Hughes attorneys asked why he had never sued for repayment, Greenspun replied, "The guy's broke. It's like suing a blank wall."

Despite the embarrassment they caused me, Hank's words helped to paint a picture. I was hardly rolling in the kind of dough that Howard Hughes had suggested I was.

When Norbert Schlei summed up the Summa Corporation's defense midway through my libel trial, he stated that I had filed suit to get revenge against Howard Hughes for my dismissal. "Mr. Maheu well knew of Mr. Hughes's phobia against public exposure and litigation," Schlei stated. "And Mr. Maheu has made certain that Mr. Hughes got plenty of both." The words hit me squarely between the eyes. Anyone who has gone through a court proceeding knows how demeaning and trying an experience it is. To suggest that anyone would endure such an ordeal for revenge is quite foolish. While Summa was officially the defendant in the case, it was my life and behavior that were being examined. If anyone was getting exposed, it was me.

Each night, I would return to my room exhausted by the trauma the testimony caused. It was an enormously difficult time, during which my sleep was sporadic. Worst of all, however, was my inability to escape the notoriety of the trial, even within the confines of the private Jonathan Club. One afternoon, while court was in recess, I was playing a game of bridge when I was paged to the phone. I happened to pass another table as my name continued to be paged and overheard a man say to some friends, "Maheu. That's the crazy old guy who's fool enough to think he can fight Howard Hughes." Despite it all, I persevered.

One of the unexpected sources of encouragement during the trial came from the testimony of Intertel president Robert Peloquin. Intertel had undertaken 425 separate investigations into my activities. There was nothing that escaped Peloquin's inquiring eye. Yet, none of these reports were entered as evidence at the trial. Peloquin had turned up nothing.

Because facts from the Intertel investigations were never introduced into evidence, my attorney was not able to cross-examine

Peloquin about them. He did, however, manage to establish the fact that during previous investigations for other clients, Peloquin had gone immediately to the authorities if he uncovered any evidence of illegal activities. When Mort Galane asked Peloquin if, based on his investigations, he reported any of my activities to the police or FBI, Peloquin had to admit that he had not. Apparently, even my fingernails were clean.

Near the end of the court case, I took the stand and testified on my own behalf. What I said surprised many people, especially my old associates. I told them I had wanted to quit my job. It was true. When Howard had backed out of the $3.5 million loan he had offered to Sidney Wyman as well as his commitment to buy Los Angeles Airways, I was left once again with egg on my face. I'd sworn to myself it would be the last time.

Judge Harry Pregerson, who was presiding over the trial, shook his head and asked me directly: "Why did you stay with this man?"

I took a deep breath and swallowed my pride. I told the judge and the court that the perquisites of the job were simply too great to give up. The huge house, the unlimited expense account, plus the $10,000 a week income. I wanted it all.

"I also stupidly believed that I could handle Mr. Hughes's misuse of power," I added. "Mr. Hughes once told me that he could buy any man or destroy any man. I didn't believe he could buy me, but I feared he could destroy me." It was quite an admission.

"So you were willing to take the thorns with the roses, is that it?" Pregerson asked.

"Judge, it turned out there weren't many roses," I answered, revealing far more than I had ever intended.

Of all the witnesses at the libel trial, the very best one for me turned out to be Hughes himself. The fact that he not only didn't appear, but failed to even supply a deposition, ultimately worked in my favor. When the judge questioned Norbert Schlei about why Hughes didn't produce answers to my attorney's written questions,

Schlei responded: "I assume it is because he chooses not to be available." It was not the answer the judge wanted to hear.

It suggested that Hughes considered himself above the court's authority. While this was unquestionably the case, Summa's attorney made the mistake of slapping the judge across the face with the fact. In subsequent arguments, he was never able to undo the damage.

Schlei argued that Howard Hughes was an "elderly, crotchety man with a one-track mind and a phobia against litigation." He made matters worse by stating that Howard was "a man to whom you cannot apply the same standards as you can to you and me." Judge Pregerson was not impressed. He instructed the jury that it could interpret Hughes's failure to appear as an indication that his testimony would have hurt his case.

In his closing arguments, Schlei characterized me as "an accomplished confidence man who has misappropriated more than a million dollars from Mr. Hughes and now wants more." He went on to say that "the issue here is not whether Mr. Hughes is a nice fellow. Mr. Hughes is not the issue—it is Mr. Maheu and what he did with the money and property entrusted to him."

Schlei, of course, was wrong. Howard Hughes was the issue in the case. More specifically, the issue was the libelous statement he had made. "Howard Hughes is a disembodied voice who did not see fit to show his face to the world as he destroyed another human being," Mort Galane said as he completed his three-day summation at the trial. "The voice emanated from a man upon whom the nation has bestowed unlimited honor, a man who has profited from the system, a man who has accepted the benefits of all the laws the nation can give him. His refusal to testify here is an act of cowardice."

In sending the case to the jury, Judge Pregerson described me as an "affable, intelligent, imaginative, articulate man" who nevertheless was "somewhat naive, artless, careless, imprecise, and overly trusting," and one whose "personal affairs were in a state of dis-array." While I thought the judge painted a rather honest picture of Robert A. Maheu during the late sixties, the attorneys for Summa took a different stance. They demanded that Judge Pregerson amend his instructions to the jury, emphasizing certain legal points dealing with embezzlement. The judge rejected the motion, turning them down flat.

The four women and two men who made up the jury took four days to reach their verdict. My heart was in my throat when I saw them reenter the courtroom on July 1. After months in that hall of justice watching these people watch me, I thought of them as long-distance friends. When the foreman of the jury stood up, there was no indication of the verdict. And then I heard it read. The six jurors had found Howard Hughes guilty of libel and had decided in my favor.

For the briefest moment, I let the verdict sink in, and then I turned to kiss Yvette, who was seated behind me. She was crying with relief. It had been a long, often lonely fight. I wanted to scream with joy that it was over. Instead, I issued a statement that said, "I feel the verdict vindicates me. I am quite pleased." Mort Galane then silenced me as we left the courtroom.

In actuality, the fight was far from over. While I had sued for $17.3 million in damages, the actual money value of the award would be decided in a separate hearing slated to begin on October 29. On Wednesday, December 4, 1974, the jury awarded me $2,823,333.30 in compensatory damages, one of the largest dam-age awards in United States judicial history. Judge Pregerson pre-viously had ruled that the jury could not award me any punitive damages. I left the courtroom a happy and excited man, one now eager to resume my life and career, finally free of the stigma of Howard Hughes's comments.

I was foolish to think that the Summa Corporation would accept the verdict. By the end of the year, Summa's attorneys had appealed the adjudication, claiming that "uncontradicted evidence regarding at least three specific incidents proves the truth of Hughes's statement." The attorneys made a point of indicating that under the laws of the state of California, Summa was not required to prove that Howard's remark was true as long as the "imputation is substantially true so as to justify the 'gist' or 'sting' of the remark."

Three years later, on December 27, 1977, the United States Court of Appeals for the Ninth Circuit agreed, and overturned the jury's damage award, sending us right back to square one. At this point, I was fed up with courtrooms and fed up with defending myself. The action never returned to the courtroom. On May 30, 1979, after more than a year of closed-door negotiations, the Summa Corporation settled out of court. While I am still obliged by law to keep the exact terms of the settlement confidential, I can say that it was substantial.

I never personally saw a penny of the settlement, however. Not a red cent. Mort Galane had taken the case on a contingency basis, and I gladly gave him his percentage for a job brilliantly done. Then there were the court reporters and other costs to be paid. The rest went to Uncle Sam. The IRS was still on my doorstep, having put a lien on my assets, and was licking its chops at the smell of cash.

After the announcement of the settlement, on dismissing the suit, Judge Pregerson said that I was now officially vindicated, thus removing any cloud still hanging over my character. But black clouds are funny things. Take them away and the sun that returns has a way of shining right in your eyes.

Chapter Ten

INTO THE LIGHT

NINETEENTH-CENTURY JOURNALIST AMBROSE BIERCE DEFINED IT best: "Lawsuit, *n*. A machine which you go into as a pig and come out of as a sausage."

During the decade of the seventies, I spent a considerable amount of my time in courtrooms in various states, and know Bierce's sentiment well. From my testimony in suits against Hughes to my deposition for the Watergate Committee, the process of litigation sapped my strength and fortune. It is one of the greatest robbers of time on this earth.

I was mentioning that truth to my Las Vegas attorney, Jim Rogers, just after Christmas in 1973. Rogers was handling my continuing battle with the Internal Revenue Service, following my instructions to cooperate fully with the government auditors. He was guiding me through the maze of forms and records that such an investigation necessitates, allowing me to concentrate on the final preparations for my defamation suit against Hughes, then two months away from being litigated. As I prepared to leave his office, however, Rogers hesitantly told me something that would take my mind away from both the IRS and civil suits.

Through sources of his own, he heard that I was about to be indicted by a federal grand jury on charges of fraud relating to the manipulation of the Air West stock back in late 1968. I was stunned. For the first time in my life, I was being accused of a criminal felony. My eyes pleaded with Rogers to tell me he was kidding. Instead, he told me to go home and wait to be served with the papers.

As I drove back to my house, my mind was hardly on the road. At one point, I realized that I should alert Yvette to the fact that process servers might soon be arriving on our doorstep. Stopping at a roadside pay phone, I placed a coin in the slot, only to realize that for the first time in my life, I couldn't even remember my own telephone number—so preoccupied was my mind.

Returning to my car, I drove the short distance to my house, my mind dizzy with the impact of the allegations against me. I had barely stepped inside the door when my worst fears were realized. I was served with papers accusing me of stock manipulation, conspiracy, and wire fraud in connection with Hughes's acquisition of Air West. Hughes himself was indicted on the same charges, along with Chester Davis and David B. Charnay, president of a Hollywood production company called Four Star International, and James H. Nall, who handled land acquisitions for Howard in Nevada. Named as coconspirators, but not indicted, were Hank Greenspun and George Crockett, one of the witnesses at Hughes's marriage to Jean Peters. It was Charnay, Greenspun, and Crockett who had sold their Air West stock at Howard's suggestion—each thinking they were helping out a friend. Undoubtedly, Charnay was indicted because he had sold the largest number of shares (19,100) and was the only one who had bought and sold shares within a twenty-four-hour period. Both Greenspun and Crockett were longtime Air West stockholders, and had merely dumped their respective 15,000 and 12,000 shares when they'd been requested to. I never really understood why Nall was indicted, but he was.

Logic would suggest that I shouldn't have been surprised by the indictment. I had been called to testify about the Air West matter by the grand jury on three occasions during the previous

November, but was convinced that nothing would come of it. I hadn't tried to hide anything about my involvement with the sale of the airline, since Chester Davis had assured me at the time that everything we were doing was perfectly legal. Obviously, Hughes had the wrong attorney.

The grand jury investigation had been led by a twenty-nine-year-old lawyer with the Securities and Exchange Commission named William Turner. He was a man with close ties to John F. Kennedy, and always held the opinion that I was somehow connected with the assassination of the president. I'm sure it didn't help my case. He had headed up the litigation for more than a year and a half before turning it over to United States Attorney V. DeVoe Heaton for possible criminal action.

As I stood surrounded by the joyous decorations of the holiday season, I knew I was in serious trouble—perhaps the most serious of my entire life. Conviction for conspiracy carried a maximum penalty of five years in federal prison and a $10,000 fine. Conviction for stock manipulation added an additional two years behind bars and another $10,000 levy. If convicted of wire fraud, I faced another five years in the pen and an additional $1,000 fine for each of four counts. It was an enormously heavy load. At age fifty-six, I was facing the prospect of another expensive lawsuit, plus the threat of thirty-four years in a federal penitentiary if convicted on all counts.

The worst part of all was that what the indictment charged was basically true. The first count said that the five defendants and the two coconspirators manipulated the price of Air West stock by dumping 46,000 shares on the market during a two-day period in December, 1968. The count went on to suggest that as a form of coercion, Howard Hughes directed Davis and me via handwritten memos and telephone conversations to bring lawsuits against the Air West directors who voted against selling the airline.

Counts two and three charged that we used the facilities of the

American Stock Exchange to do our dirty work. Count four alleged that we used the telephone to carry out our scheme, while counts five, six, and seven claimed we violated the wire-fraud statute by sending telegrams to Air West directors who opposed the sale urging them to change their votes. Since the directors had the telegrams, and since we had used the telephone in discussing the Air West takeover with Hughes, and since Charnay, Greenspun, and Crockett had sold their stock through the American Stock Exchange, I was hardly in a position to deny anything. In fact, my entire defense rested on the grounds that what we did was not illegal.

Fortunately, United States District Court Judge Bruce R. Thompson agreed and dismissed the case without prejudice a month after the indictment was served on January 30, 1974—mere days before my defamation suit against Hughes was about to be tried in Los Angeles. Judge Thompson ruled that the government had failed to "state an offense" in its case. But indictments are like flies—they seldom go away on their own. United States Attorney Heaton was out for blood, particularly Hughes's, and succeeded in gaining a second indictment on July 30, 1974—same charges, reworded. Judge Thompson, God bless him, didn't like this version any better than the first and tossed it out of court again. This time, however, he slapped our wrists as he did it. He called our actions "reprehensible and an abuse of the power of great wealth." Still, he couldn't find anything illegal in what we had done, and threw out the charges the following November.

The Justice Department disagreed and was not about to let the case drop. By this time, however, Heaton had quit doing its legal bidding and had taken a job in Saudi Arabia. No matter. The government hounds appealed Judge Thompson's ruling. For nearly two years, the case was carried on the court docket. Finally, on May 7, 1976, the United States Court of Appeals for the Ninth Circuit ruled against Judge Thompson and ordered the indictment reinstated. It was a bitter blow, one that I tried to fight by attempting to have the case reviewed by the United States Supreme Court. When the Supreme Court refused to study the case, I found myself about to face Judge Thompson in his court for a third time.

The trial was scheduled to begin in April, 1977. Fortunately, George Crockett went fishing. Having had enough of what he considered "government foolishness," Crockett had sailed his fishing boat to the waters of Sonora, Mexico, where he planned to stay, reel in hand, until the Justice Department's litigation was behind him. With one of its two unindicted coconspirators missing, the government asked for a delay. Judge Thompson, now easily as tired of hearing this case as we were of defending it, was not amused. He denied the government's motion, and once again dismissed the indictment, warning the Justice Department about wasting the time of a U.S. District Court. This time around there would be no appeal. The indictment was dropped, right along with the enormous weight that had hung heavy upon me for three and a half years. My codefendants were jubilant as well—with the single exception of Howard Hughes. He had died the year before.

In April, 1976, Yvette and I were invited to go on a cruise around the Mediterranean by orthopedic surgeon Dr. John McGonigle, a close friend. The doctor had also invited ex-Hughes physician Dr. Robert Buckley and his wife, plus Ronald Reagan's physician, Dr. John Reynolds, and his wife. I made Dr. Buckley promise that we wouldn't discuss Howard Hughes for the entire trip. It was a promise made to be broken.

On April 6, I was paged by the purser of the cruise ship. He handed me a cable from Gene Maday. Gene was an old friend who ran Leisure Industries Inc. and had hired me the previous year as a consultant for his company. Now, he was wiring me to say that the news broadcasts were carrying a story that reported Hughes had died en route from Mexico to Houston to receive medical treatment. I reacted very badly.

"I hope the son of a bitch suffered," I told Yvette. The Man had brought so much needless pain and torment to so many with his selfishness that I wanted his life to have ended in as much pain as possible. It was a childish, impulsive reaction of which I'm not particularly proud.

We continued out at sea without any further word about Hughes's passing for two days. Communication to ships in those days was very poor, so we didn't learn any details of Hughes's death until we docked in Crete. When they lowered the gangplank, Yvette and I were the first off the ship. We ran and caught a cab into the town square, where we split up and dashed from newsstand to newsstand looking for an English-language newspaper. I finally found a London paper that had a front-page story about Hughes's death—with information so shocking it gave me a change of heart.

When Yvette found me, I was seated at a table in the square, crying like a child. When she read the article she understood why. For the first time, I realized just how incredibly inhumane those bastards from Romaine Street really were. When Howard Hughes's lifeless body arrived in Houston, it weighed only ninety-three pounds. At a height of six feet four inches, Hughes was nothing more than a wasted skeleton. He had long fragments of broken hypodermic needles in his biceps. There were puncture tracks up and down his arms and legs. He had a separated left shoulder. Open bedsores were scattered across his back. An oozing tumor festered on the left side of his scalp, and his teeth had totally rotted in his mouth.

The report in the British newspaper had far more information on Howard than was being released in the United States. Officially, his formal autopsy report stated that Hughes had died of "chronic renal disease," that a total shutdown of the kidneys had allowed the body to accumulate wastes. At the same time, his body was severely dehydrated, compounding the problem.

There was no explanation of why Hughes's two full-time physicians in attendance in Mexico, Dr. Wilbur Thane and Dr. Lawrence Chaffin, had allowed the Man's condition to deteriorate to such an extent without demanding hospitalization for their patient. And while I later learned that Hughes's body contained enough codeine to have killed several normal men, there was no mention of it initially. The official autopsy said only that his body contained "minimal amounts of codeine."

When I returned home, the news media were relentless in their attempts to get me to comment. While I avoided most of them, I did keep in contact with syndicated columnist Jack Anderson. Jack was able to get Mexican authorities to search Hughes's suite at the Acapulco Princess. In fact, the Mexican police arrested some of Hughes's aides when they were found shredding documents. The papers they missed ended up with Anderson, including several which indicated that Hughes's aides continued to tell him that the case against me was going quite well—long after I had won the first round of the lawsuit and received my $2.8 million judgment against him.

These men had Howard in total isolation. And the tighter they made the cocoon, the more Hughes's version of reality existed only in his mind. By this time, of course, he was in a very, very sad mental state. Even his doctors were dangling drugs in front of him to control what contracts and papers he did or did not sign. It was disgusting.

I now saw that my lawsuit wasn't really against Howard Hughes; it was against Bill Gay, Chester Davis, and their tight little group of aides who attended to Hughes, distorted his perception, and stood by while he ruined his health. At this point, I had already won my slander suit against Hughes, but the judgment was under appeal. The details of Howard's death served to strengthen my resolve to make those bastards pay.

The most shocking allegations about the end of Hughes's life are found in a previously unpublished Plaintiff's Memorandum in a suit brought in Nevada's Eighth Judicial District Court against Bill Gay, Chester Davis, Nadine Henley, Kay Glenn, Levar Myler, John Holmes, aide Chuck Waldron, Howard Eckersley, aide Jim Rickard, and Dr. Wilbur Thain by First National Bank of Nevada, William R. Lummis (Texas temporary coadministrator of the Hughes estate), the Summa Corporation, Hughes Aircraft Corporation, and Hughes Properties, Inc.

Lummis, Howard Hughes's cousin and the coadministrator of his estate, took over the reins of the Summa Corporation shortly after his death. Lummis is a diligent attorney and an ethical businessman, and has done an admirable job at the helm of Summa. It didn't take him long to see that corporate waste was abundant within the Hughes empire, and that Gay, Davis, and Henley were the primary beneficiaries. Ridding the organization of the longtime employees was another story and took years to accomplish. When Gay, Davis, Henley, and the coterie of aides were finally history, Lummis took the entire lot to court, exposing the horrors they had perpetrated on Hughes and his company. The suit was filed by the coadministrators and three of Hughes's companies to "recover damages for an extraordinary scheme perpetrated upon Hughes and his companies by the 'Palace Guard' which surrounded Hughes for the last ten years of his life." While the aides denied Lummis's charges, the brief painted an evil picture—one, however, which was completely consistent with what I had suspected for years.

The document was based on affidavits from a number of ex-Hughes employees. Among them: aides George Francom and Paul Winn, longtime Hughes friend Jack Real, and a bevy of Hughes's doctors, including Norman Crane, Robert Buckley, and Harold Feikes. Nowhere was the Plaintiff's Memorandum more appalling than in its description of Hughes's mental health. According to the sworn testimony, during the period when Howard signed the proxy removing me from my position as his alter ego, he was hardly in a position to be making business judgments—sound or otherwise. "At the time the proxy was obtained, Hughes was seriously weakened from the second in a series of bouts of anemia, complicated in November, 1970 by pneumonia," according to depositions taken from Dr. Harold Feikes, Dr. Robert Buckley, Dr. Norman Crane, Howard Eckersley, and Levar Myler that were mentioned in the memorandum. "Dr. Feikes testified that Hughes was 'critically ill' and anemic enough to be on the verge of heart failure. Dr. Crane later described Hughes as having 'nearly died' from the 1970 bout with pneumonia." The memorandum continued:

Despite his critical illness, the amounts of codeine and Valium made available to and apparently used by Hughes during the weeks shortly before the proxy was obtained soared to among the highest levels of his life. The November 14, 1970 proxy is a curious document indeed. It gave Gay and Davis, acting together, absolute power—certainly a strange act from one who had expressed his dislike for Gay and who had authorized Maheu to fire Davis just a few months earlier. It purportedly was executed when Hughes was critically ill and under the influence of drugs. There is specific evidence that Hughes in later years was forced to approve employment contracts for members of the palace guard by his doctor's threat that he would cut off Hughes' codeine if the contracts were not approved. Given Hughes' serious illness, his mental weakness, his drug addiction and the use to which that was put on another occasion, his seclusion with aides loyal to Gay, and his prior expressions of lack of confidence in Gay and Davis, one may readily infer that the proxy was procured by undue influence. ... Moreover, the motive for the use of such influence is plain. Davis used the proxy to get rid of Maheu, lest Maheu get rid of Davis. And Gay too was threatened by Maheu's rise to power.

The proxy gave Davis and Gay the power to get rid of Maheu. But another obstacle first had to be overcome. Hughes lay critically ill and under the influence of drugs on the ninth floor of the Desert Inn. Firing Maheu inevitably would have caused a confrontation. If Hughes were in Nevada, he could have been forced to testify in any litigation over the validity of the proxy. Any court appearance or, indeed, any effort to avoid an appearance on health grounds, might disclose Hughes' addiction and other disabilities for all to see and would cast doubt on the validity of the proxy. Indeed, it could well have led to an inquiry into his sanity. The proxy therefore could not safely be used until Hughes was out of Nevada. And so Levar Myler took the signed document and put it in his safe deposit box at a bank in Las Vegas.

On November 25, 1970, Hughes flew from Las Vegas to the Bahamas. He apparently had been convinced by the aides that it was necessary to leave to avoid a confrontation with Maheu. The Court may infer that he was convinced as well that codeine would be more easily obtainable in the Bahamas.

The Plaintiff's Memorandum concluded:

Hughes' health remained poor from the time he left the Desert Inn until he arrived in London (in December, 1972). He continued taking large doses of codeine. His isolation, his peculiar rituals, his long periods of sleep, his chronic problems with constipation, and his poor diet all continued at the various hotels in which he was secluded. Then in August, 1973, while in London, his physical and mental condition suffered a further setback. Hughes fractured his hip while going from his bedroom to his bathroom. He was x-rayed by Dr. William Young in London in connection with the fracture. Dr. Young described his condition as being in a stage of malnutrition comparable to that of prisoners of war in Japanese prison camps during World War II. After the fracture, Hughes never walked again. For the rest of his life, he was bedridden and emaciated. He had increasingly long periods of unconsciousness, up to a day or more, and his days were spent sleeping, sitting in a semi-stuporous state or watching movies, some of which he had seen dozens of times before—often dozing in mid-film. He was totally out of touch with the outside world and his business affairs. The aides continued and, indeed, encouraged his isolation. Hughes' mental condition suffered a parallel decline. According to plaintiff's expert, Dr. Raymond Fowler, Hughes was mentally incompetent by August, 1973.

According to the brief, while Hughes was in his decline, and I was doing my best to keep food on the table, Davis, Gay, and Kay Glenn were living the grand life at Howard's expense. "Gay and Davis flew to Europe in 1972, ostensibly to find Hughes a new residence. While there, they chartered a private jet and flew to Nice, France, to meet Gay's wife; to Zurich to look at a watch for Gay; and to Majorca so that Davis could visit his daughter there." Additionally, according to George Francom's affidavit, two houses were purchased in the Miami, Florida area. "One was a mansion which, although in first class condition, was extensively remodeled. Although Hughes obviously had not played tennis or gone swimming for years—indeed, he had not left his bedroom for years—a tennis court and swimming pool were built. And ironically, although Hughes twice went through Miami, he did not stay at the mansion on either occasion."

The memorandum continued with page after page of testimony detailing payments by executives to friends for unknown services performed; salaries that were arbitrarily increased by $100,000 at a crack; company funds spent on the tuition expenses of the children, relatives, and friends of Gay, Eckersley, Myler, and Glenn amounting to more than $130,000; plus unpaid promissory notes, including a quarter of a million dollars borrowed but never repaid by Gay—all at a time when the Summa Corporation was losing millions of dollars per year.

While the defendants ultimately settled the case out of court, the evidence assembled for the case was cooling salve to my well-worn wounds. The defendants, of course, had not created the situation that allowed such excesses to exist. That responsibility must be credited entirely to Howard, who became a prisoner of his own design. By closing himself off from the outside world, he sealed his own fate and that of those around him. I was the lucky one. I escaped with my sanity and integrity intact, and more than a few lessons learned.

By the time that the Hughes Air West case was dismissed, it was April, 1977. Despite the fact that my slander suit was still under appeal, I felt a renewed sense of confidence. Although I was still deeply in debt, I was busy working for Leisure Industries, and my life was genuinely happy. I had been through a horror show of accusation and investigation and emerged a better man. My confidence restored, I was eager to take on new challenges. And life, as usual, didn't disappoint me.

One day in Las Vegas in November, 1977, I was eating a thick, delicious submarine sandwich—the kind that mixes assorted deli meats on a long French roll. Unfortunately, a bit of the hardened crust got wedged under my tongue and cut deep into the bottom of my mouth. At the time, I thought little of it and continued my lunch. It was only after several weeks went by and the wound didn't heal that I became concerned.

By that point, Yvette and I had traveled to Los Angeles to attend the annual Christmas party of our dear friends, the McGonigles—the same doctor and his wife who had invited us on the Mediterranean cruise the year before. John McGonigle had a tradition of throwing this party every year for the staff of St. John's Hospital in Santa Monica, and we looked forward to it with delight. During the day, I happened to mention to John that I had this sore that wasn't healing and he told me that he'd have some of the doctors look at it later that night. Since these were some of the finest medical specialists in the world, I knew I could trust their opinion.

Later that night, while the party was in full swing, I had one of the doctors take a peek inside my mouth. I was smoking at the time, and the look on his face as he examined my mouth made me put out my cigarette.

"You had better come in for a biopsy first thing tomorrow," he said earnestly. I remember worrying about his expression all night long, and was still thinking about it at 8:00 A.M. the next day when I went to St. John's Hospital and had a skin sample taken. The technician told me it would take twenty-four hours to get the results of my biopsy, and instructed me to call back the next day at 11:00 A.M.

After leaving the hospital, I drove Yvette to Newport Beach, where we were the houseguests of Jack Scudder, whose mother was Laura Scudder of potato chip fame. We had known Jack and his wife since we had our penthouse at the Balboa Bay Club, and were invited to stay in their guest house. Although everyone tried to be cheerful, my mind was on only one thing—the results of that test. By eleven o'clock the next day, I was visibly nervous.

Because the guest cottage had no phone, I had to place the call for my test results from the main house. Miraculously, everyone disappeared from the place just as 11:00 A.M. rolled around. I felt a tremendous uneasiness as I dialed the office of Dr. Robert Lee. It was as if my blood had been chilled several degrees and was tingling as it shot through my system. When Dr. Lee finally came to the phone, there was only silence—the kind of silence that communicates far better than words. I could hear him breathing, but he wasn't saying anything.

Finally, I said, "Bob, how bad is it?"

"Very bad," he said stoically. I had cancer of the mouth.

Amazingly, the first thing that came to my mind was Nat King Cole. I knew Nat slightly, and had heard how he went through five doctors before he found one who told him he did not have cancer. Two years later he was dead from the cancer that the fifth doctor told him he did not have. I knew that I had to face my problem realistically. As I hung up the phone, people started to come back into the room. They didn't have to ask me the news. They could tell that the results weren't good.

Yet, I had come too far, been through too much, to let my health kick me in the pants. Dr. Bob Buckley and I began to do intensive research into mouth cancer, and made inquiries through many of our doctor friends. Our efforts led me to the Mayo Clinic in Rochester, Minnesota, where I was examined by a doctor on December 20, 1977. After deciding that I needed surgery, the doctor told me that if I wanted to go home and relax for the holidays and come back the next month, that would be okay.

I started to laugh. I realized that with cancer growing in my mouth, I would never be able to relax, at Christmas or any other time. "Let me ask you this," I said. "If I go home for the holidays, spend Christmas, New Year's, and the first week of January there before coming back here, what are the odds that there could be the slightest additional invasion or penetration of this cancer into my mouth?"

"Oh, five million to one," he told me.

I looked at him squarely in the eyes, and told him that I didn't like the odds, not where my life was concerned. I told him to schedule me for surgery as soon as possible. I was booked for an operating room on December 22. The day before my surgery, I was sitting in an enormous waiting room at the Mayo Clinic reading *The Thorn Birds*. I was supposed to meet with the doctor one final time before he cut. My appointment was for 9:00 A.M. About quarter after nine, I heard my name being paged and went to the phone. It was the doctor's nurse. She told me that the doctor had just called her from emergency surgery to ask her to tell me that he was going to be two hours late.

Years earlier, it would have made me furious. Now, however, it wasn't a problem. Somehow, when your life hangs in the balance, a two-hour delay is incidental. I went back to my book and very calmly continued to read. Two hours later, the doctor was paging me again. This time he was on the phone personally, apologizing that there had been another delay.

"I'd like to elicit a promise from you before you say another word," I interrupted.

"What's that?" the doctor asked.

"I want you to promise me that tomorrow, when I'm in surgery, you won't leave me to go to the phone and apologize to someone else about being late. I want your full attention." He gave me his word, and he kept it. The next day I underwent extensive surgery that removed a good deal of the inside of my lower mouth. On Christmas Eve, I went to a midnight mass at the little chapel at the clinic. It was a beautiful night, with snow falling softly. Adding to the peacefulness of the evening: word that the surgeon believed he had gotten all the cancer. As we left the chapel, Yvette asked me what I had prayed for. I think she thought I would say "good health." Instead, I told her that I had asked God to allow me to be grateful. Looking at life with an entirely new perspective, it no longer mattered to me if I had money, or was successful, or achieved any of the things I'd previously held in such high regard. Now, to be grateful was all I needed or wanted.

My mouth felt like it was on fire. I refused to take any pain pills, or even the gargle that they gave me to numb my mouth. I really wanted to feel the pain to punish the culprit that had done this to me. I spent much of my time crying. It didn't stop the pain, but it seemed to help. My cancer was attributed to my extended smoking habit, and since that evening at Dr. McGonigle's house, I have never touched another cigarette. I've never even thought of it.

I arrived back in Las Vegas on December 27, 1977. As I walked through the door, Yvette by my side, our telephone was ringing. There was a reporter from the *Los Angeles Times* on the line asking me how I felt. Nobody likes to advertise that he or she has cancer, and I hadn't told anyone outside of my immediate family and some very close friends, including the Scudders. Yet, apparently, *The Times* had found out that I had been at Mayo.

"I'm fine," I told him. "Really."

"Doesn't it disturb you?" the reporter questioned.

"It's all over—why should it disturb me?" I asked. It was only then that I learned that the appellate court that very day had thrown out my $2.8 million judgment in the Hughes slander case and requested a new trial. It was quite a post-Christmas present.

As I sat down that evening to contemplate the ironies of my life, my old friend Hank Greenspun and his wife dropped by. Hank had heard about the appellate court's decision over his news wire, and expected me to be upset. I was.

"Would you have paid the $2.8 million to be free of cancer?" he asked me.

I told him, "Absolutely."

"Well, then, you have nothing to feel sorry about," he said.

Thinking about it like that, I realized that he was right. While the Mayo Clinic wouldn't give me a clean bill of health until five years later, the doctors were already quite satisfied with the results. I reminded myself of my prayer for gratitude, and suddenly felt a lot better. I had come through a life-threatening disease, the horrors and highs of Howard Hughes, the addiction of power, the very real threat of financial disaster, and criminal prosecution—I had weathered it all.

At the time, I was still happily employed as the assistant to Gene Maday, who owned Leisure Industries Inc. I hesitate to call Maday a client. He was more like a savior—giving me a job in the mid-1970s when many of my former friends were turning their backs on me. Maday was a Las Vegas entrepreneur who owned a casino called Little Caesars on the Strip opposite the Dunes Hotel, as well as two major cab companies, a car rental agency, and a string of real estate in the area. During my three and a half years working with Maday, I successfully bargained for the purchase of the marina at Lake Mead. Later, I renegotiated a long-term lease with the government that allowed for the operation of the marina on federal land. That rewritten lease allowed Maday to resell the marina at a substantial profit, much to my pleasure.

Having come through my cancer surgery, however, I found myself reevaluating priorities of life in general and work in particular. Deep down, I knew that what I really wanted was to rebuild Robert A. Maheu Associates. And to do that, I needed to part company with Gene Maday. Fortunately, my friend understood my need for professional growth and bid me well. Having cut the cord, I began to beat the bushes for new clients, putting out the word in Washington and Los Angeles that I was actively seeking business. Ironically, it fell right in my lap, and from all places—Las Vegas.

In July, 1978, I received a call from an executive at the Dunes Hotel informing me that after a lengthy illness, longtime Dunes owner Sidney Wyman had died in L.A. The hotel had chartered a plane to transport friends and family to California for the funeral services, and I was invited to attend. Having known Sidney for years and wanting to pay my final respects, I packed a dark suit and soon found myself on the plane. I was seated next to Grady A. Sanders, a stranger from Las Vegas who ran a holding company called Network One, Inc., which supplied films to area hotels. Grady happened to mention that he was going to Atlantic City the following week to investigate real estate opportunities in the oceanside resort, which had then just legalized gambling, and he asked me if I cared to come along for the ride as his guest. Investors were literally swarming into town eager to buy up property at nearly any price. I wish I could say that I sensed a business opportunity, but I didn't. However, it did sound like a pleasant trip, and I accepted the invitation.

After checking into a hotel, Grady and I were strolling down the boardwalk when I was recognized by some reporters, who began asking questions about why I was in town. Despite the fact that I had no official association with Network One, Grady made it appear as if I had, announcing that we were "here to stay in Atlantic City" and would be opening offices soon. My only quote was purposely nebulous: "We have some people interested in investing in Atlantic City, and we're trying to put together some transactions." Those words would start a ball rolling, one that would continue to gain momentum for the remainder of the year.

Returning to Las Vegas, Grady began to see that my association with his plans might be mutually beneficial. Within a month, I had been installed as president of a company called Houston Complex Inc., a shell corporation. I was paid a flat fee of a few thousand dollars for my time, and promised a variety of stock options. Several more trips to Atlantic City followed, each with a tiny flurry of news coverage. In reality, Grady did have investors who were interested in property there and we did make a run at a plot of ground next to Convention Hall—the site on which the Trump Plaza sits today.

In August, we announced plans to build a $110 million hotel and casino to be called the Regale Atlantic, and continued to pursue investors. By the end of the year, I had lined up $5 million in funds from New York real estate developers Robert K. Lifton and Howard Weingrow. If additional funds could be arranged, we had structured an agreement that gave Lifton, Weingrow, and their financing partners ownership of the hotel and casino, while Houston Complex Inc. and Network One, Inc. would manage the property. After many broken promises and unfulfilled expectations, plans for the Regale Atlantic fell through. I never exercised any of my stock options, and Atlantic City is a fond memory of mine chiefly for its delicious saltwater taffy.

By early 1980, my life had settled into a comfortable routine, one that found me spending quality time with my family. It was a luxury that I'd rarely afforded myself up until that point, and I relished our moments together. While business for Robert A. Maheu Associates wasn't booming, I eagerly pursued a variety of opportunities, admittedly to little financial gain. I missed very little, if any, of my former treadmill existence. Each day became a discovery process. I was at last at peace with myself, and perfectly content to spend my remaining days out of the limelight and the fast lane. But complacency wasn't destined to last for long.

In August, 1981, my old friend Dr. John McGonigle telephoned with a proposition I found quite interesting. He wanted me to move to Los Angeles for six months to a year in order to work on consolidating his business holdings. By this point, John was extremely wealthy and had acquired quite a lot of real estate. Unfortunately, much of it was not cohesive. While he had several properties on various blocks in Los Angeles, few if any joined one another, thereby lessening the value of the total package. He also had some zoning problems relating to development he planned, and he thought that I might be able to negotiate a solution.

As it turned out, I moved with Yvette to Los Angeles and remained there through 1984. John provided us with an apartment on the water in Marina del Rey, a set of wheels, a very nice expense account, and plenty of challenges. We arranged for a teacher to watch our house in Las Vegas, and the setup worked out quite well. Somehow that teacher would always be away when we returned home for holidays and visits with our children, who were still living in Las Vegas.

After three years, John's properties in California were finally put in order, and we returned permanently to Las Vegas. I was once again open to new opportunities, and one came knocking on the knuckles of international arms merchant Adnan Khashoggi. I received a telephone call from a friend of mine in Zurich who invited me to meet with Khashoggi and his people in Switzerland. No doubt about it, I was enticed by the prospect of working with a power broker of Khashoggi's stature, and on first meeting, he did not disappoint. Not only did he dress impeccably and have a tremendous sense of humor, he was also very, very knowledgeable about international issues. We had several discussions about public relations, as well as about what assistance I could provide him in Washington.

Later, he requested that I arrange for a well-known Middle East journalist to gain access to President Reagan for a one-on-one interview. It was a difficult assignment, as Khashoggi knew, but one which I managed to accomplish. After spending two weeks in Washington, and dealing with well-placed contacts, I arranged for the journalist to interview Reagan through the National Security Council.

Several months later, I found myself again doing Khashoggi's bidding—this time with the large international law firm of Baker & McKenzie. Khashoggi had become involved in a deal with an old friend of mine, Texas oil tycoon Mike Davis. During one point in his career, Davis had almost cornered the oil-rig market in the United States. Unfortunately, the bottom fell out of the domestic oil business, sending Mike looking for other avenues of income. His quest took him to the Sudan, where he became partnered with Khashoggi in a deal that would have given them joint rights with the government to all future oil discoveries. They contacted me when they needed to get a legal opinion on one aspect of the arrangement, and I cleared the way for the Baker & McKenzie firm to handle the project for them.

Despite my success in arranging for the one-on-one interview with Reagan, my fees and expenses had gone unpaid by Khashoggi. Also unpaid was the $2,800 bill from the Baker & McKenzie law offices. Since I had arranged the introduction with the international attorneys, I felt obligated to settle the outstanding balance, and told them so. They graciously refused my offer, stating that they would rather keep me in their debt in case they needed a future favor of influence.

As for Khashoggi, he seemed totally unconcerned by the outstanding bills—so much so that a few years ago, an associate of his called me once again for help. It was during the period when ex-Philippine President Ferdinand Marcos and his wife Imelda were being investigated for their real estate holdings in the U.S.—holdings that the Philippine government claimed were purchased with funds belonging to its people, and holdings that Adnan Khashoggi swore belonged to him. He wanted me to help him prove his legal rights to the property and to work out the details with the government in Manila. Based on his previous performance in handling accounts payable, I declined. It was a prudent move. After our conversation, Khashoggi and Imelda Marcos were indicted by a federal grand jury on charges of fraud and racketeering and stood trial in New York. Had I accepted the assignment, I might well have been seated right next to them watching the jury being selected. Although they both were subsequently acquitted of all charges, this was one lawsuit I was happy to have missed.

Looking back on that period and its ups and downs, I had two unflappable constants in my life: my devoted wife, Yvette, and my health. I had survived the years since my cancer surgery with hardly a head cold, and as I had promised myself that night in the chapel of the Mayo Clinic, I had been grateful for every moment since. Grateful, yes; careful, no. And because of that I was hardly prepared for the sudden detour my life took in the summer of 1988.

I had decided to take some time off to spend with my children and grandchildren in Newport Beach, California. Yvette and I had rented a place on the beach for two weeks, and invited the entire family to join us. By the end of our vacation, both my wife and I were ready for a rest. As much as we enjoyed seeing the family, collecting several generations together under one roof is as exhausting as it is pleasurable. Perhaps it was for that reason that as Yvette and I were packing to return to Las Vegas, I suggested to her that we delay our departure for a day and enjoy the beach one final afternoon. Luckily, Yvette went along with my plan. Three and a half hours later, I was rushed to Hoag Memorial Hospital, the victim of a heart attack. It was July 10, 1988.

Afterward, we figured that had we left as planned on our drive back to Vegas, we would have been in a town called Baker, California, at the time of my attack. Baker had a population of about six hundred, and the only place I knew in town was an eatery called Pike's Diner. I don't think they would have been equipped to handle the situation.

Not a day has gone by since that I don't thank God for my heart attack. While I'm overweight now, I was *seriously* obese then. Even though I knew I was fat and had to get on an exercise regimen, like many people I found all sorts of reasons to put it off. I was sent a message from up above and listened very well. I went into a rehabilitation program that taught me how to watch my diet (those thick steaks and Maine lobsters floating in butter were suddenly things of the past). I began to walk or swim every day as well, and have never been healthier as a result. I have made few concessions in my post–heart attack life, remaining busy doing consulting projects for firms large and small, as well as accepting speaking engagements throughout the world. Occasionally, I still uncover newspaper or magazine pieces that mention the Hughes empire, and with them come memories of a time in my life that seems curious now—more like fantasy than reality.

The fruits of wealth and power—the homes, the private jets, the helicopters, the limousines, the yachts—all came at a cost far too dear. Since the moment I realized that truth while sitting on a slab of rock on the coast of Maine in the autumn of 1971, I have never been happier or more at peace with myself. The great problem solver Maheu had learned something that, for all his wealth, had escaped Howard Hughes: No man is complete unto himself. To be truly successful, we must learn to share thoughts and kindnesses with ourselves and others.

It's hardly a new lesson. The great Greek playwright Euripides grasped the point back in 410 B.C. Speaking to hundreds of thousands of his people on the heels of a tragic war, he said, "If there is complete silence, there will be complete disaster. We must talk. As long as there is dialogue, there is hope."

Index

279